RESTRUCTURING ARCHITECTURAL THEORY

RESTRUCTURING ARCHITECTURAL THEORY

Edited by
Marco Diani
and
Catherine Ingraham

NORTHWESTERN UNIVERSITY PRESS
EVANSTON, ILLINOIS

Northwestern University Press
Evanston, Illinois 60201

Printed in the United States of America

Contents

PALENDROMY

MARCO DIANI is Visiting Associate Professor of French and Italian Studies and Sociology at Northwestern University and a Senior Research Associate at the Centre National de la Recherche Scientifique in Paris. He is editor of the forthcoming *Designing the Immaterial Society*.

CATHERINE INGRAHAM is Adjunct Professor in the School of Architecture at the University of Illinois at Chicago and a Fellow at the Chicago Institute for Architecture and Urbanism. She has published numerous articles on architecture and critical theory.

Introduction

Edifying Projects: Restructuring Architectural Theory

Let us consider architectural thinking . . .
—Derrida, *Domus*

The following remarks are a response to the almost classical invitation of Derrida's words to engage in what turns out to be a nonclassical conversation about architecture. "Nonclassical" theoretical conversations (reversals) have, of course, been going on for some time in other fields. Architecture comes cautiously to these reversals. The structuralist moment in architecture—which was worked through with rigor and insight during what can be called the "*Oppositions* years," when *Oppositions* was, at least in the United States, the main publication for architectural theory—has, as in other fields, given way to the broader scope of critical endeavors in the poststructuralist era. But it has given way with a noticeable loss of faith in the capacity of the linguistic and the philosophical model to explain architecture, and thus a loss of faith in the *transparency* promised by the "age of textuality." Perhaps this is because architecture cannot even be thought apart from "form" and formalisms.[1]

Structuralism was possible as a critical position in architecture more because of its methodological promise than because of its theoretical radicality and implications. The insatiable and complex demand for physical comfort—for the "axis," which is one of the paths "home"—in all architectural buildings (even the most austere) stands directly against experiments in building, or even thinking, the grotesque, the pluridimensional, the ideological, the sublime.

Nevertheless, architecture and architectural theory are changing.

These remarks have been organized as a series of brief encounters with only a few of the issues that currently face architectural theory. This is partly a matter of economy,[2] but we also think these concerns may be of interest to others not directly connected with making architecture "work" theoretically.

Architectural History

Unlike the literal and figurative burial grounds in remote areas that political history uses to hide its past trespasses, architecture writes its history in the center of the city. The failures and successes of architecture are heroic in scale. But it would be a mistake to think of this history as therefore fully revealed. Architecture, too, has its graveyards. Jean Baudrillard has suggested, in *Simulations* and especially in *Amérique*, that the miniaturized America of Disneyland (Fantasyland, Tomorrowland, Frontierland) formally masks the nostalgic, Disneylandlike character of all American cities.[3] One might say that architecture revises and conceals its character and genealogy precisely through such calculated displays of what it apparently is not. Sharon Willis, in her essay in this volume, "Spectacular Topographies: *Amérique's* Post Modern Spaces," criticizes Baudrillard's mapping of America as a colonization or appropriation of it. Baudrillard, in a sense, claims America in the same way a modern architect claims a site as his or her own and then erects the glass house of the simulacrum on it.

The reappropriation of architectural history in the poststructural/postmodern epoch is neither a simple matter of citing historical precedents nor a matter of resolving, bringing into one spatial

2

plane, complex layers of heterogeneity between America and Europe, between past and present, between political interests and artistic interests, between architecture and other discourses. The innocence of display—the apparently irrefutable presence of the surfaces of architecture—conceals more than it reveals. Postmodernism—linked by its name to modernism in peculiar, as yet unresolved, orthographic ways (post-modernism, post modernism, postmodernism)—is, as many people have suggested, rewriting the modernist tradition while remaining well within it—as perhaps it must.

Architecture/Philosophy

Critiques of architecture are clearly aligned with critiques of art and science underway elsewhere. And yet from a contemporary theoretical standpoint, architecture seems to be "the hardest case." It stands between art (it never becomes wholly fetishistic) and technique (it never becomes wholly technological) but not as a hinge or "point of exchange" between these two. Neither the art nor the technique of architecture is added on from outside. On the one hand, one might say that the "authority of the architectural metaphor," to use Derrida's words, in language and philosophy is, paradoxically, also the chief source of architectural authority in architecture itself.[4] But what this authority is is of course undecided. One could say that architecture does not draw its authority from some preestablished structure of materials or technique, or from some given structure of artistic meaning, but from the power granted to it by philosophy. Thus architecture builds, over and over, philosophically endorsed ideas of home, city, place—inscribing them in space much as a scribe records the words of an absolute ruler. From this viewpoint, architecture is a deeply conservative force that keeps what is philosophically, politically, and ideologically "proper" in place. From the vantage point of language, architecture thus evaporates, or melts into political, social, linguistic, philosophical analysis.

On the other hand, architecture insists on what can only be called a counterconstruction, whose form and shape are as different from philosophy as writing is different from building—which is a difference experienced in architecture as both an outrage and a solace. Derrida's use of the term "architectural thinking" seems to mute the aggressive tendencies of architecture in general. When he speaks of architectural thinking he is suggesting that a certain idea of space must be thought prior to ground breaking, in order for the ground to be split, broken in a certain way. This idea is of the same order as his discussion of the archē-violence, archē-writing that belongs always, and already, to culture.

Like a building, a piece of writing is built according to structural rules that have already cho-

reographed its place in the world: the editorial rituals of exclusion and admission choreograph a certain dance of writing. The division between the issues of language and the issues of architecture is enforced rather than relieved by writing on "architectural theory." All such essays seem to be an occupation of "architecture" by languages other than the "architectural language"—the languages of history, literary theory, philosophy, art criticism. In this regard, one might note that the presence of different languages in architecture is part of its long, albeit constantly denied, intellectual heritage. There never has been, in one sense, anything like an autonomous "architectural language" that operated in isolation from other languages, just as there is no autonomous scientific language, or natural or literal language. The search for autonomy in architecture, as in all fields, insists on final definitions and prescriptions for architectural boundaries, forms, and shapes. If the essays in this volume invade the autonomous space of architecture, they do so because the possibility of autonomy has been somehow ruined.

The "Ruins" of Autonomy

Autonomy is a project that, to borrow Daniel Libeskind's words, is in an "end condition." "I think," Libeskind writes, "that all those who practice architecture . . . feel in some way that something has come to an end."[5] This does not mean that architecture is "finished"—for clearly it is not—but that its forms of expression, its events and performances, are undergoing change, are opening. As Jeffrey Kipnis very acutely observes in his essay, Libeskind's "Lessons" were "prepared [in order] to be sacrificed . . . prepared . . . in order to teach architecture a lesson"[6]: a lesson, perhaps, about the objects of architecture or about the condition of the architect in a system that is now vulnerable, open, to multiple discourses.

However, architecture is perhaps more primary than philosophy, not as a matter of which came first (for this is unanswerable), but in the sense that Western cultures at any rate organize themselves and perhaps their theories according to master narratives of residence and space produced by architecture (home, city, center, suburb, workplace, profession, family, nations, enclaves, inside, outside). These architectural narratives, in turn, supply philosophy with the form of its discourse. It is perhaps with something like this in mind that Claude Lévi-Strauss, in his reflections about the mythical origin of writing, notices that architecture "as we know it" comes into being at about the same time as writing. If we think of writing in the Derridean sense as something "more ancient" than speech, then perhaps architecture, as Mark Taylor suggests in his various discussions of "anarchetecture,"[7] participates in some way in the "archē," the divided, fallen beginning of humankind and language.

Architecture and the Writing of Legitimation

For a profession that is actively and continuously involved with its own professionalism, it is perhaps merely fashionable to speak of an "architectural crisis." And yet, as Paul Jay suggests in his essay in this volume, the institutional territory that architecture and other disciplines have so carefully constructed for themselves is in crisis. The crisis of rationality in philosophy takes place in a society in which increasing complexity precludes planning from above and induces one to reconsider the relation between institutions and social parts, and to suggest activity that articulates, is more attentive to, their various situations. However, this requires not only that the conditions of belonging of various social groups be made explicit, but also—and this is certainly more difficult—that the latter commit themselves to the formalization of their own interests, to a form giving, a formulation process, which takes, through dialogue, the modes of thought, linguistic traditions, and value expectations of others into account. For it is not scandalous to have interests; it is scandalous to activate them without the moment of dialogic mediation. The problem then becomes a problem of the politics of planning, of how to ensure that the social entities concerned are not merely kept in mind but actively consulted and made to participate in the actual elaboration of the project. We do not believe that this is a philosophical utopia. It is, rather, one of the few ways in which one can conceive of a politics of urban space as long as no one proffers a solution that can solve all problems at once. That is, it is necessary to find different processes of legitimation, and to emphasize that these processes of legitimation not only take the interests of various groups into account but also stimulate the self-legitimation of these interests through a formalization of them within the constitution of what, after Gianni Vattimo, we can call "the hermeneutic horizon."

Such hermeneutic philosophy is not the tautological glorification of the multiplicity of cultural interests—as if to say: a foundation no longer exists; there are only many different cultural universes, many different language games; we must tolerate one another, listen to one another, and that's that. The multiplicity of cultural universes, of discourses, of interests, of fundamental conditions of belonging, is only the starting point of a process of the formation of horizons of legitimation and not the basis of an already given legitimation. There is a great difference here.

This initial multiplicity has given us a false sense of security, a false sense of heterogeneity; we have made disciplines more different than they really are. The critique of language and thought does not stop at disciplinary borders. It enters, some might say promiscuously, into institutional enclaves and dissolves certain, apparently self-evident, differences while reinstating new differences, or, rather, the problem of difference in a new way. Paradoxically, it is now institutionally legitimate to ask a range of ideological, critical, hermeneutical questions of, and within, architecture. The "act of occupation," if there was one, is already over. Perhaps it was over the moment the word *architecture* came into being. The alien beings—those who "write rather than build" perhaps—the small size of whose cadre is a matter of marvel and concern, are now in the capital city, the Kingdom of Architecture, if not exactly running the utility companies. And yet none of this suggests the collapse of architecture into the problematic of language—not even Jacques Derrida, whose tacit recognition of the difference between him, the philosopher, and Peter Eisenman, the architect, makes possible the plurivocality of "The Choral Work" at La Villette in Paris.[8]

Although some critics have understood current theoretical trends to symbolize total disconnection from the idea of historical, political, and social continuity and coherence, we are trying to suggest that the apparent lack of principles, the impossibility of strictly maintaining the "idea of the idea," might also produce a multiplication of parallel convergences. Language, Wittgenstein has said, is like a city. In architecture, then, the demise of the idea of the absolute project, of an all-inclusive plan, has been demonstrated, and theoretical reflection on existence has taken note of the dissolution of systematic thought. In philosophy, as in architectonic planning, one of the solutions that has enjoyed a certain amount of success in the last decades is that of the "parts," for which term you can substitute Wittgenstein's "language games."

The language through which we experience the world is not a finished whole; it is instead a group of expressions that fulfill quite different functions within the realm of disparate practices and fields of experience—the language games, precisely—which are governed by different rules and are always susceptible to innovation (ethics, economics, religion, are realms distinct from one another, with very different rules). In sum, the theory of language games can at least partially be understood as a subdivision of fields into ways of linguistically articulating experience, each clustered around its own system of rules.

In Wittgenstein there is no "game of games," no higher system of rules that grounds and guarantees the validity of the individual games. And this signifies two things: First, each game is only a game, in the usual sense of the word. Games are

4

not subordinated to an ultimate end; a game is played for its own sake. Second, there is something more serious than games: the very existence that games articulate. Better yet, our condition of belonging to a game must in turn be explained on the basis of rule.

There is therefore a kind of solution to the problem of the loss of centrality in philosophy in the idea of elaborating a project in parts. In both cases it is necessary to reflect on the means of escaping from the necessity of an articulation within discourses of their partialization. Theories are not denied once and for all but have, and here lies the value of the analogy, historical and changing constructions, common uses, and elementary structures. "Buildings and their arrangements," as one architectural historian has said, "are a hard historical fact, they do not let themselves be moved according to individual choice, and, on the other hand, this arrangement is completely artificial, contingent, incidental."[9] The relationship between cities and language has been only partially explored. We do not have a theory of cities that instructs us how to think.

We thus reach the point, already described by Nietzsche, at which the individual is not an individual but a "dividual," that is, the very unity of the ego is no longer a true unity: we can no longer perceive it as a unity because we are all placed in a condition of existence in which we authentically experience the ego as multiplicity. Hence the multiplicity of the spheres of value and experience renders obsolete the idea of a self-centered ego, already put into crisis by the theory of ideology, psychoanalysis, and other similar developments. These theoretical positions all put into question the hegemony of a self-consciousness that justified the unity of the ego that styles the *individuum* as already *in dividuum*, not as a shapeless chaos or an assemblage of undermen, but as an open system of multiple and overlapping pieces that derive their significance from their changing relationships to what is around them, changes the idea of the "center" to which cities and architecture have been classically oriented. The loss of the center cannot be taken as pure loss but as a necessary condition for the "requalification of the idea of the center" as a condition of multivalence, not only of external spaces but also of the interior space of the subject.

Architecture and Exile

Architecture has traditionally seen itself as coming from *somewhere*, not, as we now see language, as coming from elsewhere or from nowhere. Jean-François Lyotard suggests that for "first-world" countries, colonial desires are as strong as ever.[10] But since the gestures of colonization, the love and need of new territories, have been almost exhaust-

ed on earth, the search of first-world countries is for territory "elsewhere"—on the moon, on Mars. But the possibility of new territory beyond the perimeters of the earth has not, as yet, produced an architecture-of-elsewhere, that is, an architecture that "writes of itself from exile." On the contrary, as Giovanna Borradori notes, "the imagery of this 'elsewhere' infuses our concept of progress and technological creativity . . . . The anxiety about living 'elsewhere' animates the inner competition among western countries."[11] The elaborate architectural experiments with space colonies that provide shelter not only from the climate, but from the total environment—the air we breathe, the landscape, the "outside"—take the traditional architectural concept of shelter to its apotheosis. An architecture-of-elsewhere—what Jean-François Lyotard and Stanley Tigerman have both come to call an "architecture of exile,"[12] although they mean radically different things by this phrase—is in direct conflict with the architecture-of-somewhere (the sited, the placed, the point-in-time) that modernism, among other movements, tried to establish theoretically. The question is not so much whether we, as first-world countries, should continue to colonize, to architecturalize, the territory of earth or space (which means, in reality, "making space the earth"), although this *is* part of the constellation of the inquiry, as it is how architecture has insured itself against the amorphousness of the "elsewhere."

Architectural Propriety

The orthogonal plan is one such insurance against amorphology.

It is a conception and a technique that give architecture the illusion of escaping its inevitably metaphorical way (architecture-of-elsewhere; architecture spoken through other tongues) and entering into the way of rightness, the way of orthogonality, the proper.

What is proper to architecture is, of course, also part of its search for autonomy. And it is the "proper" that perhaps founders most profoundly in our contemporary epoch. In addition to what Mark Jarzombeck denotes as the "impropriety" of postmodernists who claim what he calls a "false historicism" for their projects, even the proper spelling (the orthography) of "architecture" has been corrupted (opened to play). The loss of an authoritative place that would, ideally, control the spelling of architecture is perhaps most indicative of its contemporary state of crisis.[13]

"Respelling," in its broadest sense, is a "restructuring."

Like architecture, respelling is a structural intervention into the city of language: it creates a space, or an edifice, where one did not exist before. It has both something and nothing "specific" to do with the "history of the city" and is both within and outside the architectural and the linguistic idiom. One might refer, in the same vein, to that most elusive of marks (made by Heidegger and others) that designates in the midst of writing a moment of interrogatory pause—the "under erasure" or *sous rature* mark—as in Heideggerean ~~Being~~. In spite of, or perhaps because of, the proliferation of this mark in certain philosophical texts and the awareness of scale it imposes, the *sous rature* is possibly the closest that language has come to revealing its "architectural markings." Like misspelling, it creates a space where no space existed before and gives to this newly created space an "aesthetic" character that wavers between the linguistic and the extralinguistic.

The implosion, or the Baudrillardian "Beaubourg Effect," of the proper spelling of architecture is academic in one sense; it happens in a context in which certain individualistic performances of language are perhaps given greater range. The Pompidou Center—the equivalent imploded architectural act, which exposes the systems by which it is being supported, much as the John Hancock building in Chicago "X's" itself out with its supporting steel cross members—does not tremble in the same way as the linguistic mark. It cannot show both the traditional structure and the disruption of that structure in the same place, or, rather, in the same materials. Like the *sous rature*, which imports a graphic mark from somewhere else (from the traditionally invisible realm of editing, or from the formal realm of graphics, where an "X" has a status and fixity apart from its status as a letter), the trembling of an architectural "implosion" can be indicated only by a different, ambiguously architectural mark, a mark made of different "materials" imported from elsewhere. This "mark" might be, conceivably, the architectural text.[14]

Architecture and Criticism

The critical project of architectural history and theory, like any other critical project, must reflect on itself and the "puzzle" of how it is made.[15] Part of this "puzzle," the combination of history, theory, and criticism in architecture, is connected to the conventional iconology of the visible, the representable, and the perspectival.

It is a curious and necessary irony of poststructural theory that, in its radical critique of structure, it creates an intoxicated desire for the same aesthetic procedures and performances that it must count, when sober, as repressive. In architectural theory this irony is felt very deeply. It is perhaps the source of architecture's current dedication to the metaphoric power of deconstruction: metaphors of rupture, fragmentation, unbuilding the

built; the artistry of demolition; the pastoral quality of the ruin; the twisted grid, have all become symbolically inscribed in contemporary architectural events. And yet these architectural metaphors, indeed this conception of metaphorization and symbolic architectural inscription, come from precisely the same impulse toward the control of architectural meaning that created the reductive structures of modernism.

Deconstruction is not so much the act of "taking apart" as it is an inquiry into what authorizes "putting together" and "taking apart" in Western thinking. In a certain sense, architecture assumes that it knows the answer to this question; it feels itself to possess the technological and artistic know-how to construct buildings, organize space, control the effects of space on people. These are the assumptions in "architectural thinking" that "architectural theory" spends most of its time questioning; this is not a matter of architectural "know-how" as a technical question, but of the epistemology that this architectural "know-how" constructs, presupposes, or gives form to. This form of epistemological thinking about architecture proceeds, in the first place, from Heidegger's statement that "inhabiting precedes building." That is: in the end, the act of building signifies the modification of the environment to which one has always belonged more than it does the foundation of a structure from scratch. And today architecture (or at least one of its trends) thinks of itself more as a restructuration of the environment than as the laying of a building in a theoretically neutral site. That in philosophy a thinker like Heidegger has maintained that memory and remembrance constitute true thought; that postmodern architecture carries out a labor of recuperation, of re-ennoblement, or even only of insertion within a previous condition of belonging; and that this is a labor of modification of the environment rather than a labor of the placing of a container in the world—all of this does not seem to us devoid of meaning.

We would not like to stretch the analogy, to exaggerate by appealing to a sign of the times, to timely elements that may have left their mark on our way of thinking. Yet when one finds similarities between fields as apparently remote as architecture and philosophy, one has the suspicion that these similarities are aspects of a more general phenomenon. Thus in the Heideggerian phrase "inhabiting precedes building" one can discern the notion of an architecture that is more conscious of belonging to and modifying a given environment.

We might then end by saying that the modernist-postmodernist debate is a false one, essentially because these two conflicting poles can exist . . . only when they exist as such, as poles, extreme elements of the same *continuum.*

On the one hand, philosophy today delineates itself, among other ways, as a leave-taking from foundational thought, in other words, as a recogni-

6

tion of the failure of the faith in the possibility of finding a first principle, a reliable and definitive reference point, on the basis of which to order experience. Now this situation, which in philosophy is called the dissolution of foundations, finds its very clear and quite striking equivalent in the transformation undergone by the idea of the project in the experience of architects and city planners. Architects, for reasons not closely dependent on or tied to those of philosophers, have experienced the demise of the idea of the plan, a demise that probably came about in the same general manner as it did in philosophy, namely, with the growth of complexities that multiply and become independent of the center. On the other hand, and this is even more important, architecture is *in short* and together with philosophy the only constructive practice, even in theory.

Edifying projects.

Notes

[1]See, for instance, the recent collection of essays in *Revisions* (Princeton, N.J.: Princeton Architectural Press, 1989).

[2]Richard Bolton, for example, suggests that the signs attached to corporate "public space" implicitly identify public space as *negative* space, "not yet absorbed by private interests." In a different vein, Michel Maffesoli recommends that we "register the existence of a multiplicity of *loci*" that secrete their own values and that "function as mortar for those who set up and are part of these values."

[3]*Simulacra and Simulations* (New York: Semiotext(e), 1983; original publication, Paris, 1981). *Amérique* (Paris: Grasset, 1985); now in English translation as *America* (New York/London: Verso, 1988). See also Louis Marin, "Disneyland: A Degenerate Utopia," in *Glyph 1*

(Baltimore/London: The Johns Hopkins University Press, 1977), pp. 50–66.

[4]"Metaphor circulates in the city; it conveys us like its inhabitants, along all sorts of passages, with intersections, red lights, one-way streets, crossroads or crossings, patrolled zones and speed limits. We are in a certain way—metaphorically of course, and as concerns the mode of habitation—the contents and tenor of this vehicle: passengers, comprehended and displaced by metaphor." "The 'Retrait' of Metaphor," *Enclitic* 2 (1978): 38. See also Derrida's "Cinquante-deux aphorismes pour un avant-propos," in *Mèsure pour mèsure: Architecture et philosophie* (Paris: Centre Georges-Pompidou, Cahiers du CCI, 1987), pp. 7–15.

[5]"Architecture Intermundium," in this volume, p. 115.

[6]In "Though to My Knowledge", p. 108, written, it must be noted, after the "consumption by fire" of Libeskind's reading, writing, and memory machines in Geneva.

[7]Mark Taylor, "Deadlines Approaching Anarchetecture," in this volume; see also his essay "Archetexture of Pyramids" in *Assemblage 5* (1988): 17–27.

[8]See Derrida's *Psyché* (Paris: Galilée, 1987), and also Daniel Payot, *Le Philosophe et l'Architecte* (Paris: Aubier Montaigne, 1982).

[9]Carlo Olmo, in a dialogue with Gianni Vattimo, "Philosophy of the City," in *Eupalino 6* (1986): 1–5.

[10]In Giovanna Borradori, "Towards an Architecture of Exile: A Conversation with Jean-François Lyotard," in this volume.

[11]*Ibid.*, p. 13.

[12]See Stanley Tigerman, *The Architecture of Exile* (New York: Rizzoli, 1988).

[13]See, e.g., Taylor's "anarchetecture," "architexture" in "Deadlines Approaching Anarchetecture."

[14]Ujjval Vyas, in his essay, "The Hidden I: A Review of Philip Johnson," places Johnson's authorship in brackets in order to investigate the problem of the architect, the writer, the builder of structures (architectural, textual), and so forth.

[15]See Patrizia Lombardo, "Architecture as an Object of Thought," in this volume.

PILOTIS

Stanley Tigerman, FAIA, is Director of the School of Architecture at the University of Illinois at Chicago. He has written extensively on architecture and is the author of two books, *Versus* (Rizzoli, 1982) and *The Architecture of Exile* (in press, Rizzoli). Tigerman has designed projects throughout the world and was the Architect-in-Residence at the American Academy of Rome in 1980.

The Measure of Architecture (a modest proposal)

In a time between times, in an "absent present," it is not unusual to have instinctually uncertain attitudes reflecting our deep anxieties about language: its ambiguities, its marginalia, its mistakes and, most significantly, its inability to find correspondence with the magnitude of contemporary problems emanating from a culture meandering and unsure about closure (philosophical, cultural, architectural).

It is not only the critical theorist who experiences pangs of uncertainty, disrupting long-held beliefs about the value of closure as the primary strategy for cultural (indeed formal) expression—it is the architect as well. Reason displaces faith, analysis dislocates synthesis, induction replaces deduction: in essence, mortality taints immortality leaving a disjunctively indelible stain. The clearly defined radiant light cast by a platonic architectural precedent loses its distinction, allowing doubt to seep in to the epochal equation denoting a permanently unresolvable quadratic remnant—a troublesome trace of an unachievable state of perfection. The erasure smudges, but does not entirely delete, every former presence of platonic perfection, so that the resulting palimpsest marks the agony of uncertainty (particularly when viewed through a rear-vision mirror reflecting the memory of an original ideal) as the site.

When narrative (linguistic as well as architectural) re-tells distantly original stories (history), the nature (or sign) of language is traditionally seen as consonant with (if indeed not subservient to) "the story line." Even though the story line of origins and history, is supported by language, current theoretical frameworks infer no "close fit"—no consonance between language and its subject—but rather a perpetual disconsonance, which gives rise to the problem in the first place. The "loss of innocence" (the biblical myth of the Garden of Eden, together with its inevitable exile and death) is reenacted innumerable times before it reaches a demarcation point, beyond which doubt creeps in; doubt, not only about narrative, but about the reason(s) why (as well as the way[s] in which) a distant original could be (and is) reiterated. Endlessly reiterative, the closure posited by repetitive, narrative circularity is finally exploded and the last Edenic boundary is breached. Faith in an "ability to return" (the reattainment of a lost innocence) is terminally shattered by irreversible doubts about the capacity of language to heal the wound of disillusionment about a present incapable of delivering us once again to Eden, and with that delivery, a return to parity with a divine being (who, in any case, was murdered long ago).

Despair resulting from "faith" emanating from the inequality, i.e., the failure to match an "original" (which is the future of mimesis), combined with the absence of the original being mimed (God), is overwhelming. After the death of God, one primary question looms large over all others: can mortals, in an epoch keenly aware of its individual and collective mortality, allow life's constituent features—death, fatal diachronicity—to infect language? Can doubt really ever displace certainty as an expressive linguistic (and formalistic) mechanism, or must language (linguistic as well as formal) be perpetually contaminated by deferential, mimetic traditions lingeringly devoted to nostalgia denoted by closure?

Is it possible to evolve a systematic marginalia—a *mistaken* mechanism corresponding to the "errors" of the day? Scientific tradition suggests a possible paradigm.

The mathematical predictability of the Fibonacci

10 series (1,1,2,3,5,...) is one-dimensional compared to Mandelbrot's "fractal" and "scaling" mechanisms (a system capable of measuring complex edges: coastlines, tree configurations, etc.). And yet, there was a time in the not-too-distant past when the Fibonacci series was mathematically broad in scope when related to arithmetic (2,4,6,8,10,12,...), or even geometric (2,4,8,16,32,64,...), progressions. In other words, complex contemporary numeric measurement methods are (and have long been) systematized so as to consistently build upon earlier models by exploding out of them. Hypothetically, linguistic, even architectural, counterparts are also possible.

Languages—linguistic, architectural, mathematical—are all unsurprisingly concerned finally with *measurement.* If languages are necessary to express the complexity of disillusionment (as seen from the apparent clarity resulting from resolution), then one instinctively anticipates correspondence between measurement, and that which is measurable. In short, systems of measurement assume this coincidence.

While new systems of measurement do not escape the problems concerned with the limitations of language, it is unreasonable to continue employing (or exploiting) traditional measurement systems based originally on ancient values no longer valid. Mythic beliefs underpinning ideal ratios such as the golden section 5 : 8, and Le Corbusier's mimetically contrived "Modulor," are platonic in origin. Hellenic concepts of "beauty" do not automatically apply to all subsequent societies: times change, and with them perceptions about such things as apparently instinctual as beauty correspondingly change. If Mies van der Rohe's 1923 explicit utterance that "architecture is the will of an epoch translated into space" transcends the particularity of Post-World War I temporality, and if Hegel's notion that the knowledge of art results only from comprehensive insights into the epoch in which that particular art evolves, then it is necessary to comprehend the values of the day so as to convincingly express them. It follows that measurement systems are concurrent with the elements measured in order to be effective. Thus, the spirit of the age, the "zeitgeist," concurs with, or defines, the elements measured.

While the values of our time appear to be clouded over by interpretation, it is precisely that exegetic operation which unpacks earlier zeitgeist notions that, in hindsight, appear to have failed (whereas during the epoch they appeared to synthesize).

Interpretation, not resolution, influences contemporary desires to revolutionize language as a means of communication sufficiently comprehensive to express the immeasurably immense complexity—and (not surprisingly) the resulting disillusionment—of our age. But, it is not only generalized interpretation within a larger order of ideal systems that is called for. After all, interpretation as a mechanism of illumination has been intrinsic to all western culture. Contemporary interpretation demands *distance* from all acculturated umbrella traditions, and hierarchical value systems. Freed from relationality, an interpretation so distanced from precedent stands in splendid isolation, detached from mimetically contrived re-iterative thinking. The independent interpretation to which I allude is then, and only then, finally, *metonymic* (the naming of a thing by one of its attributes) rather than *metaphoric* (an object likened to another by speaking of it as if it were that other).

Recent architectural interest in "fragmenting," "rupturing," "cleaving," i.e., the exploitation of disruptive strategies for expressive purposes, is a logical response to correspondingly dislocative social tendencies. That these strategies have value within the context of value systems based on hierarchical traditions is quite another matter: suffice it to say that dislocative design methodologies infect the lexicon of contemporary architectural ideation. These strategies symbolize the growing disillusionment with traditional architectural techniques originating from belief in "closure" (now seen as an inappropriate and outdated vehicle incapable of expressing the exilic nature of the day). Our contemporary period revels in open-ended strategies inadvertently displaying an inability—or at least an unwillingness—to return to closure. Curiously romantic in origin, such persuasions are not nearly as romantic as *mimesis* in its most blatant historicist re-presentation. But these persuasions are, nonetheless, romantic just as the commonly understood resistance to categorize them as constituent parts of an acceptable architectural language is romantic.

Isolated counter-reason, counter-epistemological applications of dislocative strategies denote the continuing power of traditional (and cultural) linguistic entrenchment. Instinct, desire, faith, is all that is left after closure becomes impossible. As yet, there is little evidence that social disillusionment has been sufficiently defined, so that a corresponding linguistic system capable of representing the pain resulting from disillusionment with contemporaneity appears. On the other hand, Jacques Derrida would say that language represents pain—or violence. Others would say that language is always ambiguous. We have repressed these thoughts about language in order to perpetrate our seamless narratives about the past. We have ignored the more subtle performances of language. The power, as well as the presence of culture (legitimated by the force, as well as the repetitiveness, of history), denies the potential for significant linguistic modification that could reflect the intrinsic ambiguity (as opposed to the imagined clarity) of the times. Only mute, indeed sometimes autistic challenges to verifiable cultural traditions seem plausible at this time. It may now be necessary to articulate the inarticulate—to speak, where it has not seemed possible to do so before.

Perhaps architecture can erect these more subtle performances, displaying them for all to see (and measure them as well). Architecture might be the force behind the development of a new language of measurement, for architecture knows something about silent speaking.

Architecture is not normally associated with death, or even, for that matter, pain. Its conventions are rooted in perpetual belief systems corresponding to life, or at its most elevated (and, incidentally, elegant) to life after death. Through historic tradition, architecture is inexorably linked with aspirations toward *ideals* perpetuated through reiteration, and, as such, remains reliant upon an independent truth that breathes life into it (after all, Plato says that "art is in the shadow of truth"). While it is fitting that an architecture of ideals expresses theocentric, or even anthropocentric aspirations for societies accordingly driven, when those epochal values become estranged, measurement, inevitably the expression of ideals displaced, must correspondingly change.

Death is the terminal displacement of life. Displacement needs recognition as an *autonomous* agent (autonomy is thought of here as a condition, or refusal to "play the game"), so that it can be analyzed typologically toward the end of codification. Unfortunately, displacement is dislocated from conventional judgments about such things because of an insistence on closure as an overriding measuring mechanism. And yet, when displacement is detached from cultural traditions (displacement is conventionally perceived as being inscribed in culture), it has distinct, easily definable, scientifically supportable, features. Qualities such as alterity, breaking, excising, interrupting, rupturing, severing, and shearing, are moments of displacement worth examining in isolation from the forces of culture. But it is the condition of autonomy itself that brings these examinations into being, since it is autonomy that recognizes displacement as a unique element worth setting away from cultural pressure. In other words, autonomy can be perceived as a non-systematic system of randomness (such as fractals).

Autonomy implies distance—removal. The converse of contextualism, autonomy is defined by *detachment*, rather than *attachment* to things past, or things alongside the autonomous subject. Independent of precedent, things autonomous are self-reliant, just as they are eminently vulnerable. Unsupported by history, things autonomous can only be analyzed without the burden (or blessing, depending on your view) of contextualism, which in turn reinforces dialectical reasoning. After all, the converse of a thing, however apparently oppositional, infers the original's definition by opposing (thus clarifying, while it legitimates) it.

Traditional formal mechanisms, such as axiality, symmetry, superposition, and superimposition continue to inform, indeed to dominate, architectural expression. These traditions enjoy reiteration as a sign of authenticity. Even during "modernism's"

apogee (the decades bracketing either side of World War I), the apparently contradictory condition of (a)symmetry, exploited dialectically conventional language (symmetry) to align itself with, and gain legitimacy by, the use of a cunning oppositional strategy. Precisely apprehended in the same way as "black is best perceived in the presence of white," asymmetry could thus be best understood by first comprehending symmetry. One of the results of this formal dialogue was that the socialistic, revolutionary implications underpinning such formalistic extensions were quietly, but deftly, neutralized. Such is the nature of the transitional phase of early twentieth-century expression where the exploitation of dialectical thought reaffirms, indeed perpetuates precedent as it appears to support change.

A revolutionary measuring mechanism not dependent upon metaphorical, relational correspondence to cultural verifiability for its intrinsic meaning is needed—one that is autonomous and removed entirely from antecedent legitimation.

A strategy needs to be brought into existence *precisely* to resist closure. A metonymic, rather than a metaphoric, methodology is required in order to resist the tradition of mimesis.

Distance is needed from that which is both familiar and comforting in language. Language (as we know it) is incapable of expressing the intrinsic disillusionment of the day. It is repressed when it denotes pain or violence.

This is not a plea for yet another "zeitgeist" mentality as an instrument of the forces for resolution. A new zeitgeist embodying the "disillusionment of the day" would play into the hands of the programmatic, the non-autonomous, the anticipated "new plan of domination" that this "new era" will advance. Generations of human beings have only known a strategy of resolution to express the nature of their day. The problem of "carry over" of that strategy is regressive since it retards the potentiality for a continuously interpretive mechanism that relates to epochal instability, just as it retards understanding individual, as well as collective, temporality.

Accomplishments of the magnitude suggested herein demand an understanding that the nature of this epoch is one sufficiently different from earlier periods so as to warrant mechanisms uniquely conceived to induce appropriate expressions corresponding to the extraordinary complexities of the time. A prerequisite for such an understanding is grounded in accepting *as fact* the disillusionment with the present. A position such as this rejects the nostalgia of "loss of innocence," and accepts (for the first time) the utter futility of a return to an original, guileless state, providing parity with an absent divine being. Such an acceptance is far more revolutionary than the modest proposal for a correspondent measuring mechanism: *that* result is inevitable, naturally.

GIOVANNA BORRADORI is a professor in the Faculty of Architecture at Politecnico di Milano. She was a research fellow at the Center for Twentieth Century Studies (University of Wisconsin-Milwaukee) and assistant editor for an Italian philosophy journal, *Fenomenologie e Scienze dell'Uomo*. She is the editor of *Il Pensiero Post-Filosofico* (Jaca Books, 1988) and *Recoding Metaphysics: The New Italian Philosophy* (Northwestern University Press, 1988).

Towards an Architecture of Exile
A Conversation with Jean-François Lyotard

Introduction

The broad interdisciplinary impact of *The Postmodern Condition* (1979) by Jean-François Lyotard confirms a suspicion that has animated philosophical as well as architectural debate since at least the late sixties: the suspicion that the historical cycle of modernity has come to an end, and that the right time had come to formulate again the statutes of legitimacy of knowledge, of the project, and of the project's know-how.

An *echolalia* of idiosyncrasies in the latest avant-garde movements are witnesses to a general need to de-construct the dominant codes of modernism by dis-placing, de-centering and de- mistifying the order of its meanings. The postmodern proclivity for fragmented and disconnected signs, and the deep disenchantment with every form of "totalization" —social, epistemic, poetic—push it towards the subliminal territories of *montage, collage, pastiche, paradox, paralogism, parataxis*. The dispersal of the boundaries which used to demarcate literary genres and architectural typologies, the progressive hybridization of poetics, the "de-definition" (Harold Rosenberg) of modes of representation, are some of the outcomes of this "carnevalization" (Michel Bakhtin) of modernism, that is the anarchic *ethos* of postmodernism.

By announcing—after "the death of God"—"the death of the Author," postmodern man has dissipated the traditional self and suddenly found himself submerged by a hemorrhage of signs. The assertive and subversive potentiality of modern ego has now collapsed into the self-referential labyrinth of textuality: ego itself has become part of the text, part of an immanent semiotic system. By its own textual nature the postmodern text is bound to performance. Theater isn't a poetics anymore, but the form in which postmodern culture presents itself: reality itself owns a fictional character given by the fact that, in our age, everything comes always already reproduced, linguistically mediated. "Art is everywhere for artifice stands right in the center of reality" (Jean Baudrillard). In the "society of spectacle" (Jacques Débord), the aesthetic charm is everywhere.

What kind of legitimacy is then left to knowledge? In what terms is it possible to think of knowledge as a unitary body, as a *system*, organically conceived? These are the questions which open *The Postmodern Condition*. The first answer given by Lyotard is that the function of postmodern knowledge "is to refine our sense of difference and to strengthen our capacity to stand the incommensurable." To activate knowledge means activating "differences," discontinuities, the openness of the sense towards always new interpretations—for innovation always rises from dissent. Lyotard's formulation of the social, cognitive and aesthetic notion of an "open system"—the anti- model of a stable system—is based on difference and discontinuity insofar as its role is in "generating ideas." To attempt mediation between indeterminacy and systematic control, and yet keep the notion of "open system," is a contradiction in terms. How is it possible to keep "in control" the strategy of an indeterminate system, a system which is supposed to develop, organically, around dissent and the creative potential of difference?

This question, which occupies the first section of this interview, becomes somewhat disquieting when the notion of "open system" is applied to the sociological realm, where the problem of keeping the open system's strategy in control translates itself into the problem of governability (see the entire discussion on terrorism).

In order to initially justify his idea of an "open system," Lyotard states that postmodernism is an historical category, which can be applied only to capitalist hyper-developed countries. The West has lost many of the traditional referents of modernity, such as the struggle for material welfare and the efficiency of technological development in relation to the improvement of living standards (in short, the value of "progress" for its own sake). In the West the problem of survival is no longer a biological one, but an aesthetic, ethical and moral one. This is, briefly, the irreconcilable "difference" between the West and the so called Third World countries. The question in Third World countries is how to survive on the earth; for the West the question is how "to live elsewhere." The West, according to Lyotard, bases the organization of its time and the architecture of its spaces on the category of "living elsewhere," "in exile" from earth. The imagery of this "elsewhere" infuses our concept of "progress" and technological creativity; and it orients the design of our territory, our houses and our cities. The anxiety about living "elsewhere" animates the inner competition among western countries, which is the only "true" referent left to the West. The last tasks of our civilization are no longer the "modernist" ones: the future, today, is less problematic than the past. For the Third World the future is still a basic and foundational issue.

We build, today, "in terms of the past" more than "for the future." What distinguishes our postmodern condition is thus the ineluctability of our confrontation with history, which is the radical citationality of our being. The irreducible trait of postmodern sensibility is that it is always looking for a refinement of the procedures of interrogation and interpretation of the Western historical conscience. Therefore, Lyotard examines the need for a "thought of non-control," that is, a thought that is not based on pragmatic evidence or on consensual outcomes of a conversation (Richard Rorty), but on dissent, on irreconcilable disagreements, on the silences which lie in the white typographic spacings. In other words, a thought that is able to record the incommensurability of desire by letting itself engage in an "inattentive meditation," similar to the state Freud defined as an "equally floating attention," attention that has to deal with the unconscious mechanism of free-association. Postmodern subjectivity is thus a "weak" one (Gianni Vattimo), inasmuch as it does not assume any *a priori* world vision, aesthetic project, or predetermined moral stance. "Art should listen to language," as Martin Heidegger said. This is an historic as well as a metaphysical statement. Art must "weaken," step by step, the programmatic statements of modernity.

In the arts, in philosophy, as well as in architecture we have to deal with the abandonment of the concept of "innovation" for its own sake and with the adhesion to a positive relationship to history. This is not a chance one can take or not. Looking through western history, this is, over and over again, an ineluctable process for a civilization, like ours, presently working at the complex project of a new Noah's Ark, a "Noè Arch." To this extent "building in terms of the past" is not a conservative choice, but simply what gives us the strength "to build for the future."

14   JEAN-FRANÇOIS LYOTARD is a professor at the Université Paris VIII-Vincennes à Saint Denis and a permanent visiting professor at the University of California, Irvine. Until 1986 he was Director of the College International de Philosophie in Paris. He conceived and organized the monumental exposition at the Centre Pompidou, *Les immateriaux*, in 1985. He has written extensively on philosophy and postmodernism. His books include the seminal text *The Postmodern Condition* (first published 1974; University of Minnesota Press, 1984).

Conversation with Jean-François Lyotard

Translated from the French by Giovanna Borradori

Giovanna Borradori: In your book *The Postmodern Condition* you criticize Luhmann for having based the notion of *social system* on a "terroristic" statement, insofar as by "terror" you mean the identification between the "interlocutor" of the linguistic game, and the linguistic game itself. Luhmann's assumption, which can be defined in terms of a "radical functionalism," doesn't leave any legitimacy to the critical and/or trangressive space western culture has allowed the intellectual as his proper and historical role. On the contrary, your idea of an "open system" is so entirely based on the notion of "difference," that the stability of the system itself is supposed to derive from a "paradoxical" and "paralogistic" structure whose task is "generating ideas." But if I try to translate this discourse from its pure theoretical frame into the frame of political praxis (which I see very much already in your choice of the word "system"), the whole issue concerning the creative potential of difference has to face the problem of "governability": that is, how to keep difference in control.

Jean-François Lyotard: The idea of an "open system" presupposes the capability to formulate propositions within an exchange of ideas, an exchange of words, works, "open" objects. The "openness" of the system presupposes something which seems to me to be stable by itself, that is a "social link," a communicability, *la langue même*. Particularly within a system of this kind it is interesting to insist on little "quarrels" (*différends*), being aware of the fact that this could be painful—which means that some people might not be fully understood, that some propositions will not be understood at all, that some conflicts might not be solved, or at least not in the short run. But all this has to happen *within* a system. For example, in an artistic community, let's take the community of the so called developed

countries: there can be conflicts, even very deep ones—there can be artists and art not sufficiently recognized—nevertheless all this happens within a unitary space, an open one, in which each person keeps going toward what he or she wants to achieve.

Concerning terrorism *tout court*, it is very difficult to think of it in terms of the philosophy of politics. I believe that terrorism—because it comes from that part of humankind called the Third World—is much more than political. I mean that everything seems to happen as if a *coupure* which divides humankind in two parts were already accepted; as if two totally different stakes had already been established for each one of those two parts. On the one hand there are the hyper-developed countries, which have at stake their internal competition: that is, to gain more knowledge, more technological power, to accelerate the process of appropriation of time and space, at an earthly as well as at a cosmic level. Good or bad, this kind of competition is what western civilization has been based on for centuries. It means nothing to say that it is moved by an indiscriminate will to power or desire to dominate. Simply, it is the "unconscious being" of western civilization... This is our "sense," if there is one— even if we tried to get rid of it, we wouldn't succeed. On the other hand, there is the "other" part of humankind, for whom the stakes are survival, not competition for further development. This second group of humankind has at stake something that belongs very specifically to every biological species living on earth. For instance, the larger part of Africa looks at survival as a biological problem, whereas hyper-developed countries look at it as the problem of surviving *within* technologies. We are training ourselves to evacuate earth, since we are aware of the fact that the sun will be extinguished within four million years. We are preparing our own "exile." We work on problems of human survival in space. We are building a new Noah's ark.

GB: From what you say, it seems to me that an immediate consequence can be drawn: the "other" part of humankind, the one whose values of survival are still somehow tied to a biological horizon, hasn't yet lost the "referent," which would imply that post-structuralist notions—such as Baudrillard's "hyperreal"—are historical-geographical notions that apply only to our western reality.

JFL: Yes, I do believe that for the Third World the problem is *vivre/survivre* on earth, whereas for the West it is *vivre/survivre* somewhere else. I think that terrorism is somehow connected with the awareness that it is already too late and that the difference/discrepancy between the two parts of humankind will continue to grow. It is as if terrorism expressed the terror of being lost. When one is lost, there is nothing left to lose.

GB: This discussion makes me think of two definitions you present in your book (*The Postmodern Condition*). In the first place I think of your idea of subjectivity as a merely "linguistic" knot within a communication system. In the second place, I think your assumption of the multiplicity of language games as "linguistic heteromorphism"—a notion in which you root the possibility of "freely" conceiving the relation between culture and reality—is not *a priori*, that is, fixed within an ideological framework. Going back to the radical difference between the West and the Third World (if it is possible to interpret it in linguistic terms): each one of the two cultures enacts its discourse within a different language game, but both discourses act within a unitary open system. In the same way different language games establish their interrelation on the basis of a quarrel (*différend*) which cannot be solved through a discursive explanation. Do you think that terrorism can be interpreted as an extreme form of *différend*? Is it allowable to think of it in terms of the most radical form of *différence/différend* within a common open system (implicitly, this would legitimize it theoretically)? Is your notion of *différence/différend* an epistemological or an ethical one?

JFL: The *différend* presupposes a peculiar organization of discourse—an organization that allows the coexistence of many types of discourse. The political expression of this organization is "tolerance," and its political space is the "republic": a linguistic space where types of discourse (and their different versions) can engender themselves. It can happen that some of them aren't recognized, or even refused, but conflicts can't end up in the death of one of the interlocutors. Nobody has to die. This is the privilege of our contemporary societies, and it also embodies their very high level of complexity. If you take, for instance, Iranian society, this level of complexity is totally excluded. Any *différend* is excluded. Everybody has to play the same language game. This is terror.

GB: I would like to investigate a little more your notion of *différence/différend* as an epistemological means "to generate ideas," or, as you say, to keep the system "open." When you try to explain the "openness" of the system on an epistemological level you bring up the notion of "free association," which also refers to the idea that "sense" comes to the surface -without being predicted or predetermined—in the process of thinking, during the process of experiencing. I would like to understand how you connect the notion of "system" itself (which, even if open, implies the issue of "control"), and the notion of indeterminacy, somehow intrinsic to your definition of free-associating differences.

JFL: The *différend* between the West and the Third World is rooted in the fact that, since the Renaissance, the West has played within that specific language game called "techno- science." Us, the intel-

lectual class, after reading Nietzsche and Heidegger, Plato and the Sophists, feel ourselves to be, at the same time, in a passionate and in a timorous position. We keep issuing warnings by saying that the techno-science game is a totalitarian language game based on terror, which compels everyone who does not want to be thrown out of the system to be performative. This is true. But it is also true that we couldn't have enacted this criticism if we weren't ourselves "products" of this same system. Heidegger says this in his essay, "The Question Around Technique." It is from within this specific concern that I speak of free-association, indeterminacy, etc. For the Third World the only alternative would be to take possession of the techno-scientific discourse. And this is hard to imagine: we are always tempted to be a little simplistic in this regard. Africa and the Orient cannot be thought of as a Heideggerian "poetic modality" of *Dichtung*. When Edward Said says: "be careful this is orientalism," he's right. It isn't that simple. Even Heidegger's conversation with a Japanese, which I love very much, well, I think we should be a little suspicious of it: this is also orientalism.

Anyway, I believe that in our world it is very important for the intellectual class to advocate something like free- association. For instance, it is clear that behind the whole notion of postmodernism many people see just the performative criteria, that is, the rising hegemony of techno-scientific discourse in fields where it didn't use to be hegemonic at all: such as the body, sexuality, feelings, nature. All this has become part of the dominion of techno-scientific understanding: only what is relevant and performative (how well it works) becomes important.

GB: On both sides of the ocean, it seems to me that the suspicion toward technology as a foundational category is becoming more diffused. Increasingly, technology, as such, appears to be an obsolete materialist category which asks to be redefined through the new patterns given by the "society of spectacle" (Jacques Débord).

JFL: I think that the "spectacle" has been a brief moment. As a matter of fact, this represents the main difference between Baudrillard and myself.

GB: Still, at least from my Italian point of view, I look at the problematic of the "image" as a very crucial one. Probably this has to do with the fact that, within the world role assignments, Italy, and perhaps France, have been given an "image-maker" role model.

JFL: Image and spectacle are the forms in which Mediterranean civilization has been able, throughout history, to transform technologies, to make the "beautiful." This is a very old tradition... But I believe that the crucial change we are staring at today depends on techno-scientific skill. It is possible to create a brand-new universe (this is the new

16 media) of images—musical, visual, spoken ones, which can be rapidly diffused. But the constitutive trait of this universe is the relation it has with time and space: which means, "as soon as possible," "in the shortest time," "the largest amount of space covered." Basically, this is what happens to the book as an object today: booksellers buy books strictly according to the law of supply and demand. Publishers want to be sure, before a book comes out, that a certain number of copies can be sold within the first six months. This has an influence on the way we think of the problem: this is technology, not spectacle. This is the strength of "capital" itself.

GB: The word capital leads me to ask you your opinion about the neo-pragmatist invitation to recuperate a socially active role for culture, given the refusal to think of culture through the Habermasian "emancipative" perspective.

JFL: Right now in Europe there isn't any synchronicity among political movements. But in the long run I think that Europe will progressively orientate itself toward the "center"—socialists as well as the extreme right. What does the center mean? It means that everybody agrees on the main issues. In France, for example, the last socialist government expressed middle-of-the-road politics at every level—social, financial, cultural. Most people would say there was no alternative. As a matter of fact there are alternatives, but they concern only a small piece of the national budget. The problem is: either we decide to devote this fringe to theatre, film studies, publications, or we decide to build up new prisons, new cars for policemen...

GB: To some extent it is true that the "center" as such is neo-pragmatist, at least because the Rortian notion of conversation is what the center has actually to do with. However, I think that an important point should be clarified, especially if our discourse is allowed to invade the socio-political realm: given the difference between the neo-pragmatist "continuous," or negotiative, strategy and the "localistic" and discontinuous form of postmodern thought, how can these two positions legitimately interact?

JFL: From the socio-political point of view Rorty is right: we have to enact a conversation. There isn't anything better to do. Obviously, this means to enact a conversation on various topics: such as human rights, freedom, security, etc., and therefore on the use of wealth. The political strategies of the French socialist government have been a catastrophe, as well as those advocated by the French communist party: there is no alternative at this macro level.

I do believe that the task of the intellectuals—if there is one, and if there are still intellectuals around—is to "push" toward conversation. I think that the system needs us for this purpose. What the system does not need is to fall asleep during our conversation, which risks becoming a discussion about the 2% or 3% of the budget which can be devoted to educational expenses, etc. This position can be defined as the "totalitarianism of conversation." Rorty doesn't want to understand this. I think, rather, that our task is to always provoke new quarrels and differences (*différend/différences*); to say no, to point out what belongs to the order of thinking I call "thought of control." Our task is to cultivate a "thought of non-control," which lets itself emerge from things, from ideas, from associations, from those images which can look odd, dangerous, certainly disquieting, but which are the true resources of thought. I see our task in being "present," which means pointing out that there is something "other" and someone "other." Certainly we converse with one another, but there is always something "other" (*autre*) which cannot be confused with the others (*autres*).

GB: What you think about the "thought of non-control," which lets itself emerge spontaneously from things, is interesting, particularly if related to the question of technology. In order to let thought come out of things, one can just "float," as you said, somewhere else, in between them, without positing any sort of dialectical conversation with them. But in our postmodern moment the distinction between natural and artificial, *façon* and *contrefaçon*, nature and technique cannot be detected so easily. If thought has to come out of things in order to be abandoned to the destiny things lead it to, thought itself must also be abandoned. It then becomes a rhetorical partner of technology—it legitimates technology.

JFL: This is true. But is there something beyond rhetorics? Anyway, I do not understand the verb to float (*flotter*) as you do. In my use it does not have any conversational meaning. I think that the Freudian notion of "equally floating attention" is by no means conversational. The link between a passion and its unconscious referent isn't conversational at all; rather, it means loneliness and anxiety. The *libraiment flottent* I am speaking of doesn't refer to the good mood implied by conversation, but rather to the restlessness of the sense: in other words, it reveals the orientation of desire, if this is possible.

To some extent no species of thought belongs to the order of conversation. Conversation—to listen to one another—exists already by itself. When Gianni Vattimo speaks of "weakness" (*debolezza*), I think he means what we assume from and through free-association: the effort not to enact a conversation, but rather to listen to something that you can't really "hear" in a conversation.

GB: What you're saying about weakness is also related to the refusal to assume the "strong" constitutive attitude of the subject toward reality, theorized by phenomenology.

JFL: From this point of view, weakness is good because to be weak means actually to be strong... in relation to the "other." The relationship you can have with technology isn't a conversational one: if you speak to machines, well, you end up doing what they have been programmed to do. On the contrary, one should try to have a "weak" relationship with them, in Vattimo's words. For example, I love Godard because he looks exactly for what I'm saying now: through rhetorical means, of course. Some of his decisions are rhetorical, but it is a rhetoric based on the weakening of control over the image.

GB: If an artist had to interpret what you're saying about weakness and technology, do you think he or she would use citation as a foundational expressive means? How would this sort of "quotationism" be related to the modernist concept of "innovation"?

JFL: The concept of innovation is itself a wrong one, for it is an industrial and not an artistic concept. The true artwork is never based on innovation, but rather on re-sumption, re-commencement. The artwork does not want to say: "I will do better," but "I will do something else, reflecting upon what has already been done." Malraux used to say that "a painter is a man who looks at paintings": in the same way, a writer is a man who reads books.

Editorial note: The title of this article coincidentally corresponds to the title of a forthcoming book by Stanley Tigerman, *The Architecture of Exile*. Lyotard's discussion of "survival elsewhere" is an uncanny analogue of Tigerman's concept of "exile on earth."

MARK C. TAYLOR is the William R. Kenan, Jr. Professor of Reglion and Director of the Center for Humanities and Social Sciences at Williams College. His most recent books include *Erring: A Postmodern A theology*, *Deconstruction in Context: Literature and Philosophy*, and *Alterity*, all published by the University of Chicago Press.

Deadlines
Approaching
Anarchetecture

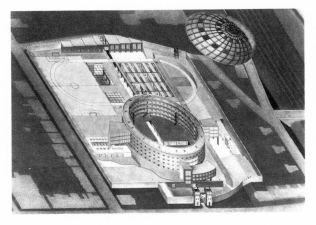

Figure 1
Rem Koolhaas with Stefano diMartino
Project for alterations to Arnheim Prison
Netherlands, 1979

[Dead Lines]

"Sometimes she is far away, very far away," she said, *making an impressive gesture with her hand.*
"In the past?" I asked timidly.
"Oh, much farther away!"
I pondered, trying to discover what could really be farther away than the past. Meanwhile, she seemed all of a sudden afraid that she had thrown me slightly beyond the limits.

When the Time Comes, Blanchot

Prison
House

What is a deadline? Is it temporal? Or spatial?
Temporal: A time limit, as for payment of a debt or completion of an assignment.
Spatial: A boundary line in a prison that prisoners can cross only at the risk of being shot.
Neither simply temporal nor spatial, the deadline is "the becoming-time of space and the becoming-space of time."[1] As the intersection of time and space in which time is spaced and space timed, the deadline is a THRESHOLD, an irreducible threshold that is never present as such. To cross the threshold of the deadline is to run the risk of being shot dead.

But what is the prison that the deadline surrounds? Who or what is the jailer? Perhaps, but only perhaps for in this case insiders *cannot* know, the prison house is language and the jailer the penal eye/I of reason. The eye of reason that guards the prison house of language must be panoptical.

Bentham's *Panopticon* is the architectural figure of this composition. We know the principle on which it was based: at the periphery, an annular building; at the center, a tower; this tower is pierced with wide windows that open onto the inner side of the ring; the peripheric building is divided into cells, each of which extends the whole width of the building...All that is needed, then, is to place a supervisor in a central tower and to shut up in each cell a madman, a patient, a condemned man, a worker or a schoolboy.[2]

If the prison house is constructed by securing the deadline, then can the gaze of reason really be panoptical? Or is such vision but a dream—a dream of the master who is never really master even in "his own" house? What if the circle of prison house is redrawn as an ellipse without a penal tower in its midst? Is the figure of the ellipse the (re)inscription of unavoidable ellipsis and/or vice versa?[3] Is the ellipse/ellipsis what the deadline surrounding the prison house of language is constructed to erase?[4] Is the ellipse/ellipsis the blindspot that drives reason mad by exposing its impotence? Might this impotence be traced by decapitating the prison rather than the prisoners...as when Bentham is refigured by Koolhaas and diMartino? In such a prison house the gaze would always be the castrating gaze of Medusa.

Are such deadlines (simply) graphic? Or are they inevitably elliptic—even cryptic?

The Present/Presence of the Modern

Modernity is preoccupied with the presence of the present and the present of presence—the *hic et nunc, ici et maintenant.* The word "modern" derives from the Latin *modernus,* which means "just now." The modern is of the present and not of the past. The present/presence of the modern is affirmed by the negation of the past. Rupture is announced in the dictum: "Make it new!" Or so it seems. It is, of course, possible for the repressed to return unexpectedly. What if the presence of the modern, which seems to arrive in the break with tradition, turns out to be the culmination of the tradition itself?

The search for the new is the search for originality. The original is not derivative; it is primary not secondary, independent not dependent...on an Other/other (O/other). In different terms, to be original is to be present at an origin or an *arche* that is nothing O/other, or more precisely, is nothing other than oneself. So understood, the quest for originality has always been the dream of Western theology, philosophy and art. As Heidegger points out: "What characterizes [Western] metaphysical thinking, which grounds the ground for beings, is the fact that metaphysical thinking departs from what is present in its presence, and thus represents it in terms of its ground as something grounded."[5] During the modern era, the quest for grounding presence takes the form of the search for a subject that is truly original. Descartes' inward turn to the subject reaches a certain closure in Hegel's dialectical philosophy. According to Hegel, the subject comes to completion in and through "pure self-recognition in absolute otherness." In this panoptical gaze, subject and object achieve perfect transparency. The logos of the object and the logos of the subject join to form a consciousness that is, in fact, self-consciousness. The subject becomes *present* to itself *here and now* in everything that seems to be other than itself. When every difference returns to identity, the subject is grounded in nothing other than itself. The self-grounded subject is original. Such originality has been the end of the

Western tradition from the beginning. Sometimes, however, the end is not the end.

The modern philosophy of the subject extends into the 20th-century in forms of reflection as seemingly different as phenomenology and structuralism. Following Hegel, Husserl regards philosophy as a "universal science" that seeks perfect clarity and certainty by uncovering the "absolute foundations" of knowledge. A phenomenon, for Husserl, is an entity *as it appears to consciousness.* The task of the phenomenologist is to *describe* all being as being-for-consciousness. Through this description, it becomes apparent that every object of experience is the product of a constituting subject. This subject is "the transcendental ego" that projects the world of experience through its "intentional" activity. In examining the object of consciousness, the phenomenologist does not look for empirical data but seeks the ideal logos which, having been constructed by the transcendental subject, constitutes the objectivity of the object. Husserl labels the essential structure of the object its *eidos.* The eidos is the unchanging form that secures the spatial and temporal presence of the object. The phenomenological eidos is reinscribed in the patterns and codes uncovered in structural analysis. For the structuralist, the object of investigation, be that object a text, a work of art, or psychological and historical processes, is essentially formal. Interpretation moves toward something like eidetic vision in which the knowing subject sees the formal structure that is *present* in the known object. This unifying vision presupposes the isomorphism of subjectivity and objectivity. In a manner reminiscent of Hegel, a structuralist like Levi-Strauss insists that knowledge must become encyclopedic.

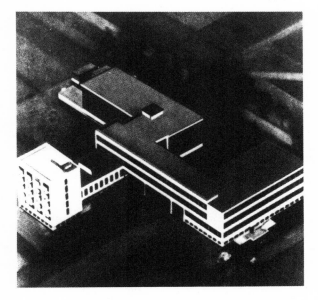

Figure 2
Walter Gropius
Bauhaus, Dessau, 1927

20 It would be a mistake to think that the modern philosophy of the subject that seems to reach closure in Hegel's System resurfaces in this century only in philosophy and the social sciences. It is possible to understand the formalism of abstract art and high modern architecture as the refiguration of philosophical phenomenology and linguistic structuralism. As the phenomenologist attempts to bracket the natural attitude of consciousness and the structuralist struggles to suspend historical supplements in order to discover the essential form of the object, so the modern architect seeks to manifest the transparency of structure by erasing historical reference. In the absence of quotation, the structure of the architectural object is supposed to be self-referential. The self-referentiality of the created object is the perfect reflection of the reflexivity of the creative subject. The arche of the modern *archetect* is nothing O/other than the creative subject of modern philosophy. The erasure of history in the construction of pure form represents an effort to secure a present/presence that is undisturbed by the past. The search for this "now" is what defines modernism. What most modernists do not understand is that the present/presence of this "now" remains thoroughly traditional. The repressed returns to establish continuity where there had appeared to be discontinuity. Just as an end sometimes is not an end, so a beginning sometimes is not a beginning.

Presence of the Past

In 1980, Paolo Portoghesi, Charles Jencks, and others organized the Biennale of Architecture in the old Arsenale in Venice around the theme "The Presence of the Past." More recently, Heinrich Klotz mounted a more extensive exhibition, first shown in Frankfurt, entitled "Die Revision der Moderne: Postmodern Architecture 1960-1985." These two shows amply illustrate the remarkable changes architecture has undergone over the past two decades. Gone are the simplicity and formalism of the International Style. Instead of structure purified of decoration and ornamentation, we discover forms, sometimes irregular or even fragmented, cluttered with details that are historically allusive. The shift from the modern to the postmodern involves a return to or of history. Rather than trying to affirm the present by breaking with the past, the postmodern gestures of citation and quotation repeatedly invoke the presence of the past. Tradition returns but with a difference. In their writings, Jencks and Klotz have done much to illuminate the complex relationship between modernism and postmodernism.

As early as 1978, Jencks defined postmodernism as "double coding: the combination of Modern techniques with something else (usually traditional building) in order for architecture to communicate with the public and a concerned minority, usually of other architects."[6] The strategy of communicating on different levels at the same time represents an effort to overcome the inadequacies of modernism. "Modern architecture," Jencks maintains, "had failed to remain credible partly because it didn't communicate effectively with its ultimate users...and partly because it didn't make effective links with the city and history."[7] By joining past to present and present to past, the postmodern architect constructs a double code, which, according to Jencks, is intended to communicate in different ways to different people. The polymorphous perversity of architectural forms generates a polysemy that is creative rather than destructive. Such plurivocality undercuts the possibility of all univocality. It is important to understand the precise nature of the polysemy Jencks identifies. Each message in the double code is, in principle, understandable. The duplicity of meaning results when different messages are conjoined. Jencks' double code, therefore, simultaneously multiplies meaning and *controls* its proliferation.

When plurivocality is radicalized, single-mindedness becomes impossible. Equivocality displaces univocality and truths that once seemed certain begin to appear undeniably fictive. Anticipating much of Jencks' argument, Klotz contends that postmodernism represents "an architecture of narrative, symbolism and fantasy."[8] Klotz recognizes that the rehistoricization of architectural form through supplementary details and ornaments involves neither a reactionary response to modernism nor a nostalgia for the simplicity and security of earlier times. The past that returns in historical citation is transformed through its reinscription. When quoted by the postmodern architect the past is, in effect, rewritten as fiction. The past that is present as fiction is never simply represented. Rather, representation itself is refigured in and through repetition.

The implications of the refiguration of representation, which prepares the way for the presence of the past in postmodern architecture, can be seen by noting central insights that emerge in contemporary semiology. Signs, we have learned, do not represent objects or events that once were present. To the contrary, the sign is always the sign of a sign. Forever entangled in the play of signification, we never have access to things themselves and thus cannot penetrate naked reality. What we often naively take to be objectivity is actually nothing other than a sign or set of signs whose signature has been forgotten. Inasmuch as we deal only with signs and never with "reality" as such, our knowledge is inescapably fictive. Unlike (almost all) his predecessors, the postmodernist not only recognizes but gaily embraces the fictions among which he is destined to err. It is, of course, Nietzsche who is the most prescient precursor of this postmodern understanding of understanding.

Against positivism, which halts at phenomena—"There are only *facts*"—I would say: No, facts is precisely what there is not, only interpretations. We cannot establish any fact "in itself": perhaps it is folly to want to do such a thing...Insofar as the word "knowledge" has any meaning, the world is knowable; but it is *interpretable* otherwise, it has no meaning behind it, but countless meanings. —Perspectivism.[9]

Nowhere have the implications of Nietzsche's fragmentary account of interpretation been more artfully expressed than in the poetry of Wallace Stevens. In a poem entitled "Asides on the Oboe," Stevens rereads Nietzsche's perspectivism in terms of poetic fiction.

> The prologues are over. It is a question, now,
> Of final belief. So, say that final belief
> Must be in a fiction. It is time to choose...
> The impossible possible philosophers' man,
> The man who has had the time to think enough,
> The central man, the human globe, responsive
> As a mirror with a voice, the man of glass,
> Who in a million diamonds sums us up...
> It was not as if the jasmine ever returned
> But we and the diamond globe at last were one.
> We had always been partly one. It was as we came
> To see him, that we were wholly one, as we heard
> Him chanting for those buried in their blood,
> In the jasmine haunted forests, that we knew
> The glass man, without external reference.[10]

Postmodern fictions are as fragile as the glas(s) man who makes them. This fragility is the result of the recognition of fiction as fiction. In the postmodern world, belief is both impossible and unavoidable. The fictions we fabricate do not refer in any straightforward way to things or events "out there" in the "real" world. That world, like Kant's thing-in-itself, is completely inaccessible and hence functionally nonexistent. In different terms, the concept of reality or the notion the true world is nothing but another fiction that we invent (usually unknowingly) to check and balance the signs from which there is no exit. Stevens summarizes the complex interplay between fiction and belief in an important posthumous text: "The final belief is to believe in a fiction, which you know to be a fiction, there being nothing else. The exquisite truth is to know that it is a fiction and that you believe in it willingly."[11]

If one follows the leads of Nietzsche and Stevens, it becomes apparent that it is not only the past that is fictive. If signs are always signs of signs, then, in the final analysis (but, of course, there is no final analysis for analysis is inevitably interminable), everything is fictive. The recognition of the inescapability of fiction issues in what can best be described as *ironic self-consciousness*. Rather than nostalgic or reactionary, the presence of the past in postmodern architecture is ironic. Irony, as Kierkegaard citing Hegel insists, is "infinite and absolute negativity."[12] As such, irony is a paradoxical strategy of relationship to the world of experience in which one simultaneously sustains a certain attachment while remaining somewhat detached. In the ironic gesture, one distances oneself from that to which one nonetheless relates. The duplicity of this negativity renders it infinite or absolute. Never merely negative, irony harbors a positivity that results from doubling negation. While realizing the fictiveness of the signs with which he deals, the ironist acknowledges their necessity. Signs that are negated as real or true are reappropriated as fictive, which is not to say false.

The positivity involved in absolute negation, however, is more profound than the return of the sign as sign. Irony, I have suggested, is a form of *self-consciousness*. From his own point of view, the ironist's self-consciousness is *more complete* and thus *higher* than nonironic awareness. It is precisely the sophistication of ironic consciousness that transfigures the past in its quotation. The ironist "knows" something that those he cites do not know or did not know: he "knows" that he believes and that he can believe in nothing other than fictions. The negation and reappropriation of the past is, therefore, the assertion of the subject's own ironic self-consciousness. The performance played out on the postmodern stage unexpectedly displays a subject that affirms itself in and through a negation that is absolute or infinite.

If, however, the negativity of irony is the covert positivity of subjectivity, then are the fabrications of "the glass man" really different from glass constructions in the International Style? As modernism unwittingly perpetuates the tradition from which it struggles to escape, so postmodern architecture (as traditionally understood) is actually an extension of the most basic philosophical presuppositions of modernism. The end of both modern and ironic self-consciousness seems to be Stevens' glass man, without external reference. Contrary to expectation, when everything becomes transparent (the) all becomes obscure. To be without external reference is to be locked up in a prison house. For the ironic postmodernist, as for the visionary modernist, this prison house is *language*. With this insight, apparent opposites collapse into a surprising identity. Fictive perspectivism becomes indistinguishable from absolute idealism. The idealist's claim that objectivity is truly subjectivity and vice versa, returns in the ironist's confession that signs are signs of signs. Though seemingly partial, the gaze of the ironist is, in its own way, panoptical. Affirming itself in every negation, the ironist extends rather than subverts the modern philosophy of the subject. In seeing through everything, the glass man *sees himself*—sees himself more truly than anyone before him.

> He is in the transparence of the place in which
> He is and in his poems we find peace.
> He sets this peddler's pie and cries in summer,
> The glass man, cold and numbered, dewily cries,
> "Thou art not August unless I make thee so."
> Clandestine steps upon imagined stairs
> Climb through the night, because his cookoos call.[13]

"August": the cry of a subject still too august.

22

Future
of
the
Past

The threshold...sustains the middle in which the two, the outside and the inside, penetrate each other. The threshold bears the between...The threshold, as the settlement of the between, is hard because pain has petrified it. But the pain that became appropriated to stone did not harden into the threshold in order to congeal there. The pain presences unflagging in the threshold, as pain.

But what is pain? Pain [tears or] rends [reisst]. It is the [tear or] rift [Riss]. But is does not tear apart into dispersive fragments. Pain indeed tears asunder, it separates, yet in such a way that it at the same time draws together everything to itself. Its rendering, as a separating that gathers, is at the same time that drawing, which, like the pre-drawing [Vorriss] and sketch [Aufriss], draws and joins together what is held apart in separation. Pain is the joining agent in [tearing]/rending that divides and gathers. Pain is the joining [or articulation] of the rift. The joining is the threshold. It delivers the between, the mean of the two that are separated in it. Pain articulates the rift of difference. Pain is difference itself.[14]

Of this pain, the ironic subject knows nothing. The tears of the pain of difference rend the subject of modern philosophy and architecture. This *Aufriss* not only "draws and joins" but also draws and quarters. The *Riss* of difference is a deadline. This deadline marks the threshold of the prison house of language. Neither the classical modern nor traditional postmodern architect dares transgress this limit. To entertain such transgression, one would have to imagine the cryptic drawing of deadlines.

The failure of modernism is undeniable in Ibaraki. As Heidegger maintains, the atomic age is the inevitable end of the Western philosophical tradition. The bomb is the actual embodiment of the struggle for mastery that comes to a devastating conclusion in the modern subject's will to power. If irony is interpreted as an extension of the will to power in which the self affirms itself through infinite and absolute negation, then Hiroshima and Nagasaki might be understood as the end of modernity and the anticipation of the end of postmodernity. In the flash of the bomb, calculative-technological reason turns on its own creator with tragic consequences. What can possibly rise from such ruins?

Ibaraki represents an attempt to answer this urgent question. But the "answer" is a failure; in the attempt to erase the past, the errors of modernity are repeated. In contrast to many towns, villages and cities of the past, Ibaraki has neither a definite center nor obvious boundaries. Near what might once have been the center, the planners of the new city placed the Temple of Reason: the university. This university quickly became a place of death. Young people, in distressingly large numbers, began committing suicide on the university grounds. Having become concrete, the lines of the modern city became all-too-literally

Figure 3
Ueli Berger
Riss
Bern, 1970

deadlines. How, asked city-dwellers, can such terrifying deadlines be erased without leaving a trace?

Though atomic fission seems to make fusion unachievable and centeredness impossible, for many people some kind of center appears necessary to human survival. Yet any simple return to a past center or orientation is impossible. The center that once seemed secure must be redrawn in such a way that it can simultaneously be affirmed and denied. In his Tsukuba Center Building, 1979-1983, Arata Isozaki attempts to accomplish this double gesture by a non-nostalgic return to the past. He refigures the decentered city around a *fictive* center established by historical citation. In the midst of Ibaraki, Isozaki recreates the center of the world. More precisely, he reconstructs the center of the center of the Eternal City—Rome—by replacing the Place of Death with a representation of the Campidoglio. In this return, the past is supposed to be refigured so as to transfigure the present.

But Isozaki seems uncertain about the success of his "solution" to the problem of the destruction of modernity. He offers a *supplement* to his "Center Building." This supplement is a painting that reinscribes (which *is not* to say represents) the reconstruction of the reconstructed city. The title of the supplement is *The Future City*. The city of the future is a city in ruins. Isozaki gives no explanation ...just an image. In his painting, the city is precariously perched on the brink of a cliff. The buildings—even

Figure 4
Arata Isozaki
"Future City," Tsukuba Center Building, 1985

the obviously postmodern buildings—are all decap- itated. Through the middle of the reconstructed center runs a deep *Riss* or fissure. This fault, which extends through the buildings, past the limit of the city, to the edge of the cliff, and beyond, is *black*. What is this tear? What future does it portend?

The ruined city of the future, Isozaki implies, has been struck by a strange disaster. Unlike the catas- trophe wrought by the bomb Isozaki's uncanny disaster does not destroy everything but, in a certain sense, leaves things unchanged. What kind of a disaster is both destructive and non-destructive? In his extraordinary text, *L'Ecriture du déastre*, Maurice Blanchot suggests a possible answer to this question.

The disaster ruins everything, all the while leaving everything intact. It does not touch anyone in particular; "I" am not threatened by it, but spared, left aside. It is in this way that I am threatened; it is in this way that the disaster threatens in me that which is exterior to me—an other than I who passively becomes other. There is no reaching the disaster. Out of reach is he whom it threatens, whether from afar or close up, it is impossible to say: the infiniteness of the threat has in some way broken every limit. We are on the edge of disaster without being able to situate it in the future; it is rather always already past, and yet we are on the edge or under the threat, all formulations which would imply the future—that which is yet to come, that which has put a stop to every arrival. To think the disaster (if this is possible, and it is not possible inasmuch as we suspect that the disaster is thought) is to have no longer any future in which to think it.[15]

...on the edge of disaster without being able to situate it in the future...always already past...on the edge or under the threat, all formations which would imply the future...that which is yet to come—if the disaster were not that which does not come...that which has put a stop to every arrival. The disaster that is the future, Blanchot suggests, is inseparably bound to an extraordinary past that has never been and can never be present. Forever eluding any form of presentation, this past repeatedly approaches as a future that never arrives. In the absence of arrival, the presence of the present is interrupted. This never- present past, which is always on the edge of the present as the never-present future, Blanchot describes as the "terrifyingly ancient." The disastrous impli-

cations of this *future antérieur* can be clarified by examining the relationship of Blanchot's "terrifyingly ancient" to what Emmanuel Levinas describes as the "unrepresentable before."

Much of *L'Ecriture du déastre* is written in response to Levinas. In his most philosophically astute work, *Otherwise than Being or Beyond Essence*, Levinas develops an indirect critique of the structuralists' tendency to concentrate on synchronic form rather that historical and temporal development by form- ulating a complex analysis of diachrony. Rather than envisioning past and future as modalities of the present, Levinas points toward an irreducible past that was never present. He labels this past *"anarchie."* This anarchy is an *anarche* that signals a "deep formerly" (*profond jadis*), which is not a "'modification' of the present"[16]

Incommensurable with the present, unassemblable in it, it is always "already in the past" behind which the present delays, over and beyond the "now" that this exteriority disturbs or obsesses.[17]

Like the Lacanian unconscious, which is something other than the Freudian preconscious, the trace of Levinas' anarche is a past "more ancient than every representable origin, a pre-original and anarchical *passed.*"[18] Instead of an absolute origin (arche), the anarche, which is *toujours-déjà*, renders impossible every origin and all originality. In the wake of the trace, everything, and everybody is ever after, i.e., never primary, always secondary. In contrast to the presence of the past in postmodern architecture, Levinas' nonoriginal anarche cannot be re-presented. "Immemorial, unrepresentable, invisible, the past that bypasses the present, the pluperfect past [*plus que parfait*] falls into a past that is a gratuitous lapse. It cannot be recuperated by reminiscence not because of its remoteness, but because of its incom- mensurability with the present. The present is essence that begins and ends, beginning and end assembled in a thematizable conjunction...Diachrony is the refusal of conjunction, the nontotalizable, and in this sense, Infinite."[19] Immemorial, unrepresentable, and invisible, this elusive anarche can never be captured in the prison house of language. To attempt to think this unthinkable "thought" is to transgress the deadline drawn by reason.

Developing insights advanced by Levinas, Blanchot tries to take this impossible *pas audelà*[20] by writing something like (a) *Death Sentence.*[21] *When the Times Comes*, which, of course, it does not, we can lapse into reflection and reread dead lines:

"Sometimes she is far away, very far away," she said, making an impressive gesture with her hand.

"In the past?" I asked timidly.

"Oh, much farther away!"

I pondered, trying to discover what could really be farther away than the past. Meanwhile, she seemed all of a sudden afraid that she had thrown me slightly beyond the limits.[22]

24 Never present, anarche is always yet to come. "It is without present, just as it is without beginning or end; time has radically changed its meaning and its flow. Time without present..."[23] Anarche...Disaster. Perhaps this terrifyingly ancient anarche is the future inscribed in the dark fault of Isozaki's *Future City*. But why did he draw or paint this future of this past as a supplement to a city he had rebuilt? Why didn't Isozaki construct the *Riss* that is the deadline marking the limit of the modern and its return in the postmodern?

The *Riss* that inscribes the deadline cannot be *constructed* but can only be *deconstructed*. Never present and yet not absent, the anarche that faults every modern and postmodern construction can never be figured as such. *If* the past that approaches in the disastrous future is to be solicited, it must be *between* lines that remain irreducibly cryptic. Fault is always dark—as dark as the night beyond night whose darkness cannot be dispelled by day.

Postmodernism, at least in architecture, is, in a certain sense, over before it begins. Rather than reversing the assumptions of modernism, the postmodern return to the past actually extends the modern philosophy of the subject. Nothing O/other can happen until contemporary architects begin to reconceive space by rethinking time. In anarche, time is spaced and space is timed. This anarchic threshold harbors a space without presence and a time without the present. Architects—classical, modern, and postmodern—can never represent this unrepresentable before. Anarche can be figured, if at all, only in anarchetecture. Rather than resecuring foundations and reestablishing centers, the anarchetect makes everything tremble...even if ever so slightly.

But where has [anarchetecture] led us? To a time before the world, before the beginning. It has cast us out of the power to begin and to end; it has turned us toward the outside without intimacy, without place, without rest. It has led us into the infinite migration of error.... It ruins the origin by returning it to the errant immensity of an eternity gone astray.[24]

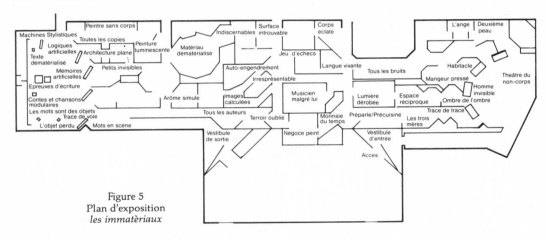

Figure 5
Plan d'exposition
les immatèriaux

Why hasn't it been built?

Can it be constructed?

Only deconstructed?

Time will tell.

If, that is,

time can

tell

.

.

.

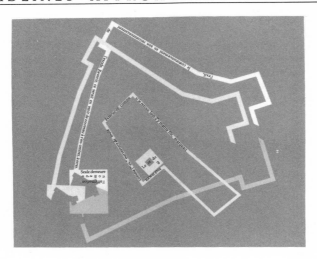

Figure 6
Peter Eisenman
Romeo and Juliet Palace in Verona *Moving Arrows, Eros, and Other Errors*[25]

Notes

[1] Jacques Derrida, "Differance," *Margins of Philosophy*, trans. A. Bass (Chicago: University of Chicago Press, 1982), p. 8.

[2] Michel Foucault, *Discipline and Punish: The Birth of the Prison*, trans. A. Sheridan (New York: Random House, 1979), p. 200.

[3] Somewhere Lacan suggests that the significance of the Freudian revolution might best be understood in terms of the shift from talking in circles to thinking in ellipses.

[4] "...the return of the book is of an *elliptical* essence. Something invisible is missing in the grammar of this repetition. As this lack is invisible and undeterminable, as it completely redoubles and consecrates the book, once more passing through each point along its circuit, nothing has budged. And yet all meaning is altered by this lack. Repeated, the same line is no longer exactly the same, the ring no longer has exactly the same center, *the origin has played*. Something is missing that would make the circle perfect." Jacques Derrida, "Ellipsis," *Writing and Difference*, trans. A. Bass (Chicago: University of Chicago Press, 1978), p. 296.

[5] Martin Heidegger, "The End of Philosophy and the Task of Thinking," *On Time and Being*, trans. J. Stambaugh (New York: Harper and Row, 1972), p. 56. In order to stress the intersection of theology and philosophy, Heidegger describes the Western tradition as "ontotheological."

[6] Charles Jencks, *What is Postmodernism?* (New York: St. Martin's Press, 1986), p. 14.

[7] *Ibid.*, p. 14.

[8] Heinrich Klotz, "Das Pathos des Functionalismus," *Werk Architheses*, March 1977 (with reference to a symposium held in Berlin in 1975). See also *Moderne und Postmoderne: Architektur der Gegenwart, 1960-1980* (Braunschweig: Friedr. Vieweg & Sohn, 1985).

[9] Friedrich Nietzsche, *The Will to Power*, trans. W. Kaufmann (New York: Random House, 1968), p. 267.

[10] Wallace Stevens, *Collected Poems* (New York: Alfred Knopf, 1981), pp. 250-51.

[11] Wallace Stevens, *Opus Posthumous* (New York: Alfred Knopf, 1957), p. 163.

[12] Soren Kierkegaard, *The Concept of Irony*, trans. L. Capel (Bloomington: University of Indiana Press, 1969), p. 349.

[13] Wallace Stevens, *Collected Poems, op. cit.*, p. 251.

[14] Martin Heidegger, "Language," *Poetry, Language, Thought*, trans. A. Hofstadter (New York: Harper & Row, 1971), p. 204.

[15] Maurice Blanchot, *The Writing of the Disaster*, trans. A. Smock (Lincoln, NE: University of Nebraska Press, 1986), p. 1.

[16] Emmanuel Levinas, *Otherwise than Being or Beyond Essence*, trans. A. Lingis (Boston: Martinius Nijhoff, 1981), p. 9.

[17] *Ibid.*, p. 100.

[18] *Ibid.*, p. 9. Levinas' "trace" either recalls or anticipates (genealogy is, as always, uncertain) Derrida's "trace." For an elaboration of Levinas' trace, see his article, "The Trace of the Other," *Deconstruction in Context: Literature and Philosophy*, ed. Mark C. Taylor (Chicago: University of Chicago Press, 1986), pp. 345-59.

[19] *Ibid.*, p. 11.

[20] See Maurice Blanchot, *Le Pas au-delà* (Paris: Gallimard, 1973). *Pas* can be translated as either "step" or "not." Thus Blanchot's ambiguous title might be rendered: *The Step Not Beyond*.

[21] See Maurice Blanchot, *Death Sentence*, trans. L. Davis (Barrytown, NY: Station Hill Press, 1978).

[22] Maurice Blanchot, *When the Time Comes*, trans. L. Davis (Barrytown, NY: Station Hill Press, 1985), p. 48.

[23] Blanchot, *The Writing of the Disaster*, p. 15.

[24] Maurice Blanchot, *The Space of Literature*, trans. A. Smock (Lincoln, NE: University of Nebraska Press, 1982), p. 244.

[25] The text superimposed on Eisenman's drawing is from Blanchot's *Le Pas au-delà, op. cit.*, p. 49.

PAUL JAY is an associate professor in literary criticism and theory at Loyola University in Chicago. Author of *Being in the Text: Self-Representation from Wordsworth to Roland Barthes* (Cornell University Press, 1984), he has written numerous essays on contemporary theory and criticism. He is the editor of *The Selected Correspondence of Kenneth Burke and Malcolm Cowley, 1915-1981* (Viking, 1988).

Critical Historicism and the Discipline of Architecture

The word "architecture" refers, of course, to the art and science of constructing buildings. It also, however, refers to a discipline within the fine arts and, more generally, to a social institution that orders and regulates the nature of buildings and how we think about and experience them. Although recent critical theory—particularly structuralism and deconstruction—has had an impact on the construction of buildings (Peter Eisenman's work comes particularly to mind), it has had a more pervasive impact on the nature of critical discourse within the academic discipline we call "architecture," and to a lesser degree, in more public discussions of architecture as a cultural and social institution. It is now easy to chart, beginning in the early seventies, the successive effects of phenomenology, formalism, structuralism, semiotics, deconstruction, and Marxism (often mixed with a heavy dose of Foucault's analyses of the relation between knowledge and power) on both the practice and the style of architecture criticism.[1] One result of the importation of critical theories developed in linguistics, literary criticism, political science, philosophy, and history into the domain of architecture criticism has been the blurring of the clear lines which have traditionally separated the discipline of architecture from these other disciplines. Architecture criticism as a discursive practice—the "reading" and analysis of specific buildings, the analysis of the work of particular architects, and the marking off of historical periods in architecture, etc.—has begun to be transformed by critical theories developed in other disciplines. But along with this transformation, though it has received less notice, has begun the transformation of the discipline or institution of architecture itself.

That such a transformation is in fact the inevitable outgrowth of the kinds of theoretical questions posed within the discipline by contemporary critics is made clear by Jacques Derrida in a recent discussion of "architectural thinking" in *Domus*.[2]

For some time, something like a de-constructive procedure has been establishing itself, an attempt to free oneself from the oppositions imposed by the history of philosophy, such as 'physis/teckne, God/man, philosophy/architecture.' Deconstruction therefore analyzes and questions conceptual pairs which are currently accepted as self-evident and natural, as if they hadn't been institutionalised at some precise point, as if they had no history. Because of being taken for granted they restrict thinking.

While often misconstrued as a radically ahistorical form of linguistic and philosophical freeplay, Derrida reminds us here that deconstruction is in fact a form of historical analysis that focuses on the *institutionalization* of key "conceptual" pairs that organize, delimit, and authorize the nature and bounds of discourse within organized fields of knowledge.[3] To "institute" something is of course to give form, order and organization to it, to regulate and control formlessness and difference. Hence the (Foucauldian) link between *institution* and *discipline*: to institute or discipline is to institute a regulative form of control over something—in our case, an evolving body of knowledge and critical practice. Derrida's deconstruction of the role of metaphor in western philosophical thinking, for example, is precisely an analysis of the history of the institutionalisation of conceptual pairs which, their metaphorical status having been repressed, ignored, or forgotten, came to seem fixed, natural and "self-evident," thus disciplining the institution of philosophy to proceed in a certain kind of way. In this sense, deconstruction charts the institutional history of philosophy.

What is most significant about Derrida's observation is that it suggests the inevitability of deconstruction's close attention to language at the textual level carrying over to an analysis of the institution within which that language is used. Because deconstruction focuses on the process whereby conceptual pairs (nature/culture, theory/practice, natural/supernatural, organic/built, etc.) become institutionalized as self-evident regulating concepts, that process leads inexorably to a critique of the discipline in which it takes hold. This phenomenon is most clearly at work in literary criticism, where deconstructive readings of literary works—the first wave of deconstruction's impact on the American critical scene—have given way successively to deconstructive studies of the language and concepts of literary criticism, and then to studies of the history of the institution of literary studies itself.[4] In fact, Derrida has insisted that it is deconstruction's ultimate focus on "material institutions" that marks it off from analysis or criticism:

It is by touching solid structures, 'material' institutions, and not merely discourses or significant representations, that deconstruction distinguishes itself from analysis or

"criticism." And to be pertinent, it works...with...institutional conditions and forms of teaching and learning.[5]

Because deconstruction—if it is "pertinent" in the sense Derrida means it to be—analyzes the foundational, often unexamined, assumptions that define and delimit fields of study and how scholarship and criticism in those fields must proceed, it moves in a logical way from textual and linguistic analyses to an analysis of institutional forms. For, just like the conceptual pairs Derrida spoke of in the short passage I quoted, academic disciplines represent divisions of knowledge and procedures "which are currently accepted as self-evident and natural, as if they hadn't been institutionalised at some precise point, as if they had no history." Because deconstruction insists on analyzing the metaphorical and figurative nature of philosophical language, it has had the effect of collapsing the distinction between philosophy and literature. This has also been the case in other fields of study where poststructuralist theory has taken hold. Because Hayden White's appropriation of the study of fictional narratives focused attention on how "history" was in fact plotted in narratives, the distinctions between history and literature have blurred;[6] because Lacan was able to use structural linguistics to show how the unconscious is structured like a language the distinctions between psychoanalysis, linguistics, and literary narratives have also blurred; and because semiotics, especially in the hands of a critic like Roland Barthes, has shown us how sign-systems are at work in similar ways in the worlds of literature, advertising, wrestling, fashion and the cinema, the clear distinction between so-called academic disciplines and institutions and practices usually relegated to "popular culture" has also blurred.

Such rigorous boundaries are of course one of the legacies of modern culture. Jurgen Habermas has argued that a key aspect of modernism was its tendency to divide and separate intellectual work into autonomous spheres. Habermas recalls that for Weber "cultural modernity" began when there was a separation of knowledge and the pursuit of knowledge into the separate spheres of science, morality and art, spheres that came to be "differentiated because the unified work-views of religion and metaphysics fell apart."[7] The clearest instance of this, of course, is the rise of the modern university, with its "rigorous" organization into divisions and disciplines. The institutionalization of such separate spheres during the rise of cultural modernity resulted in the autonomy of academic disciplines and the effective separation of philosophical, moral, scientific and aesthetic discourses. The result, as Habermas notes, was that "each domain of culture could be made to correspond to cultural professions in which problems could be dealt with as the concern of special experts." Thus what developed in the modern period was something like a "professionalized treatment of the cultural tradition." This had a double

28   result: the separation of knowledge into specialized disciplines, and an increasing distance between "experts" and the "larger public." Thus "the differentiation of science, morality and art has come to mean the autonomy of the segments treated by the specialist and their separation from the hermeneutics of everyday communication."

As we have already seen, poststructuralist theory has had the effect of undermining the kinds of divisions Habermas discusses, and as such constitutes a critique of the modernist impulse to compartmentalize fields of knowledge. It is in this sense that poststructuralism, as a critique of high modernist culture and aesthetics, is often linked with postmodernism. Habermas himself rejects such a linkage, arguing that theorists like Bataille, Foucault and Derrida are simply "young conservatives" who "recapitulate the basic experience of aesthetic modernity." Though they recapitulate such experience they produce in their work what Habermas insists is an "antimodernism," since it seems to him to be "emancipated from the imperative of work and usefulness" (p. 14). However, the literary critic Fredric Jameson argues not only that these theorists have done useful work, but that that work has had the effect of overturning the modernist separation of knowledge into separate disciplines. Far from being "antimodern," then, Jameson specifically links poststructuralism with postmodernism because contemporary theory constitutes an "effacement of the older categories of genre and discourse."[8] Recalling the changes that have taken place in the academy in the last generation he unconsciously echoes Habermas:

A generation ago there was still a technical discourse of professional philosophy...of political science, for example, or sociology or literary criticism. Today, increasingly, we have a kind of writing simply called "theory"(p. 112).

This theoretical discourse, in its collective form, is for Jameson one of the "manifestations of postmodernism." It is thus in terms of its *institutional impact* that Jameson deems poststructuralism postmodern; for him, such an impact seems a function of theory's being postmodern in just the sense Habermas would want it to be, for it has become an instrument that not only "negates" the separate spheres of cultural modernism, but begins to reconstitute the pursuit of knowledge along what we are used to thinking as interdisciplinary lines. Such a negation, such a reconstitution, Jameson seems to be arguing, is just the kind of useful work Habermas is looking for.

Jameson's position on the relationship between poststructuralist theory and postmodernism is not without its detractors. In addition to Habermas, other important theorists of what has come to be called "the postmodern condition" have argued that poststructuralist theory is merely the last gasp of a debilitating form of modernist aesthetic free-play. Andreas Huyssen, for example, in his book, *The Great Divide: Modernism, Mass Culture, Postmodernism*, insists that contemporary theory "is primarily a discourse of and about modernism,"[9] that is, that it focuses too exclusively on the analysis of classical modernist texts, and that its concerns are purely aesthetic. Modernism, he argues, has simply been "reinscribed" in contemporary theory. Poststructuralism, because it insists "that there is nothing outside the text," and because it "privileges" aestheticism and language, offers an *"archeology of modernity"* rather than a *"theory of postmodernity"* (p. 209).

How are we to account for the disparity between these two positions (a disparity all the more striking for the fact that both Jameson and Huyssen are critics on the Left)? Huyssen wants to salvage postmodernism from its identification with neoconservatism by defining a version of postmodernism that is *oppositional* rather than simply preoccupied with style and performance: "we explore the question whether postmodernism might not harbor productive contradictions, perhaps even a critical and oppositional potential" (p. 200). However, his conception of poststructuralist critical theory as a form of aesthetic modernism and textual and linguistic *jouissance* means that it does not embody the critical and oppositional potential he is looking for. This narrow definition of poststructuralism effectively precludes its incorporation into an oppositional postmodernism. Huyssen isolates a particular strain of poststructuralism which seems apolitical and performative,[10] and then he makes it stand for the dominant tendencies of poststructuralist theory *per se*. He ignores the oppositional thrust of deconstruction emphasized by Derrida in the passages we reviewed earlier, a move which has the effect of repressing its powerful role in analyzing the material history of social and cultural institutions. Too quick to embrace Habermas' equation of French poststructuralism and neoconservatism, he misses the role of contemporary theory in deconstructing ordered and well-disciplined fields of knowledge.

Perhaps because he has been actively engaged in transgressing this order in his own interdisciplinary theoretical work, Jameson recognized the oppositional potential of contemporary theory, both in its general tendency to ignore conventional divisions of knowledge and in its potential to contribute to a form of ideological analysis. In this respect, his analysis of the relationship between postmodernism and poststructuralism is both more acute and more constructive than Huyssen's, for it focuses on the *link* between critical theory, the critique of ideology, and the nature and role of academic institutions. Jameson's position, in fact, has come to be held by an increasing number of critics writing on architecture, where the elaboration of a form of "oppositional postmodernism" and what I will call "critical historicism" has emerged. This development can be dated from two recent collections of essays, *The Anti-Aesthetic: Essays on Postmodern Culture* (1983), and *Architecture, Criticism, Ideology* (1985).[11] In his Preface to *The Anti-Aesthetic*, Hal Foster writes that there are essentially two "standard positions to take on postmodernism: one may support postmodernism as populist and attack modernism as elitist or, conversely, support modernism as elitist—as culture proper—and attack postmodernism as mere kitsch."[12] He then goes on to identify a third, emerging alternative, what he calls a "postmodernism of resistance":

In cultural politics today, a basic opposition exists between a postmodernism which seeks to deconstruct modernism and resist the status quo and a postmodernism which repudiates the former to celebrate the latter: a postmodernism of resistance and a postmodernism of reaction.

Such a postmodernism, he continues, would be "concerned with a critical deconstruction of tradition, not an instrumental pastiche of pop- or pseudo-historical forms, with a critique of origins, not a return to them" (p. xii). In Foster's version of postmodern criticism, deconstruction has an instrumental role, one based on his understanding that any form of cultural critique needs something like a theory of reading and that deconstruction offers such a theory.

Foster's reference to "deconstruction" in the above passage, it should be noted, has about it that kind of characteristic vagueness such references often have in the popular press, where the word is stylishly used as a euphemism for "taking apart" or "falling apart." Nevertheless, his reference to deconstruction's role in analyzing "tradition," and in generating a "critique," rather than a reverential or ironic return to "origins," is reminiscent of Derrida's emphasis on the historical and institutional focus of deconstruction. Foster's "critical deconstruction of tradition" suggests a form of historicism postmodern in its attempt to distance itself from either an uncritical digesting of canonical works and the cant about them, or from a simple parody or pastiche of the past. Recall again Derrida's description of deconstruction as a "procedure" that "analyses and questions" the *historical* and *institutional* context of forms and arguments we may otherwise take to be natural or self-evident. Such a procedure is anything but "conservative," nor does it represent the atrophying of "an earlier aestheticism." Rather, it suggests a critical mode of reading which, while it begins at the rhetorical and linguistic levels in its analysis of discourse within academic disciplines like architecture, inevitably works its way toward a critique of the institution that sustains—and is sustained by—that discourse.

It is in this sense that Foster's notion of an oppositional form of postmodernism is conceptually related to that movement within architectural criticism I have called "Critical Historicism." Its emergence, as I noted earlier, can be dated from the publication in 1985 of *Architecture, Criticism, Ideology*, a collection of essays by Demetri Porphyrios, Thomas Llorens, Frederic Jameson, Alan Colquhoun, and Manfredo Tafuri (among others) which sketch out historical methods in architectural criticism influenced variously by Marx, Foucault and Derrida. This collection of essays gives a kind of cohesion to a movement within architectural criticism dating from the mid-seventies, one which can be traced in essays by Tafuri, Anthony Vidler, Alan Colquhoun and others in the journal *Oppositions*. I want to look briefly at one of these articles, Tafuri's "The Historical Project" (1979), and at one of the essays from *Architecture, Criticism, Ideology*—Demetri Porphyrios' "On Critical History." Taken together, these two essays constitute two representative examples of a Critical Historicism in architectural criticism influenced by deconstruction, but more emphatically and explicitly oriented toward a Marxian critique of ideology than Derrida's work. They also demonstrate the ways in which such theories have led to a rethinking of architecture as a separate discipline, and to an analysis of its constitution as such.

In his essay, Tafuri announces what had by that time become a familiar "focus": "the language of architecture."[13] By this term, however, he does not mean what Peter Eisenman or Charles Jencks mean, or meant, by the term (that is, using it simply as an elaborate metaphor for formal relations). Rather, he uses it to refer specifically to "architectural writing" as an institution, a kind of writing unfolding in what he insists is the wake of structuralism's failure— the impossibility of "translating architecture into linguistic *terms*." Tafuri insists that the criticism of architecture needs to move away from a self-referential, ahistorical formalism toward a kind of historicism that is focused on ideological analysis. He wants to move architectural criticism back toward an engagement with history, but with a notion of "history" transformed by the insights of contemporary theory. "History," for Tafuri, is not some fixed, static "thing" itself which is lying there for us to comprehend. Rather, it is a written, textual production, what he calls a "provisional...analytical construction." "History," he writes, "is both determined and determining: determined by its own traditions, by the objects it analyzes, by the methods it adopts; also determining its own transformations as well as those of the reality it deconstructs" (p. 56). That is, what we call history is both something that is determined by "what happened," and something that is determined by the *methods we use* to determine what happened. The methods of the historian always in part determine the kind and quality of historical transformations he or she "sees." History, Tafuri insists, is an analytical construction precisely in the sense that Freud's versions of his patient's pasts were: they organize, explain and interpret, but they do not necessarily represent verifiable objects of knowledge.

History, like quintessential Freudian analysis—is not just therapy. Calling into question its own materials, it

30 reconstructs them and continuously reconstructs itself (pp. 66-67).

The problem with conventional concepts of "history," as Tafuri points out, is that they tend to think of the category "historical" in an objectivist, logical-positivist fashion, as if the "history" we have access to somehow exists outside our own textual formations of it. In this way, we have, until recently, tended to distinguish "history" from "interpretation." But this is precisely one of those distinctions which deconstruction has helped us to question. As a narrative construction, "history" is inseparably linked to the narratives we produce when we interpret something—and to the interpretations we produce when we *narrate* something.[14] The point is not a facile one, i.e. that history somehow does not exist, but simply that history is constructed textually and rhetorically, not as the mirror of "what happened" but as an assertion. "History" is a kind of writing about the past that, in representing it in a certain way, takes a position in the present.

Tafuri wants his form of historical criticism to focus on the taking of such positions, that is, to be explicitly ideological—but not in the sense of ideology as simply "false consciousness," i.e., those bad ideas the other guy has. By "ideology," Tafuri means the set of assumptions about the nature of reality and behavior that any given culture accepts uncritically as natural or self-evident but which are, as we saw Derrida insist earlier, the actual products of history, argument and the forces of institutional power. "Historical interpretations of ideologies," Tafuri writes, would allow for analyses of the past that would, by their critical thrust, constitute "concrete interventions" in the present that the past has helped to construct (p. 69). Here Tafuri makes explicit his interest in a kind of Critical Historicism which would be consistent with Foster's vision of an oppositional postmodernism that incorporated deconstruction in a theory of reading that focused on ideology, one that reads critically in order to intervene in institutional and cultural discourses. As such, Tafuri's "Historical Project" looks forward to Demetri Porphyrios' conception of what he calls "Critical History."[15]

His essay (1982), influenced by the work of Michel Foucault, treats architecture as "discursive practice." For Porphyrios, "architectural discourse is a form of representation that naturalizes certain meanings and eternalizes the present state of the world in the interests of a hegemonical power" (p. 16). While Derrida would never use the phrase "hegemonical power," in other respects Porphyrios' description of architectural discourse mirrors Derrida's description of what a deconstruction produces when it analyzes the institutional and historical contexts of the kind of naturalization Porphyrios refers to. The marriage here, of course, is one arranged between Marx, Derrida and Foucault. For Foucault, to represent something is always to present it in a certain way and for a particular purpose. "Representation" in

this sense is not what literary critics call "mimesis" (after Aristotle)—the carefully realistic presentation of reality, the attempt to mirror it. Rather, representation in the Foucaultian sense refers to a discursive practice that cannot and does not faithfully mirror what already happened, but which, in narrating a "reality," constructs it.

As a discursive practice, architecture and its criticism is, for Porphyrios, an "ideology" (in that it "reflects the manner in which the agents of an architectural culture live the relations between architecture as production and architecture as institution"). His aim is to delineate a critical method able to deal with architecture as such. He calls it "Critical History" —which he distinguishes from a less critical and supposedly more disinterested kind of historiography—in that it is "concerned with the project of constituting" and critiquing the "imaginary coherence" that architecture gives reality (p. 16). "Imaginary" and "coherence" are the operative words here, especially in terms of Porphyrios' focus on the rhetoric of historiography in architecture—which is his central concern in the essay. In his view, historical criticism in architecture can too often create a "coherent" explanation of the past which, while it carries the import of that authoritative phrase, "this happened," fabricates an imagined coherence. Conceived as a practice that would analyze the language of such criticism in order to reveal "the way in which architecture as ideology naturalizes and dehistoricizes a historically created reality" (p. 16), Porphyrios' critical history seeks to blend an essentially deconstructive method of reading with a neo-Marxist interest in ideology and power relations. In a phrase, critical history wants to "grasp the concept of architectural ideology as a process of mythical destructuring that aims at the reproduction of relations of power" (p. 19) at the disciplinary and institutional levels. Critical Historicism examines previous histories in order to show where they mythologize rather than report, and to try to see how such mythologizing fits into, or is complicit with, specific forms of cultural and political power. Treating architectural criticism as a discursive practice which utilizes a rhetoric that naturalizes and mythologizes material and social conditions, Critical History becomes, in part, a critique of the idealist language of architectural criticism itself, and thus of the discipline it sustains.

A brief analysis of the following short passage from Nikolaus Pevsner's Introduction to *An Outline of European Architecture* can suggest how such a critique would proceed:

Architecture is not the product of materials and purposes— nor by the way of social conditions—but of the changing spirits of changing ages. It is the spirit of an age that pervades its social life, its religion, its scholarship and its arts. The Gothic style was not created because somebody invented rib-vaulting; the Modern Movement did not come into being because steel framed and reinforced concrete construction had been worked out—they were worked out because a new spirit required them.[16]

In this passage, Pevsner fashions a theory that attempts to account for changes in architectural styles, a theory meant to provide *coherence* to a complex series of historical changes. At what expense is this coherence purchased? Not simply by discounting the role of material and social forces in historical change as opposed to spiritual ones, but by insisting on a kind of absolute opposition between material and social forces. His argument is founded on a classic binary opposition between material and spirit. The rhetorical strategy at work in this passage is thinly veiled by Pevsner's uncritical use of the phrase "spirit of an age," which is employed as if it referred to something as concrete and identifiable as a chair or a table. Pevsner's absolute division between material conditions and "spirit" begs the question of the complex *interrelationship* between material, social and spiritual forces. The coherence Pevsner's passage claims for historical change is based on the uncriticized assumption that the "spirit of an age" is unrelated to material and social conditions, and that social conditions and changes that result from innovations in the use of material do not have a role in giving shape to what he calls the spirit of an age. The passage also begs the question of whether there is in fact such a thing as a "spirit of an age," and whether that spirit has any kind of existence outside of the mind of the historian who postulates it.

What Pevsner has produced in his passage is precisely the "imaginary coherence" Porphyrios suggests the Critical Historian needs to analyze in the language of architectural criticism. Pevsner's "spirit of an age" is not a thing existing out "there" in the world, but a figure of speech, a metaphor, deployed in his passage in order to give shape to a "reality" it does not reflect, but interprets. The passage has an ideology, contained in the position it takes about the primary importance of "spiritual" over material and social forces in the shaping of historical change (suggesting that such change does not come from social action, but by the workings of some transcendental force). Such an ideology drives what Porphyrios refers to in his essay as a "process of mythical structuring" in which "relations of power" are reproduced. Pevsner's passage perpetuates the idealist notion that power comes from an indwelling of spirit rather than from control of material conditions and the institutions that oversee them.

Because Pevsner's theory of historical change is based on eliding the metaphorical status of its key term, the Critical Historian would want to examine the role of that metaphor in Pevsner's discourse rather than go outside it in an attempt to locate his "spirit of an age." The point is not that Pevsner's phrase is meaningless, but rather that its meaning is a function of its relationship to other elements of his discourse, not of its relationship to something that actually exists outside of it. The important question for the Critical Historian would not be "what are the spiritual qualities of this age," but rather, "what is the function of the metaphysical conception 'spirit of an age' in Pevsner's argument, and in support of what view of the world is it being made?" Moreover, the Critical Historian would probably want to argue that however an "age" might have conceived of its spiritual values, those values are best studied as a *part* of "social conditions," and that they need to be viewed in light of their relationship to material relations and conditions.

Such an analysis of Pevsner's passage—which might be extended over the entire book—suggests how the kind of critique Porphyrios and Tafuri elaborate must inevitably affect the discipline of architecture at the institutional level. To read Pevsner's passage in this way is to reorient both the focus of architectural criticism and the conventional conception of what a course on the history of architecture would be like. Critical Historicism insists that the procedures and assumptions that guide the historian and critic must become part of the subject matter of such courses, that any "history" of architecture must incorporate within itself (whether it is a course or an essay) a critique of the theories and methods whereby it proceeds. The *language* of architectural criticism must, from this point of view, become part of its own subject matter. This change will inevitably lead, as we have already seen, to a critique of the ways in which "architecture" has been constituted as a discipline and as a separate sphere of knowledge. As critical theories from other disciplines create more and more of an impact on architecture, the separation between these disciplines will continue to dissolve. As Jameson suggests, Critical Theory is emerging as a distinct field, but part of what is distinctive about it is precisely that it cuts across as it inhabits and takes roots in disciplines as disparate as literature, philosophy, legal studies, sociology and history. In each of these fields analysis has come to focus on the very grounds that constitute these disciplines as separate institutions, so that Critical Theory has fostered a wholesale rethinking of their shape and the critical procedures that regulate them. The more theory comes to focus on the traditional disciplines as specifically *discursive* forms, the more we will see architectural criticism changed by, and contributing to, the evolution of a broad-based study of the interrelationships between academic fields of knowledge and the culture they both embody and perpetuate.

32   Notes

1 For a brief overview of such developments see Mary McLeod's Introduction to *Architecture Criticism Ideology* (Princeton: Princeton Architectural Press, 1985), pp. 7-11.

2 Jacques Derrida, "Architettura ove il desiderio puó abitare," *Domus* 24, April 1986.

3 In speaking of deconstruction in this way I do not mean to be suggesting that such a description covers the whole range of Derrida's work. What has come to be called "deconstruction" constitutes only one aspect of the Derridean project. Gregory Ulmer, in *Applied Grammatology: Post (e)-Pedagogy from Jacques Derrida to Joseph Beuys* (Baltimore and London: Johns Hopkins University Press, 1985), has for example drawn a distinction between deconstruction and grammatology in Derrida's work. He emphasizes that while deconstruction is a mode of analysis, grammatology is a mode of writing. While his division is a little too neat (since Derrida's reliance on puns, wordplay and miming, and the performative element of his writing is meant finally to do *analytical* work) it is a helpful one to keep in mind, for when we talk about "deconstruction" we are not talking about the whole of Derrida's work.

4 Recent examples include Gerald Graff's *Professing Literature: An Institutional History* (Chicago: University of Chicago Press, 1987), Paul Bove's *Intellectuals In Power* (New York: Columbia University Press, 1986) and Samuel Weber's *Institution and Interpretation* (Minneapolis: University of Minnesota Press, 1987).

5 Jacques Derrida, "Le Parergon," in *La Vérité en Peinture* (Paris: Flammarion, 1978), pp. 23-24. The English translation of this passage is Samuel Weber's (see *Institution and Interpretation*, p. 19).

6 See Hayden White's *Metahistory: The Historical Imagination in Nineteenth Century Europe* (Baltimore: Johns Hopkins University Press, 1973).

7 Jurgen Habermas, "Modernity - An Incomplete Project," in *The Anti-Aesthetic: Essays on Postmodern Culture*, ed. Hal Foster (Port Townsend, Washington: Bay Press, 1983), p. 9.

8 Fredric Jameson, "Postmodernism and Consumer Society," in *The Anti-Aesthetic: Essays on Postmodern Culture*, p. 112. All further references to this work appear in parentheses in the text.

9 Andreas Huyssen, *The Great Divide: Modernism, Mass Culture, Postmodernism* (Bloomington and Indianapolis: Indiana University Press, 1986), p. 207. All further references to this work appear in parentheses in the text.

10 Huyssen rather predictably chooses as his example Roland Barthes' *The Pleasure of the Text*. See *After The Great Divide*, pp. 210-212.

11 *Architecture Criticism Ideology*, Joan Ockman, ed. (Princeton: Princeton Architectural Press, 1985).

12 Hal Foster, *The Anti-Aesthetic*, p. xii. All further references to this essay appear in parentheses in the text.

13 Manfredo Tafuri, "The Historical Project," *Oppositions* 17 (1979): 55. All further references to this work appear in parentheses in the text.

14 The most important source for this view of history and historiography is Hayden White's *Metahistory*. Much of what Tafuri says in his article echoes White's analysis there.

15 Demetri Porphyrios, "On Critical History," in *Architecture Criticism Ideology*. All further references to this essay appear in parentheses in the text.

16 Nikolaus Pevsner, *An Outline of European Architecture* (New York: Penguin Books, 1983), p. 17.

ZONES

MICHEL MAFFESOLI is Professor of Sociology at the University of Paris, La Sorbonne, Director of the Centre d'Etudes sur l'Actuel et le Quotidien (CEAQ), and editor of the international journal *Sociétés*. He has written several books, among them: *L'ombre de Dionysos. Contribution à une sociologie de l'orgie* (1985); *La connaissance ordinaire. Précis de sociologie comprehensive* (1985); *Le temps des tribus* (1987).

"Affectual" Post-Modernism and Megapolis

The Community of Fate

A close bond exists between space and daily life. Space is the conservatory of a "sociability" that can no longer be ignored. This is what numerous studies of the city show and what H. Raymond's question expresses in his foreword to the work of Young and Willmott: "Must we think that in some cases urban morphology and the worker's daily life achieve a harmonious whole?"[1] Such harmony exists, of course. It is, really, the result of what I propose to call the "community of fate." For anyone familiar with the *Courées* (common courtyards) of Northern France, or with the ramshackle buildings (*bâtisses*) found in the mining villages of Southern and Central France, no doubt lingers that such a morphology constitutes a crucible as the diverse groups adjust to one another. Obviously, and this point cannot be stressed enough, any harmony has in itself a certain amount of conflict.

A community of fate is an adaptation to the natural and social environment, and, as such, it must come face to face with heterogeneity in its many forms. With reference to the Simmelian metamorphosis of "the bridge and the door"—that which connects and that which separates—putting the accent on space and on territory makes of rational man a mixture of openness and of reserve. It is well known that a certain type of graciousness is the indication of a powerful "as for me." All of this seems to indicate that "proxemy" in no way means unanimism—that it does not postulate, the way history does, rising above the contradictory, rising above that which is or those who are in the way.

As the trivial saying goes, "one must make do." This calls for an *appropriation* of existence, albeit a relative one. Indeed, not assuming a perfect life to be possible, not counting on a heavenly nor on an earthly paradise, *one does with what one has*. It is true that beyond the diverse and often very empty declarations of intention, the protagonists of everyday life are extremely tolerant toward the other, toward others, toward whatever happens. That is why, paradoxically, it is possible for an undeniable and existential richness to spring forth from economic misery. Taking proxemy into account may be the right way to rise above our usual attitude of suspicion in order to appreciate the deep personal and interpersonal investments that express themselves in the tragic side of everyday life.

It is with this in mind that the expression "proxemy" is used here. Relationships built on proximity are far from restful. To repeat a well known term, "urban villages" have relationships at once deep and cruel. Indeed, always knowing something about another person, without intimately knowing him or her, does not fail to have remarkable consequences for the modes of everyday life. Contrary to a concept of the city made up of free individuals cultivating primarily rational relationships—it suffices to remember the well-known claim that the spirit of the city is liberating: *Stadtluft macht frei*—it would appear that contemporary megapolises give rise to a multiplicity of small enclaves founded on absolute interdependency. The autonomous "individualism" of the bourgeois mode is being succeeded by the heteronomy of tribalism. Whatever name is used for them: districts, neighborhoods, interest groups, or networks, one sees a return to the affective, to a passional investment, the structurally ambiguous and ambivalent side of which is well documented.

I am describing here a matrix "die." The passional affectual tendency forms an "aura" in which one floats, but which can also be expressed in a pointed

36 manner. This also has its cruel side. It is not contradictory, as Hannerz says, to see "brief and rapid contacts" take place in it[2]. Depending on the interests of the moment, and on the tastes and occasions, passional investment will lead toward one group or another, toward one activity or another—something that unavoidably brings about adhesion and separation, attraction and repulsion, heartbreaks and conflicts of all sorts. One truly *feels* here; and this is a characteristic of contemporary cities in the presence of a mass versus tribe dialectics, masses being the embracing pole, tribes the pole of individual crystallization. Social life is organized around those two poles, in an endless motion: a motion more or less rapid, more or less intense, more or less "stressful," depending on the location and people.

In a certain way the ethics of the moment brought about by this ceaseless motion makes possible a reconciliation of the static "spaces, structures" with the dynamic "stories, discontinuities" that are generally considered as antinomic. Besides civilizational groups that tend to be "reactionary"—favoring the past, tradition, spatial inscriptions—and "progressive" groups that tend to emphasize the future, progress and the race toward what is to come, one can consider social aggregates that ally these two points of view in a contradictory manner and which consider the "conquest of now" as their main value. The mass-tribe dialectics may also serve to express that coincidence (*cum-currire*)[3].

To use a thematic that, since G. Durand and E. Morin, no longer leaves intellectuals indifferent, one should recognize the existence of an endless process that goes from the culturalization of nature to the naturalization of culture. This leads to an understanding of the problem both in its social and in its natural milieu. In this respect, it is necessary to pay attention to the changes taking place in our societies. The purely rational and progressive model of Western civilization, which has enjoyed world-wide acceptance, is on the verge of saturation. One sees cultural interpenetrations that remind one of the contradictory third group (the group "of the now") just discussed. Side by side with Westernization that, since the end of the last century, has been moving forward at a gallop, one can notice numerous indications which send one back to what might be called an "Orientalization" of the world. The latter is expressed in specific lifestyles, in new fashion, new attitudes with regard to the use of space and toward the body. On this last point especially, one can call attention to the multiplicity of "parallel medicines" and to the various "group therapies." Research in progress shows that far from being marginal these practices constitute a capillary system running through the entire social body. That, of course, is on a par with the introduction of syncretic ideologies which, decreasing the importance of the classical body/soul dichotomy, surreptitiously are fashioning a new *Esprit du temps* to which the sociologist cannot remain indifferent. It would appear that the process that is starting is no longer reserved for an elite and, especially, that it is developing in those small tribes which, by concatenations and various intercrossings, take on the appearance of a culture.

The main characteristic of the signs that have just been pointed out is, in truth, a new "given" in the space-time relationship. To go back to the ideas suggested at the beginning, *importance is accorded to what is near, to what is "affectual"*: what unites one to a particular place, a place that is experienced with others. As a heuristic illustration, I shall refer here to A. Berque who states "that it is not impossible for certain present aspects of Western culture to fall in line with certain traditional aspects of Japanese culture."[4] Now, if his analysis of this point is carefully followed, it will be noted that the main points of that overlapping territory deal with accentuating the "global," the natural, the rapport with the environment—all things which lead to a behavior of the communication type: "the nature/culture relationship and the subject/other relationship are indissolubly connected to the perception of space" (p. 35). To remove oneself as little as possible from one's milieu, which here must be understood in its broadest meaning, sends one back, strictly speaking, to a symbolic vision of existence, a vision of existence in which "immediate perceptions" and proximate references (p. 37) will be favored. The connection between the spatial, the global, and the "intuitive-emotional" (p. 32) falls completely within the forgotten, the denied, the discredited tradition of sociological holism, organic solidarity and founding whole-being, which may never have existed, but which nonetheless remains the nostalgic basis, either directly or *a contrario*, for most of our analysis. The concept of *Einfuhlung* (empathy) which comes to us from German Romanticism, best expresses this line of research[5].

As paradoxical as it might appear, the Japanese model could be a specific expression of that holism, of that mystical correspondence which strengthens what is social as *muthos* (myth, story, narrative). Indeed, whether within a company, in daily life or during leisure, few things appear to escape the Japanese model. It so happens that the contradictory mix resulting from it is not without consequences today. At whatever level—political, economic, industrial—the Japanese model exerts a clear fascination for our contemporaries. Should we speak, as Berque does, of a "Japanese paradigm"? It is possible. Especially since the term "paradigm," as opposed to "model," suggests a flexible and perfectible structure. What is certain is that this paradigm accounts for the mass-tribe dialectics which occupies me here; and for that endless and somewhat undefined motion, that "die" without center or periphery in which all things are made up of elements which, depending on the situation, adapt themselves into changing figures according to a few pre-set archetypes. That swarming, that culture broth, is enough to cause our individualistic and individualizing minds to reel. But after all, is this so new? Other civilizations have been based on the ritual games of the de-individualized "persona," on collectively lived roles, something which has not failed to produce solid and "relevant" architectonics. Let us not forget that the affectual confusion of the Dionysian myth has produced important civilizational pinnacles. It is possible that our megapolises are serving as a frame for their own renaissance.

Tribes and Networks

Spatial accentuation is not an end in itself. If meaning is given back to the *quartier*, to neighborly practices and to the affectual that does not fail to emanate from them, it is first of all because they permit networks of relationships. Proxemy essentially sends one back to the very bottom of a succession of "we's" who constitute the substance of any "sociability." Continuing what has been said, I would like to stress the fact that the constitution of micro-groups, of the tribes that punctuate spatiality, starts in the feeling of *belonging*, as a function of a specific ethics, and within the framework of a communication *network*.

These three concepts can be summarized by speaking, metaphorically, of a "multitude of villages" that criss-cross one another, oppose and help one another while each one remains itself. We now have a few speculative analyses from field studies that support this point of view[6]. The city object is a succession of territories where people, in a more or less non-systematic manner, take root. People fall back upon, and seek protection and safety within these territories. By using the word "village" I made clear that I was dealing with a metaphor. Indeed, the village may of course be a concrete space, but it may just as well be a "*cosa mentale*," a symbolic territory—whatever its type, it is just as real. In this respect it suffices to refer to the "fields" that intellectuals cut out and turn into hunting preserves, in order to understand that the metaphor of the tribe or of the village is not without heuristic interest. In all fields therefore, whether intellectual, cultural, "cult-ual," commercial or political, one observes the existence of these rootings that enable a social "body" to exist as such.

It so happens, in addition, that the tribal feeling of belonging can be strengthened by technological development. Speaking of the "electronic galaxy," A. Moles (with a few reservations it is true) suggests what might be the "model of a new global village."[7] Indeed, potentially, "cable," the computer delivery companies (ludic, erotic, functional) are creating a communication core within which there arise, grow, and die, groups that have diverse forms and diverse objectives, groups which do not fail to call to mind the archaic structures of tribes and of village clans. The sole appreciable difference, characteristic of the electronic galaxy, is the short lifespan peculiar to these tribes. Indeed, contrary to what the concept of tribalism generally evokes, the tribalism under consideration here may be completely ephemeral: it organizes itself as the occasions present themselves. To recover an old philosophical concept, this tribalism exhausts itself in the action. As may be seen from several studies, more and more people live alone, but the fact of living *alone* does not mean living *in isolation*. Depending on the opportunities that present themselves—especially through informational ads suggested by "Minitel" (a French system of electronic communication)—the "single" person becomes involved with this or that group, this or that activity. Thus, through numerous oblique paths (Minitel is one among many), sports, friendships, sexual liaisons, religious groups, or others, "tribes" are formed. Each one has a different lifespan which depends on the degree of investment of their participants.

Just as successive truths exist in love relationships, and just as science is built from sequential approximations, it is possible to imagine a participation in these various "forms" of sociability which is itself differentiated and open. This has been made possible by the speed of the offer-demand circuit inherent in computer procedure.

It is nonetheless still true that even though these tribes are stamped with the seal of a seasonal quality, and with a tragic dimension, they control the mechanism of belonging. Whatever the field, one is more or less under the obligation to participate in the collective spirit. Integration or rejection will depend on the degree of "feeling" experienced either by the group or by the person wishing to enter it. Later, that feeling will be reinforced or weakened by acceptance or rejection of the diverse initiation rituals. Whatever the lifespan of the tribe, these rituals are a necessity and they occupy a more and more important place in everyday life. More or less imperceptible rituals exist that enable one to feel at ease, "to be a regular" in a certain bar or nightclub. The same is true if one wishes to be served well by the tradesmen of a neighborhood, or wants to take a walk on such and such a street. The rituals of "belonging" are found also, of course, in offices and in workshops, and the socio- anthropology of work is paying closer and closer attention to them. Finally, it may be recalled that mass leisure or tourism are based almost entirely on rituals[8].

It would be possible to multiply the examples that support this point of view, but it is sufficient to indicate that side by side with the renewed importance of the image and of the myth (a story which each group tells itself) in today's world, the rite constitutes an efficient technique which forms the ambient religiosity (*religare*) in our megapolises. It is even possible to state that the ephemeral character of these tribes, and the tragic side that is specific to them, emphasizes the exercise of rituals. Indeed, rituals by their very repetitive nature and the attention they pay to that which is small, reduce the anguish characteristic of "presentism." At the same time, as the "project," the "future," the "ideal" no longer serve as society's mortar, ritual, by reinforcing the feeling of belonging, may fill that role and thus make it possible for groups to exist.

It is necessary to indicate, however, that at the same time as it favors attraction, even a plural one, the feeling of belonging proceeds if not by exclusion at least by exclusiveness. Indeed, the very characteristic of the tribe, which stresses that which is near (persons and places), has a tendency to close up on itself. Here is found again the metaphor of the door dear to G. Simmel. The abstract universal is making room for the concretized state of the particular. Hence the existence of those "localisms" that have surprised many an investigator. In the very core of neighborhoods one finds a series of clubs—groupings into associations—that take place within a very precise perimeter. Peregrination itself is circumscribed by a limited number of streets. This phenomenon is well known in the cities of Southern Europe, but the investigations of Young and Willmott reveal it is also true for the city of London[9]. Localism favors what one might call the "mafia spirit": in the search for lodging, work, and small daily privileges, priority is given to those who belong to the tribe, or to those who are drawn to its circles of influence. Generally, this process is analyzed within the framework of the family, but it is certainly possible to extend it to the larger family—the group that is based on family relationships and also on the numerous relationships of friendship, patronage or of reciprocal favors.

The expression "bond" (family, association) must be understood in its strongest sense: that of necessity, what the medieval trade guild system categorized as "the obligation." Mutual help in its various forms is a *duty*, the touchstone of the honor code, often unexpressed, that rules tribalism. This is the cause of that exclusivism that, in many respects, mistrusts everything unfamiliar. In their investigation of the "everyday-life villages" Young and Willmott quote a remark that underlines this phenomenon: "they are newcomers: they have only been here 18 years." The paradox is an apparent one only. These "newcomers" have created other bonds, other networks of mutual help; they belong to other groupings and they function according to their own proxemy. This is a reality that is especially obvious in large cities but which is, as with all self-evident considerations, worth being remembered. The group, for its own safety, shapes its natural and social environment and at the same time, *de facto*, forces other groups to constitute themselves as such. In that sense the marking of the territory, both the physical territory and the symbolic territory, is structurally the foundation of numerous "sociabilities." Besides direct reproduction, an indirect reproduction exists that does not depend on the will of the social protagonists but rather on that structural effect: "attraction-repulsion." The existence of a group—the foundations of which rests on a strong feeling of belonging—requires that other groups be formed according to requirements of the same nature.

The manifestations of this process are rather trivial after all. It suffices to observe the frequenters of a particular cafe, the specificity of some neighborhoods, or even the clientele of such and such a school, show place, or public space, to become aware of the pregnancy of that structure. Inside these diverse locations it is possible to notice other groupings, just as exclusive, that rest on the subtle but deeply rooted consciousness of a feeling of belonging and/or of a feeling of being different. Maybe one must see in this situation, as suggested by C. Bouglé, "traces of the caste spirit."[10] What is certain is that, beside an apparent egalitarianism a highly complex social architectonics has always existed, the diverse elements of which are both entirely opposed and necessary to one another.

It is possible to see that a *de facto* recognition of these groups among themselves does exist. As I have indicated, *exclusiveness does not mean exclusion*. Therefore, such recognition brings about a specific mode of adjustment. Conflict may exist, but it is expressed as a function of certain rules; it can be perfectly ritualized. Let us remember the *paraxystic* metaphor of the mafia: the division of the territory generally is respected and the war of the "clans" or of the families occurs only when, for some reason, the "honorable society" equilibrium is broken. If this model is applied to city tribes, one observes the existence of highly sophisticated regulation mechanisms. The role of the "third party," very well described by political sociology (Freund, Schmitt) finds its application here. In this respect, a system of differentiated alliances results in the fact that one of these tribes always occupies the position of a mediator. The pointed aspect of these alliances makes the system a constantly shifting one, which, at the same time, remains perfectly stable. The role of the third party is not reserved for a single person. It may be filled by an entire group that acts as a counterweight, or intermediary that, very simply, "carries the weight of many" and thus strengthens the equilibrium of a given body.

This can be compared to the "proxemic" function that existed in the ancient city. It is the function of an intermediary; the problem is to develop a bond among the diverse ethnic and national groups that constitute the city. Playing with words, it is possible to say that the *proxène* (the close one) makes one close. It is that *perdurance* (enduring through) that enables the foreigner, while remaining a foreigner, to be a real part of the city and have a place in its social architectonics. Is it accidental that, as M. F. Baslez reports, the poet Pindar, who plays the part of a *proxène*, is, at the same time, the one who writes the Dithyramb in honor of the city? It is indeed possible to imagine that the celebration of the city as a city reminds one of the power it has to tame and integrate the stranger[11].

Thus the recognition of diversity, and the ritualizing of embarrassment that this fact creates, lead to a specific adjustment that to some extent uses disagreement and tension as equilibrium factors useful to the city.

Here one finds again the contradictory logic, often analyzed (Lupasco, Beigbeder, Durand), that refuses both binary structures and the dialectic process as too mechanical or limiting. The diverse urban tribes "form a city" because they are different and at times even opposed to one another. Any restlessness is a structurally constructive activity. This is a basic sociological rule which, of course, did not escape Durkheim; the main thing is knowing how to use that restlessness, how to ritualize it. One good way, in the logic of what has just been presented, is to let each tribe be itself, the resulting adjustment thus being more natural. As I have already explained elsewhere, *coenesthesia* of the social body is to be compared to that of the human body, i.e., as a general rule, functioning and dysfunctioning complete and balance each other. The problem is to make the particular "bad" serve the global "good." Fourier placed that homeopathic procedure at the base of his phalanstery. Thus, he intended to use what he called "small hordes" or small bands, even anomic ones, to the best of their capabilities: "my theory limits itself to using passions (condemned ones) as nature gives them, without changing anything. That is the entire black book, the whole secret of passionate attraction."[12]

It may be that Fourier's careful calculation, somewhat utopian in his time, is in the process of becoming reality today. Heterogeneity being the rule, pluriculturalism and pluriracialism being the best characterizion of today's large cities, one may be lead to think that *consensus is more the result of an a posteriori "affectual" adjustment than it is that of a rational a priori regulation.* In that sense, we need to pay great attention to what, in too convenient a manner, we are calling marginality. The latter certainly is the laboratory of future lifestyles; the renewal of the group initiation rites that have been discussed is only taking the place of the ancient rites (which one no longer dares call by that name), empty of meaning for having been rendered uniform. Hasty condemnation is not sufficient, nor is condescension. Such rites really deserve a specific analysis. Their vitality, in fact, underlines the point that a new form of social binding is in the process of arising; it may be difficult to conceptualize it, but with the help of ancient images one certainly can draw its contours. Hence the metaphors of tribes and tribalisms that have been suggested.

It so happens that such a metaphor really translates the emotional point of view, the feeling of belonging and the conflictual atmosphere brought about by that feeling. At the same time, it makes it possible to pin-point, beyond that structural conflict, the search for a more hedonistic way of life, less determined by "what one must be" and by "work." All of these things were clearly observed by the ethnographs of the Chicago School several decades ago already. The "conquest of the present" shows itself informally

in the small groups that spend "the best part of their time erring and exploring their world."[13] This, of course, leads them to experiment with new behaviors among which the "trip," the movies, sports and "fast-fooding" occupy a place of choice. Moreover it is interesting to note that, with the help of age and time, small bands become stable; they become clubs or even "secret societies" with a strong emotional component. It is this passage from one form to another that pleads in favor of the protective aspect of tribes. They do not survive, of course, but the fact that some of them pass through the various steps of socialization transforms them into a social "pattern" of organization, a pattern that is flexible, somewhat bumpy, but which satisfies, *concreto modo*, the diverse contingencies of the social environment and of that specific natural environment, the postmodern city. From this point of view, the tribe may lead us to define a new social logic that presents the danger of shattering a number of our safety-inducing analyses. Thus, what appeared as "marginal" a little while ago no longer qualifies as such. Even before the Chicago School, Max Weber noted the existence of what I am calling here a "tribal romanticism" that enhances the value of the affectual life and of experience lived through. It seems to me that Weber's analysis of small mystical groups contains *in nuce* numerous elements that enable us to understand what we are observing today. In this respect, the prudence of Jean Seguy no longer appears acceptable to me because, beyond reservations that specifically apply to his time, the description of what escapes a rationalizing of the world is in perfect congruence with the *non-rational* that underlies the deep movements of urban tribes[14].

We must insist on this point: the non-rational is not the irrational, it does not take its place in relation to the rational; it uses another type of logic than that prevailing since the Age of Enlightenment. It is more and more accepted now that the rationality of the eighteenth and nineteenth centuries is only one of the possible models of reason at work in social life. Parameters such as the affectual or the symbolic may have their own rationality. Just as the non-logical is not the illogical, so it is possible to agree on the fact that the search for shared experiences, the gathering around eponymous heroes, non-verbal communication and body language, rest on a non-efficacious rationality, which in many respects is broader and more generous. This calls for a generosity of mind on the part of the social observer. That generosity can only make us attentive to the multiplication of tribes that are not marginal but which constitute inscriptions on a nebula that no longer has a precise center.

Let us register the existence of a multiplicity of *loci* that are secreting their own values and which function as mortar for those who set up and share those values. Nineteenth century rationality referred to history, to what I shall call an "extensive" (ex-tension) attitude. This rationality announces itself as proxemic,

40 "intensive" (in-tension) and it is organized around a pivotal point (guru, action, pleasure, space) that binds individuals while leaving them free. It is both centripetal *and* centrifugal. Hence the apparent instability of tribes—the "belonging coefficient"—is not an absolute one and each person can belong to a large number of groups, investing into each one a large part of the self. This fragmentation is one of the main characteristics of social organization that is taking form. Paradoxically, it allows us to postulate, on the one hand, the existence of two poles, the mass and the tribe, and, on the other hand, their constant reversibility—a back and forth motion between the *static* and the *dynamic*. Should this be related to the "objective chance" dear to the Surrealists? It is certain that each person (persona) is increasingly fenced in by the closed circle of relationships while he or she always remains capable of receiving the *choc* of the unexpected, of an event, of an adventure. Hannerz qualifies the essence of the city as: "the fact of discovering something by chance while looking for something else."[15] This applies also to our discourse: although defined by territory, tribe and ideology, each person can easily break into another territory, into another tribe, into another ideology.

This is what leads me to consider as passé individualism and its numerous theoreticians. Each social actor is less acting than acted upon. Each person defracts him or herself *ad infinitum* depending on the "Kairos," the opportunities, the situations which may arise. Social life, then, is a stage where, for a moment, crystallizations take place. The play can then take place. But once the play has ended, what formed a whole becomes diluted until another node emerges. Such a metaphor is not extravagant; it helps us understand that the succession of "presents" (with no future) is the best characterization of the atmosphere of the moment.

Notes

1 H. Raymond, Foreword to M. Young and P. Willmott, *Le Village dans la Ville (The Village within the City)* (Paris: G. Pompidou Center, C.C.I.), p. 9.

2 Cf. U. Hannerz (Paris Minuit: 1983) on the "Villages Urbains" ("Urban Villages"); H. Gans, *The Urban Villagers* (New York: Free Press, 1962). On attraction, see P. Tacussel, *L'Attraction Sociale (Social Attraction)* (Paris: Mèridien, 1984).

3 Regarding this theme and its main categories, see my book: M. Maffesoli, *La Conquête du Présent (The Conquest of the Present)* [Paris: PUF (Presses Universitaires de France), 1979].

4 A. Berque, *Vivre l'Espace au Japon (Living Space in Japan)* (Paris: PUF, 1982), p. 34. Cf. analysis, pp. 31-39.

5 I am calling attention to the fact that I have suggested reversing the Durkheim concepts of "organic solidarity" and "mechanical solidarity," Cf. M. Maffesoli, *La Violence Totalitaire* (Paris: PUF, 1979). Japanese translation: *Koseisha-Koseikaku* (in press).

6 The expression "multitude of villages" which is closely related to the Chicago School in this case is borrowed from J. Beauchard, *La puissance des Foules (The Power of Mobs)* (Paris: PUF, 1985), p. 25; regarding neighborhood relationships and their conflicts or solidarity, refer to a paper by F. Pelletier, "Quartier et Communication Sociale" ("Neighborhood and Social Communication") in *Espaces et Sociétés* 15 (1975). More recently, see the poetic analysis of an ethnologist, P. Sansot: *La France sensible (Sensible France)* (Champ Vallon: 1985), p. 45. See also F. Ferrarotti, *Histoire et Histoires de Vie (History and Life Stories)* (Paris: Mèridien, 1983), p. 33.

7 A. Moles, *Théorie Structurale de la Communication et Sociétés (Structural Theory of Communication and Societies)* (Paris: Masson, 1986), p. 147 and following.

8 E. Hall, *Au-delà de la Culture (Beyond Culture)* (Paris: Seuil, 1979), p. 67, gives in this connection the example of Japanese factories. Regarding tourism, I am referring to the article (and to the research in progress) of R. Amirou, "Le Badaud approche du Tourisme," ("The Stroller comes close to Tourism"), in *Sociétés* no. 8, (1988).

9 M. Yound et P. Willmott, *Le Village dans la Ville, op. cit.*, pp. 137, 138. 143 and passim.

10 B. Bouglè, *Essais sur le Régime des Castes (Essays on the Cast Regime)* (Paris: PUF, 1969), p. 5.

11 I am freely interpreting, here, an analysis of M. F. Baslez, "L'Etranger dans le Grece Antique" ("The Stranger in Ancient Greece") *Les Belles Lettres* (1984): 49 and passim. With respect to the role played by the "third party," see J. Freund, *L'Essence du Politique* (Paris: Sirey, 1965), and J. H. Park, *La Communication et le Conflit dans le Mode de Pensée Coréen (Communication and Conflict in Korean Modes of Thinking)* (Dissertation, Sorbonne-Paris V). Regarding the territories of the Mafia, see J. Ianni, *Des Affaires de Famille (Family Business)* (Paris: Plon, 1978).

12 Cf. Fourier, *Oeuvres Completes* (Paris: T.V. Anthropos, p. 157). See also E. Durkheim, *Les Formes Elémentaires de la Vie Religieuse* (Paris: PUF, 1968). Regarding the use of violence, I gave my own explanation in M. Maffesoli, *Essais sur la violence banale et fondatrice (Essays on trivial and constructive violence)*, second edition (Paris: Meridien, 1985).

13 See the analysis of ethnographists done by U. Hannerz, *Explorer la Ville (To Explore the City)* (Paris: Seuil, 1983), pp. 59-60. Regarding the theme of the present, I refer the reader to my book, M. Maffesoli, *La Conquête du Prèsent* (Paris: PUF, 1979). As for the model of what is secret, cf. G. Simmer, *Les Sociétés Secrètes (Secret Societies)* in *Revue Française de Psychanalyse* (Paris: PUF, 1977). About the rites of adolescent groups see L. V. Thomas, *Rites de Mort (Rites of Death)* (Paris: Fayard, p. 15).

14 It may be noted, moreover, that the normative reservations of M. Weber are found more in *Le Savant et le Politique (The Scientist and the Politician)*, a collection of "educational" texts, than in *Economie et Société*. Cf. M. Weber, *Le Savant et le Politique* (Paris: Plon, 1959), pp. 85, 105 and following. Regarding the "emotional community" see *Economie et Société (Economy and Societies)* (Paris: Plon), pp. 478, 565, and J. Seguy, *Rationalisation, Modernité et Avenir de la Religion en M. Weber (Rationalization, Modernity, and the Future of Religion in M. Weber)* in *Archives de Sciences Sociales des Religions* (Paris: CNRS, 1986), p. 132 and notes. Regarding the climate in which M. Weber was writing on *l'orgiastique* and his closeness to the "Ecole des Prêtres de Baal" and to the Cosmic circle of Klages, see W. Fietkan, *A la Recherche de la Révolution Perdue: Walter Benjamin* (Paris: Editions du Cerf, 1986), p. 291 and following.

15 Hannerz, *op. cit.*, p. 154.

RICHARD BOLTON is an artist and writer living in
Boston. He is the series editor for "Men and Society,"
a collection of texts on social issues in mass media
and art production published by the University of
Minnesota Press, and teaches at the Massachusetts
Institute of Technology in the Visible Language
Workshop. He has written extensively on photography
and contemporary criticism and is the editor of *The
Contest of Meaning: Critical Histories of Photography*
(forthcoming, MIT Press).

Figments of the Public: Architecture and Debt

AT & T Building, plaza marker
(Philip Johnson John Burgee Architects)

PUBLIC SPACE

Owned and maintained by AT&T, 550 Madison
Avenue, New York City. Complaints regarding this
public space may be addressed to The Department
of City Planning or The Department of Buildings
of the City of New York. This building is accessible
to the physically handicapped.

*Plaza marker at the AT&T Building, 550 Madison Ave-
nue (Phillip Johnson John Burgee, architects)*

In the present-day city, public space is conceived
of as a commodity, as a volume with an explicit
market value. Civic-minded politicians and investors
claim to give up this potentially profitable space for
the greater good, for the needs of society. Into this
public space will be placed all the necessary activi-
ties which do not immediately produce revenue:
lunchtime daydreaming, traffic, crowd control, free
speech. Since it is assumed that we inhabit a democ-
racy, it is assumed that any open space can be put to
democratic use, and so it is the responsibility of the
architect only to provide this space, to give over
enough volume that the social might live. But profit-
taking is never far from anyone's mind; in fact,
public spaces are designed to prevent any challenges
to this profit-taking—the efficient functioning of
the system remains paramount. The social is defined
as a financial question rather than a philosophical
one, and so public experience is seen as an engineer-
ing problem rather than the political issue that it is.
The terms of economic efficiency inevitably reflect
the interests of the patron rather than the public,
and since architects by and large accept these terms,
the city offers the public little opportunity to con-

struct complex and critical social experience. Public space remains only *negative space*: space awaiting the plans of developers, hollow space not yet absorbed by private interests. The "public realm" is only an irregularly-shaped volume, its boundaries formed by fences, walls, zoning ordinances, traffic patterns, real estate contests and deals over air rights.

Such concern over profits creates a view of the public as a collection of natives who must be moved around the land: relocated, persuaded, accommodated and swindled so that capital can be generated. Even worse, it means that our public selves, like the spaces of social experience, exist only in the negative. We are produced only as a mass, a potentially profitable one. We await annexation to private interests. Like other commodities, we must be stored until our moment in the arena of exchange arrives. Architecture undertakes the storage of the public, constructing more-or-less elegant warehouses for the masses and so bringing order to the workforce. On one side of the curtain wall, the corporation is organized. On the other side, the social is organized, warehoused according to the logic of the corporation.

The metaphors of economic exchange upon which I base my analysis here are not just "metaphors," for they reveal how thoroughly the structure of exchange has invaded our experience. They reveal how completely the circulation of capital and authority has rewritten our views of architecture and the public life that architecture allows. For all mass-produced reality, including the reality of architecture, is created by corporations. These corporations choose not to secure their realm by the blatant exercise of power (at least not at home—when abroad, the powerful become more adventurous); instead the corporation *legitimates* the system through rhetorical persuasion. We meet the system through the corporation. By means less strident than out and out propaganda the corporation hopes to convince us of the universality of the system's model of exchange. Architecture is one of these means.

Architecture facilitates economic exchange and the exercise of corporate authority. To understand this we must enlarge our understanding of "functionalism." In the traditional sense of this term, the building is seen as a work of engineering—it functions as a machine. Design decisions reflect the pragmatic needs of the client, and smooth and profitable operation of the company is the goal. The building is a basic tool for organizing productivity— architects help to construct the reality of labor by designing the spaces where work takes place. But architecture also functions rhetorically, fulfilling the *ideological* needs of the client, or the client-state. Architecture can create a rhetorical spin that sustains the company—the company is presented as a glossy symbol to the masses beyond the door. This symbol abstracts labor and product, helping to create the image of work and exchange most conducive to the company's goals. Capital itself is portrayed as

an abstract force. In this way, the material reality of the corporation is made invisible; the corporation is emptied of specific content, and becomes instead a series of flourishes, an image, a free-floating signifier, a sign of utopia and freedom. This signifier is the ultimate product of the corporation. As architecture's "public," we are given over to this signifier; we are delivered to sit and worship before the image of power. "Public space" is but a ringside seat to a carefully-controlled corporate spectacle. (Such is the circumstance with all authority in America— leaders exist in image only.)

Further, architecture generally keeps order; it categorizes and polices experience. Buildings define activity, and as one might expect, office space replicates the logic of the corporation. But public space also follows the corporate model of controlled access. The public space allows only what the architecture and the patron will permit. To mention one case: the IBM Plaza Garden, a public space certified by the city of New York, is filled with mystical light and bamboo, but it is also filled by surveillance cameras, guards, and sliding walls that can seal off the space immediately if necessary. What kind of activities can occur there? Only rest, contemplation, the quiet consumption of food and literature. The only active experience allowed is the *purchase*, and the not-too-animated conversation. The "social" exists here in name only: a collection of people happen to inhabit the same space, but they are utterly detached from one another. The Plaza Garden is merely a warehouse, or more succinctly, a *showroom* of the social.

There are many, many spaces that function in the same way as the Plaza Garden. Through the uncritical design of the workplace, through an apolitical approach to public space, through the purposeful creation of corporate icons, architecture helps to control the flow of authority, information, commodities and capital upon which corporations and governments depend. For maximum efficiency, all potential challenges to corporate reality are eliminated: dissenting histories are erased, multi-income dwellings and rent control are discouraged, as are low business rents for the small business owner. Competing realities are wiped away, and subcultures, workers and neighbors are prevented from gaining any understanding of their common interests. In place of social complexity, the public is offered such amenities as the concrete bench, the bubbling fountain and the ennui of the "planned" public space.

Both the federal and local governments have been selling off public properties and services to the highest bidder for many years now; oil leases, forest areas and information technologies have made their ways into private hands, out of the reach of government regulation. Even the National Weather Service has been considered for possible sale. This drive toward privatization has affected the urban environment directly. City governments find it easier to ignore their responsibilities to the citizenry. Deals are struck,

44 city space is placed under corporate control, and an urban plaza is built as token compensation. These plazas are ironic monuments to a diminished, disappearing social sphere. Here stands a final frontier, a frontier turned inward upon the city and the citizen—a raid upon the negative spaces of the social and the self. Architecture marks the site of loss: the loss of the self to authority, the loss of the public to private control, the loss of democracy to oligarchy, the loss of social participation to a new feudalism. Once the overly-idealized source of social possibility ("Architecture or Revolution. Revolution can be avoided," wrote Le Corbusier optimistically), architecture now works in reverse, diminishing an already exhausted social world.

PUBLIC SPACE

This urban plaza is accessible to the physically handicapped. To ensure compliance with the requirements regarding this urban plaza, a bond has been posted with the comptroller of the city of New York. This urban plaza is owned and maintained by 40 West 53rd Partnership, 31 West 52nd Street, New York, NY 10019. 212-969-4954. Plaza trees required: 6. Street trees required (53rd St.): 9.

Plaza marker at the Hutton Building, 31 West 52nd Street (Kevin Roche, John Dinkeloo, & Associates, architects)

Earlier in this century, architects restricted their practice, calling for the use of unit shapes, universal designs and materials, flexible generic plans, and uniform methods of construction in an effort to increase the flexibility of architecture, to allow architecture to fulfill myriad functions with the same basic vocabulary. Progressive architecture, and its "reasoned" view of the world, was to be made available to everyone. But utter simplicity also proved quite profitable, and the architect was conscripted into the service of the patron class. Heroic modernism became but a small part of heroic capitalism. But after several decades of this progressive simplicity, as the environment filled with cheap and banal buildings, the working population grew demoralized

and the city grew sterile. The symbolic order was faced with the loss of its rhetorical power. When capitalism itself underwent a crisis in the 1970s, an entertaining new architecture showed a way to a cure. Through figuration, quotation, pun, allusion and illusion, a "user-friendly" architecture was established, and was soon put to work rebuilding the image of the threatened system. At first perhaps unwittingly, but eventually quite cynically, the architect provided a new voice for the powerful. Released from the tyranny of the modern, released from the heroism of limitation, the architect could now indulge in the heroism of excess. The festooned building of postmodernism characteristically has served as a site of fascination and distraction, of big talk and big effects. The building has taken on the function of a fetish, posing itself as a gleaming substitute for the lack in social consciousness, magically compensating for the pieces missing from public life.

Perhaps the building has served as a fetish throughout this century. Even if this is true, the nature of this fetish has changed. In the first half of this century, rationalism was the fetish of choice; the building was intended to be a rarified site of control and organization, of rational development and consumption, of a sublimity born of science. Our time prefers a more immoderate, extravagant fetish. The building is glamorous, a spectacle of uncontrolled consumption and unabashed narcissism, with a sublimity borrowed from advertising and fashion. This fetish more perfectly suits our "postindustrial," "workless" economy, where labor and community have been rewritten as forms of entertainment, where reality has been replaced by publicity.

Wages are insufficient compensation. The citizen also hopes to make some contribution to community reality. We hope to play a role in the explanations of reality that are produced by our culture; we want to participate in the symbolic order of our society. Citizens look to the symbolic order, to this collection of common explanations, for stability; unfortunately, the symbolic order usually is not formed communally, but by a minority with power. The powerful have the means to initiate and conform representations, to control usage, to establish interpretive contexts, and to define invention. Some-

times this powerful minority considers the good of others, but more frequently it does not. We may try to contest this monopoly by countering authorized images and readings with "illegitimate" ones. This task is made difficult by the powerlessness of our position, and by the nature of the symbolic order itself. For in our "postindustrial" society, the symbolic order is formed through corporate-owned and corporate-sponsored information production, most specifically through the production of publicity. Publicity is manifest most obviously in advertising, but the logic of publicity also informs fashion, journalism, television production and the cinema. Magazines tell stories about fashion and the fashionable, and films and television weave commodities into their narratives. The publicity apparatus is all-encompassing.

OPEN TO PUBLIC

This urban plaza, its landscape of 12 trees, 384 linear feet of permanent seating, and the adjacent sidewalk landscape of 16 trees are provided and will be maintained for the enjoyment of the public by Park Tower Associates, 499 Park Avenue, New York, New York 10022. 212/355-7570. Complaints regarding this urban plaza may be addressed to Park Avenue Tower Associates, The Department of City Planning, or The Department of Buildings of the City of New York. This urban plaza is accessible to the physically handicapped.

Plaza marker at the Park Avenue Tower, 499 Park Avenue (I.M. Pei Associates, architects)

The image of architecture is very useful to the publicist. Routinely used in advertisements as a backdrop for new commodities and fashions, architecture helps to communicate the power and pleasure these products can provide. For architecture is an authoritative, even stereotypical symbol of culture: through association, architecture legitimates the advertised product. But it is not enough to talk about how architecture is used in advertising. It is important to recognize that architecture has become a *form* of publicity. Not only buildings, but *all* commodities are marked from the earliest stages of design by the rhetoric of publicity. For from the beginning, products are considered as both commodity and sign. Semantic meaning receives as much attention as does humble function, and eventually semantic meaning eclipses all other aspects of the product. Design facilitates the product's voyage from factory to market and on into the image-world of publicity—a world of advertisements, commercials, appearances. To do well in the marketplace, the product must function well in the image-world. If the product is extremely successful, the rhetoric of the product will seem more real than the product itself. In fact, the object may disappear from reality entirely, as the laws of publicity overtake the limitations of physical existence. Commodities begin to shimmer like mirages, to speak to us like phantoms. The building is such a commodity-sign, offered as a spectacle for consumers. And like all other phantasms of publicity, the illusions of architecture are insistent ones: they constantly interrupt our lives, constantly remind us of the power of the system, constantly seek to amaze and persuade us.

Once again: to remain loyal to the system, one must feel some participation in its symbolic order. In our society, where wealth is the greatest goal, everyone must be convinced, if not of one's *actual* wealth, then at least of one's *proximity* to wealth. Since the symbolic order is manifest in commodities, this order can be made available for sale; one can either obtain the commodities themselves, or bask in the publicity generated for these commodities. Of course there are other reasons to purchase products. Certainly they speak to human needs: to hunger and the need for shelter, to romantic and erotic desires. But this motivation of need must be seen next to the opportunistic nature of the commodity-sign. For the sign is arbitrary; its chief goal is to be authoritative, and any specific content for the sign is chosen with this authority in mind. The commodity-sign speaks to human needs only because this is the easiest way to circulate the sign, the easiest way to empower it. For these signs have a great deal of work to do. Exchange is the primary vehicle by which the messages of capitalism circu-

late; the commodity-sign must regulate this exchange, stimulate production, and otherwise establish order. Signs must be both naturalized and generalized if they are to do all these things effectively. Thus they usually refer to human need, and also—to avoid controversy—to dominant opinion, all the while maintaining a crucial arbitrariness.

This process of sign production and circulation has created great changes in our ideas about authenticity. This is easily seen by examining the workings of fashion. Fashion establishes an original, and turns this original into an origin. A changeable commodity is cloaked in ontological certainty; being is centered upon a purely arbitrary choice. (Subsequent contradictions are held at bay by the sheer force of the production system, or else these contradictions are rationalized through a kind of knowledge called "taste.") The original must be rare—if it is to sit at the center of being, only a few must be able to afford it. For those who cannot obtain this original, fashion allows proximity to this rarity by establishing a language—a style—which is spread throughout the culture. One either buys the original, the *real* fashion, the mark of *real* difference, or one approximates the original by adopting its style, achieving a less expensive simulation of the real. Everyone chases after the original, and some obtain it. Others achieve a sense of proximity to the original, and so a proximity to the symbolic order.

In short, authenticity has come to be located precisely at the heart of artificiality, in the heart of culture. (Advertisers at times illustrate this quite literally, linking the product to some natural setting: new automobiles within a leafy forest, alongside a bubbling brook, and so forth. Playing upon our belief in the authenticity of nature, this tactic is meant to persuade us that an equal authenticity can be found in commodities and publicity.) If we can be convinced of the legitimacy of the symbolic order, then the system can more easily eliminate or assimilate "illegitimate" outside positions that might be used for critical ends. From the system's point of view, all authenticity that is not clearly at one with the symbolic order is a threat. Origin must be locked securely within so that all attempts to locate it will confirm the reality of the system. In fact, just as the system works to bring outside positions under control, it also invents a new authenticity, an apparently unprejudiced reality that is written entirely according to the system's needs. Through a highly sophisticated manipulation of artifice, the ideology of the system is naturalized. In short, the system strives to simulate authenticity. This authenticity is rendered in the terms of the artificial, and then this artificiality is ignored.

Movement and conflict between the artificial and the authentic have informed bourgeois culture for a very long time. Critics of the status quo have often sought an authenticity outside dominant reality to best expose the inauthenticity of cultural life. But we have grown to recognize the degree to which all our notions of authenticity *depend* upon the artificial. We form the authentic in and with our language and culture; in a disturbing way, we *invent* the authentic, that is, we give the authentic to ourselves. We no longer trust that authenticity can be found *outside*. This is particularly true from the viewpoint of postmodernism, which emphasizes the role language and other forms of social mediation play in establishing reality. Inauthenticity lurks behind every appearance; the real depends entirely upon contrivance.

It has been thought that this postmodern skepticism would provide the critical means to contest the naturalizing ideologies of the powerful. Postmodern artists have not tried to invent an authentic reality wholly outside culture, as this would contradict their very argument. Instead, they have attempted to invent new perspectives that do not have recourse to authenticity. Attention has been drawn to the many ways the mediated reality of the system is naturalized, in the hope that skeptical analysis will generate new positions within the field of power. For if the commodity-sign can be made specific, if it can be placed within history, if its rhetorical strategies can be exposed, then the sign will become too controversial, and the closed circulation of authority will break down. The system will be open to critique, its ideological manipulation apparent.

This is why the system must both produce and reproduce itself—the system must prevent any breakdown at any level of its formation of reality. It would seem then that we have a model antagonism—ideology constructs, and criticism deconstructs. But as the last few years have shown, the system has resisted this method of attack successfully, taking critical work and *re*constructing it in a way that further fetishizes and legitimates the very forms of signification and authority criticized. Critical works of art have become commodities in their own right, and many once-radical artists endorse consumer goods and pose for publicity stills, allowing this lionization to overwhelm their initial critique. Works once thought media-critical now seem media-obsessed, extensions rather than criticisms of publicity's reality. Adjustments in the system have neutralized postmodernism's critical approach, and deconstruction now *sustains* the very ideological forms it once hoped to take apart. The symbolic order is empowered precisely by postmodernism's inability to suggest any kind of authentic life outside the forms of the system. For the system will always put forth a powerful revised version of the authentic in an attempt to recoup its losses. With no utopian possibility, and with no alternative vision of social life, postmodernism has been easily assimilated into a reformed dominant reality.

This transformation is much more obvious in architecture than in art, since architecture is more closely tied to patronage and market forces. What began in architecture as a critique of dominant artificiality quickly became a narrow argument over a new *style*. Architecture began to present critical *effects* rather than critical effectiveness, and even these critical effects soon disappeared. Postmodern architecture's final contribution has been the creation of new enjoyable commodities stripped of critical possibility. Audiences marvel at these flashy new buildings, but it is only conspicuous consumption that astonishes them. Postmodernism is now but a disguise, an "historicized" alibi, a stunning garb that robes naked power. The symbolic order has not been subverted; it has been rewritten in a powerful new way.

---

535 MADISON AVENUE

This open space landscape of 15 trees, seating of 30 movable chairs, and food service are provided and will be maintained for the enjoyment of the public by Madison Tower Associates. To ensure compliance with requirements regarding this open space, a bond has been posted with the New York City Planning Commission. This open space is accessible to the physically disabled.

Plaza marker at the 535 Madison Avenue Building (Edward Larabee Barnes Associates, architects)

Architecture reinforces the forms of rhetoric and exchange that characterize our economic system. As do advertising, fashion, and entertainment, architecture accepts publicity as its model of public discourse. Architecture, as engineering and as publicity, organizes the social, and generates these effects: the abstraction of the public and the abstraction of labor, the development of means of control and surveillance, the privatization of the public sphere, the creation of rhetoric and fetish objects, a confusion between artifice and authenticity. But in addition to all this, we also find in architecture the most nagging crisis of our present system—deficit. Debt is everywhere. It is the flip side of every attempt to construct our very expensive symbolic reality. Recent government accomplishments—economic stability, a booming market on Wall Street, the defense of our system through military buildup, control over developing nations—have all contributed to a massive national deficit. It is a measure of the success of our present order that this debt has come to seem natural, the inevitable cost of a "stronger America." The problem, however, does not end here. Debt is required for *all* participation in the social. At the individual level, everything from transportation to education depends upon loans. Once these loans are obtained, the individual is committed to becoming successful within the system in order to pay off these debts. Our system offers a symbolic order well beyond the means of most individuals and most other countries, an order even beyond the means of our system itself. Well-qualified candidates who can be depended upon to play the game are loaned the funds neces-sary for participation. These candidates are given contingent entrance to the symbolic order. These *arrivistes* are well-dressed but in debt. The system continues as before. All deficits, personal and national, are masked by rhetoric and fine wardrobes, by illusions of authenticity, by the extravagant messages of mass media and architecture.

Meanwhile, in place of community life there appears only negative space, a public deficit. This deficit is the result of our very concept of the social, a concept promoted to satisfy the needs of the corporation and the state. This concept is manifest in the way architecture constructs both work environment and public space as social warehouses. The entire city has been commodified, the public realm monopolized and privatized. Access to public life has been restricted according to the rules of economic exchange.

In the realm of the self there is only silence, a personal deficit. Public speech has been overrun by publicity, by the commodification of the symbolic order, by the privatization of communication. To obtain proximity to this commodified symbolic order—to be able to *speak*—an entire generation of workers lives beyond its means, in hock to the system. Debt has become a means to stabilize this class of workers, in the same manner that debt has been used to stabilize the entire American economy. Our private self has been colonized by commodities, by publicity, by architecture. It is almost impossible to recognize a self outside of this ever-widening circle of commodification. Can an uncommodified self be identified? Can critical speech be written and maintained? Can critical forms of work be developed? Can critical public experience be encouraged?

Within this structure of commodification, there appears again and again the structure of deprivation. Something is always promised, then withheld: origin, wealth, community. That which is manifest and made available to the public is mere appearance, phantasm, mirage. Within the self, within the social, can be found a web of repression: silence, alienation, deficit. On the surface, at the level of publicity, all seems well. But on any other level, reality is hard to discern: the social is only negative space, the self only emptiness and debt. This debt gradually blurs into a kind of death. We find ourselves with no public life outside of publicity, no community experience outside of commodities, no privacy outside of deprivation. And as the self dies, rhetoric lives. We are witnessing the beginning of another life, one framed completely by the rhetoric of the system.

PUBLIC SPACE

Open to public 8am to 10pm.

Plaza marker at the IBM Plaza Garden, 590 Madison Avenue (Edward Larabee Barnes Associates, architects)

PAUL WALTER CLARKE is an architect and assistant professor in the School of Architecture at Miami University, Oxford, Ohio. His publications include "Notes on a Critical Theory of Architecture" (coauthored with Thomas A. Dutton) published in *The Discipline of Architecture: Inquiry Through Design* (ACSA, 1986), and *Residential Rehabilitation Handbook: An Instrument for Neighborhood Decision-Making* (1977).

The Economic Currency of Architectural Aesthetics

My objective is to argue that the shift in architectural philosophy from modernism to postmodernism reflects a profound transition in advanced capitalism and accordingly in the production and control of space and space relations. It is a simple assertion that architecture costs money and occupies space. It is therefore integral to the production of space and the spatial configurations of the urbanism of our political economy. Not so simple is the assertion that architectural theories and aesthetics themselves possess political and economic significance. In other words, phenomena like modernism and postmodernism are political agendas; each confronts us not simply as a style, but rather as a cultural evocation which promotes and propels a range of very different urban phenomena.

This objective raises immediate questions: How do changes in the economy become manifest in the urban landscape? What was the engine that powered modernism and what now is the engine that propels postmodernism? The response to these questions demands an examination of urban, economic and architectural history. What follows are descriptions, first of the destructive tendencies of capitalism; second, how these tendencies facilitated the change from the industrial city to the corporate city and the role of modernism in this capitalist transition; and third, the further evolution of the corporate city with the requisite, ongoing destruction of its previous self and the role of postmodernism in this urban reorganization.

Before proceeding, certain caveats must be stated. Not all cultural production today is "postmodern"; neither postmodernism nor modernism is a holistic, homogeneous phenomenon. I will not attempt to make absolutely explicit, "stylistically," what is modern and what is postmodern. I do not consider either to be just an architectural "style" but to be cultural dominants that have architectural manifestations. Every era has contained within it the seeds of the subsequent era. I believe that the cultural phenomena of postmodernism was physically expressed in the "modernist" style. Hence I will be confusing what are typically considered distinct architectural styles. The argument I present is tentative, not plenary. My intention is neither to embrace modernism or postmodernism as a capitalist necessity nor to promote any argument for economic determinism. Subtleties and complexities characterize the physical and spatial operations of any society. The practice of architecture may be economically contingent, yet it is also capable of autonomous developments engendered by struggles, conflicts, innovations, contradictions and ambiguities.

Creative Destruction

A common perception is that the architecture of postmodernism arose from the failures of modern architecture. This is, at best, a naive truth; a simplistic formula for a complex reaction. Modernism concerns more than an architectural movement. Indeed, modernism radically changed the urban landscape of twentieth century capitalism. In that regard, modernism was a resounding success. However, this success was the result of its relationship to other parts of society. Success is seldom absolute. The awe inspired by our urban skylines is inhabited by a sense of dread. The forces that wrought these grand constructions are still in motion. As these buildings replaced earlier landscapes, so too will the newest architecture fall. Intentional destruction of the built environment is integral to the accumulation of capital. The emergence of postmodernism does not signal the demise of this "creative destruction."

"Built environment" is a simplistic title, of credible utility, for a complex assemblage of various constructions (roads, buildings, transit systems, utilities); each produced within specific conditions and according to various regulatory and financial strictures. The built environment is long-lived, difficult to alter, space specific, and absorbs large aggregates of capital. Its value must be maintained throughout its life in order to amortize the immense costs it entails. A proportion of this environment is at times used in common by capitalists and consumers. Nevertheless, even those elements privately appropriated (houses, shops, factories) are situated and utilized within an economic context and contribute immensely to the flow of capital. This suggests that the constellation of various elements that comprise the urban landscape must function as an ensemble. This characteristic, plus all the aforementioned characteristics, has implications for capitalist investment.[1]

The elements of the built environment serve as a vast investment field for surplus capital. Consequently, through the process of capitalist development, urban form will be more and more affected by the exigencies of capitalist accumulation. If this argument appears tautological, it is presented because typically we have tended to view urban form fatalistically, as an inevitable corollary of advanced industrial (or now, "post-industrial") society. From this perspective, patterns of movement and settlement (from countryside to city, from center city to suburbs, from suburbs to "gentrified" center city) and spatial divisions of work and home, of commercial and residential districts, of upper-class and lower-class neighborhoods, of even week and weekend, appear to be politically neutral, forged outside of the economic system by pragmatic necessities. Such an impression has been an enduring myth until recently. It is being exorcised by a growing popular awareness, wrought by "deindustrialization" and massive loss of employment, that cities will atrophy if not redeveloped to facilitate and reinforce capitalist production and consumption. Otherwise investment will move elsewhere. This is not new and has been integral to the "free market" economy since before the inception of industrialization. Capitalism has a demonic appetite to build and to rebuild. Each new construction adds value to the urban matrix. The built environment both expands and expends capital. Construction in central city areas forces other enterprises and occupancies to the periphery. Construction in outlying areas gives greater worth to the center.

Buildings occupy space. If the location, not the building, becomes more valuable, then the existing building prevents the realization of that value. Under these circumstances, it is only through the destruction of old values in the built environment that new values can be created. With a voracious appetite, capitalism bites its own tail.

Capitalist development has therefore to negotiate a knife-edge path between preserving the exchange values of past capital investments in the built environment and destroying the value of these investments in order to open up fresh room for accumulation. Under capitalism there is, then, a perpetual struggle in which capital builds a physical landscape appropriate to its own condition at a particular moment in time, only to have to destroy it, usually in the course of a crisis, at a subsequent point in time. The temporal and geographic ebb and flow of investment in the built environment can be understood only in terms of such a process. The effects of the internal contradictions of capitalism, when projected into the specific context of fixed and immobile investment in the built environment, are thus writ large in the historical geography of the landscape...[2]

Modernism is credited with the destruction of the traditional city and of its older neighborhood culture. But this destruction was inevitable. Haussmann could have died at birth, but Paris would still have had to be changed if capitalism was to be accommodated. If Le Corbusier had remained a watch engraver, corporate capitalism would have found a utopian image other than the *ville radieuse* with which to remodel its cities. Again I do not wish to portray an economically determined manifest destiny, but rather to illustrate that in all epochs, whatever the significance

50

of his or her role, the architect has been subject to the "reason" of those in power.[3]

The pathos of all monuments is that their material strength and solidity actually count for nothing and carry no weight at all, that they are blown away like frail reeds by the very forces of capitalist development that they celebrate. Even the most beautiful and impressive buildings are disposable and planned to be obsolete, closer in their social functions to tents and encampments than to "Egyptian pyramids, Roman Aqueducts, or Gothic cathedrals."[4]

Capitalist cities are cities of constant flux. If the physical world offers a frame of reference for what is "constant," then the latent power of the physical ordering of the world must be contradicted, even destroyed. This was essential for the success of modernism and the legacy of this constant destruction has contributed to the essence of postmodernism: a tenuousness, a new superficiality, a "depthlessness."[5] The critical question for architects is what processes of legitimation arise to mask this violence?

Modernism and the Crucial Value of Image

By mid-nineteenth century, the dominant economic character of cities shifted from centers of commerce to centers of production. What followed was the era of emerging monopoly capitalism, of robber barons, and the extension and refinement of the factory system. The transition from commercial accumulation to industrial accumulation wrought immense urban upheaval. No capitalist city escaped some change and most underwent radical and traumatic alteration. Huge factories were concentrated in downtowns near rail and water heads. Working class housing districts emerged in central locations, segregated in various districts by class. The middle and upper classes fled from the center city as fast and as far as their affluence permitted.[6] Many pieces of literature describe the horrific conditions of the land speculation that preyed upon the working class in the industrial city: from Dickens, to Riis, to Engels.[7] Only the most desperate of conditions forced the laboring classes to submit to capitalist exploitation. While the hegemony of industry left a minimum of opportunities for manifestations of independence, there was resistance, urban riots and unionization.

The Industrial Revolution could hardly proceed without Labor. The working class had to be accommodated, at least to the point of their compliance. The subsequent, bourgeois, urban reform movement that followed was to prove more pro-capitalist than pro-labor. Gordon very convincingly argues that the fundamental transformation of our cities from industrial to corporate in character came not so much from the obvious innovations in technology that allowed production to leave the center city, or

from the economies of administrative agglomeration that warranted the geographic separation of administration from production; but from the capitalist drive to control labor.[8] The co-optation of labor occurred, in part, through the mediations of newly formed professions; among them, law, medicine, social work, and germane to this discussion, architecture. The requisite urbanism for industrialization gestated modernism, which, in turn, was instrumental in the later urban reorganization that produced the corporate city of the mid-twentieth century. This period also brought the full flowering of the professionalization of architecture. These are not unrelated phenomena.

The architect is, by convention, identified with the ruling powers of society. The ruling power has universally been the only force capable of amassing and supplying capital, materials, land, and the authority to act; typically considered prerequisites for architecture. Prior to the Industrial Revolution, architects, for the most part, came from the ranks of the ruling elite. They designed for their own class. Architectural objects had as their subject the architect's own class. This changed with the rise of industrial accumulation and this change had great significance in the formation of the architectural credos of modernism.

Typical of an avant-garde, the early modernists of the 1920s attempted to divorce themselves from the practices of the dominant regime. Their program called for the elimination of concepts of form in the sense of fixed or traditional types. Formal ordering methods of the Beaux Arts and other historical architecture were scorned as the architectural representation of an exploitive and moribund society. Historical styles were also viewed as having been made obsolete by innovations in techniques and materials. The modernists sought a vernacular of modern technology that would address and satisfy the shelter crisis of the new concentration of urban populations. Furthermore the new architecture was to be *functional*, developing out of the exact determination of needs and "practical demands."[9] The struggle was to evolve a language of form premised upon a minimum of costly ornamentation and traditional labor-intensive construction.[10] The geometric play of proportions, new materials and color would give significant richness to the new architecture. The intended economy of means gave credence to the exhaltation of spareness as a style. Having dismissed previous architectural paradigms, the modernists substituted their own: universal space, column grids, moveable wall planes, and an asymmetrical and nonhierarchical orientation; all signifying an architectural intent to create an egalitarian society.

Modern architecture is surely most cogently to be interpreted as a gospel...its impact may be seen as having very little to do with either its technological innovations or its formal vocabulary. Indeed the value of these could never have been so much what they seemed as what they signified...they were didactic illustrations, to be apprehended not so much for themselves but as the indices of a better world, of a world where rational motivation would prevail and where all the more visible institutions of the political order would have been swept into the irrelevant limbo of the superseded and forgotten....its ideal...was to exhibit the virtues of an apostolic poverty, of a quasi-Franciscan *Existenz minimum*...one definition of modern architecture might be that it was an attitude towards building which was divulging in the present that more perfect order which the future was about to disclose.[11]

Unfortunately, the new style as an image supplanted the initial social intent. While a new architecture was created, it proved to have a negligible effect on the social order. Housing for the masses became confused as mass housing. The aesthetic of pure geometry—the unadorned cube—was mistaken as a desired end unto itself. The opposition to ornament became a pursuit of new visual patterns and not, as was initially proclaimed, the elimination of visual determinants of design. The agenda of social reform was divested. The concern that a building *employ* rational methods in its design was eclipsed by the concern that a building *appear* rational.

The style of the pure and unadorned object has enigmatic corollaries. It signifies that the object is separate from social meaning. The object has no history and continues no history. It is ahistorical. Meaning and form are independent; the object has only to refer to itself to be legitimate. The purity of the object is untainted because the object has no subject. All of these are futile assertions, the stuff of myths.

However, if as stated earlier, modern architecture was a resounding success, it was because its mystifications were essential for an economy that was destroying in order to create. It was an economy which appropriated the practice of architecture and which alienated the very act of *dwelling* and called it *housing*. The architect was no longer designing for her or his class. The housing, factories, schools, "public" libraries, warehouses, and other new building types were commissioned by the capitalist class, but not occupied by them, and certainly not occupied by architects. The subject of these objects was not the working classes, although indeed, they inhabited them. The subject was capitalism. The modernist architects were the first to have disenfranchised "clients." Objectified by a mode of production, the laboring masses were further objectified by an architectural philosophy which did not respect history, that rebelled against notions of class and thereby refused to recognize the continued relations of class. It was a philosophy of universal norms, unconcerned with aspects of existing culture since its proposed architecture was the vanguard of a new "emancipating" culture. The major success of the modernists was the creation of a model of utilitarian construction and a rationale for it. This model was then appropriated and debased by the very economic forces from which the model was to be the salvation.

The so-called Modernist architecture...devoted itself to the cultivation of the fantasy that the *appearance* of lifeless objects could gratify man [or woman] and relieve him [or her] from the anxiety and terror of oppression. By ostracizing the ornament and emphasizing the significance of the surface structural relations as the vessels of contained functions, it was thought that the building could be made a rational product, that the consumer was obtaining indeed a utility, a real one, and not a signifier of value. However, the exposure of the structural skeleton, the articulations of functions, the adoption of elementary geometric forms, did not in the least make the skeleton more effective or improve the contained functions; these were all attempts to build up a new visual vocabulary for a language that now had a new purpose, the temporary abandonment of power to the producer of rapidly obsolescing products.[12]

Modernists, like any avant-garde, ignored existing material. In fact, they encouraged its destruction on the basis that it was decadent, obsolete, a fetter to real progress and true creativity. The early modernists appropriated the technology of modern capitalism and, in so doing, also embraced the social logic of that technology regardless of how neutral they considered it. The modernist movement was utopian in aim but wasn't, and couldn't be, within capitalism. It was a utopia of objects—a revolution of objects. The failure of modernism was not simply in the architecture, but in the social logic behind it. That logic was that the object is neutral; outside of social relationships.

Ultimately the modernist stance was defensive and insular, a trait still endemic to an architectural culture which prefers "to deduce from its own centre what could have only been found by a complete and unprejudiced analysis of the ways in which the mythical *society* being addressed decodes, distorts, transforms, makes factual use of the messages launched by the *builders of images*."[13]

The modernist city has yet to be built as the shanty towns of Brasília painfully illustrate. Nevertheless, it was under the cosmetic of modernism that the corporate city arose from the contradictions of the industrial city. To be sure, industrial activity continued within the corporate realm which ultimately depended upon the production and realization of value. A new distinction was that these operations and tendencies were guided by the decisions of fewer and much larger economic bodies which sought legitimations in various forms, not the least of which was architecture. Equally crucial was that economic production increasingly included the production of space and long-term investments in land improvements. The "builders of images" were integrally involved as the centers of cities became more and more dominated by central business districts comprised of towering corporate skyscrapers.

While the corporate city and the skyscraper were epiphenomena of the same economy—a roughly tuned engine and its hood ornaments—it is paradoxical that, symbolically, the two were mutually antagonistic. The corporate city was distinguished

52 from the industrial city by several characteristics. Administration and production became geographically separated. Manufacturing moved rapidly away from the center of the city rather than being concentrated at its center. Corporate icons spiked the landscape of the central business districts, the chosen locale for key control and command functions of business and high finance. It was also critical that the city became politically balkanized, fragmented into hundreds of separate urban and suburban jurisdictions. This trait is significant in that manufacturing was able to escape, across legal fences, the conflicts and contradictions brought by the centralization of large masses of labor in the industrial city. What had previously proven efficient had become a liability.[14] The city and its hinterland were being reorganized as a single realm for corporate efficiency. This efficiency was not complete; there was some confusion between the dancers and the dance. The skyscraper was emblematic of the paradox that, while each phase of capitalism has engendered a commensurate form of urbanism, certain factors of urbanism operate, at times, in an autonomous fashion. Land speculation and the production of space are prominent examples.

The skyscraper was an "event," as an "anarchic individual" that, by projecting its image into the commercial center of the city, creates an unstable equilibrium between the independence of the single corporation and the organization of collective capital.

The single building operations within the city, as speculative ventures, entered into conflict with the growing need for control over the urban center as a structurally functional whole. In the face of the problem of ensuring the efficiency of the central business district in terms of integrated functions, the exaltation of the "individuality" of the skyscraper in downtown Manhattan, already dramatically congested, was an anachronism. The corporations, still incapable of conceiving the city as a comprehensive service of development, in spite of their power, were also incapable of organizing the physical structures of the business center as a single coordinated entity.[15]

In a corporate world, architecture is image. The skyscraper is the epitome of the centralization of power. It is also sunk capital which must have credentials in the marketplace. As a building program, the office tower consists of accretions of cellular spaces or open, continuous, modular spaces. It is a building type that has remained stubbornly the same.

Being of recent origin, this building type lacks a well established iconography deriving its legitimacy from precedents, and unlike the town hall, the museum, or the railway station, it is endlessly repeated within our city centers. Paradoxically a lot of its success will rest on its distinctiveness from its surroundings, inasmuch as it is meant to represent and advertise the power of corporations or of commercial organizations. Therefore, the office building as a semantically neutral type is yet most likely to be dressed in a seductive image.[16]

The Tribune Tower competition of 1922 documented the inventory of architectural skins and the construction almost proved the inelasticity of neoclassicism as regards height. A more pliable skin for this urban metamorphosis was Art Deco; an aesthetic of industrialized art nouveau (to turn the eye of the elder avant garde while the younger still struggled for legitimacy), a machined "Arts and Craft" (labor, if not accommodated, must at least be heralded), the last aesthetic gasp of the Beaux Arts that recognized much of the modernists' formal agenda despite the chiseled surfaces.

The shift in seductive images, from Deco to the pure modernist skin of taut, Miesian, graph-paper facades enveloping Platonic volumes, bridges a chasm of infinite tears: the Depression and the second World War.[17] The trauma of these years further deteriorated urban conditions and fostered, within popular consciousness, the rejection of the traditional city. The Great Depression was considerably more than a crisis of underconsumption. However, it appeared as such and the capitalist class responded to it as such. Despite the New Deal, the Depression was ended by the defense spending of World War II. Fear of the Depression (among other fears) has since maintained defense spending in the subsequent Cold War. Thus appeared a corollary of the corporate city; the Keynesian city.[18] This response was another transformation of the urban process, one in which corporate accumulation forged a new spatial dynamic. Shaped as consumption artifacts, the social, economic, political and physical attributes of capitalist cities depended upon state-backed, debt-financed consumption. Several features warrant discussion since they contributed to the increasing dependency upon image.

The Keynesian City

First, federal policies, the zoning practices of the politically fragmented, metropolitan regions, the uneven, geographic investment patterns of banking institutions, the real estate developers and the construction industry all contributed to the creation of sprawling, extensive, single-family housing developments in the 50s and 60s. The massive increase of single-family homes intensified the isolation and separation of individual families from their communities and class. The consequence of this was that the search for identity was collapsed into innumerable consumer choices ranging from the prestige value of house and neighborhood to "better schools for the children." Architectural images were just one mode of these distinctions. New enclaves of class exclusion and racial segregation underwrote the suburban dream.

Second, the sprawling, circumferential development of the Keynesian city was reinforced by the energy, auto and highway construction industries.

Auto and highway development accentuated the disadvantages of the older central cities and further reinforced people's isolation within the metropolis.

Third, when manufacturing employment moved outside of the center city, financial and real estate interests and city governments ("coalitions for growth"), intent upon maintaining the value of municipal investments in infrastructure, realized that their mutual interests could be advanced only if more and more corporate headquarters located in their central business districts. The modernist program became bureaucratically operational in "urban renewal." "Decaying," "blighted," "slum" districts were "cleared" for "redevelopment." Demolition and renewal occurred to an extent previously unknown. These programs of renewal had the effect of pushing the poor into more crowded quarters and, in many cases, vacating vast downtown tracts of land for long ghostly periods of "incubation."[19]

These three traits illustrate how powerful growth coalitions promoted their own interests through urban renewal and suburbanization. Creative destruction became geographically disparate. The suburbs were created as the neighborhoods of the center city were destroyed. New instrumentalities were forged in the practices of finance capital and federal, state and local government. The consequence was ideological control "to ensure that consumer sovereignty was sovereign in the right way, that it produce rational consumption in relation to accumulation through the expansion of certain key industrial sectors (autos, household equipment, oil and so forth)."[20] By the sixties, America had very different-looking cities of low-density sprawl, with distinctive spaces of consumption (rural to suburban to center-city) premised on "strange significations of life-style and social status etched into a landscape of unrelieved consumerism."[21] Many of these traits of "demand-side" urbanization would prove even more invidious in the next phase of capitalism.

The Spread of Modernism

What of modernism? Why did this imagery, fashioned and championed in the twenties and thirties, become so widely subscribed to by corporations in the fifties and sixties? The skyscrapers of the fifties were exemplary in that, while still emblematic of corporate values, they appealed to ideals higher and more widely respected than those of business. In that decade, modernism was not the credo of an avant garde but was the anthem of a rebuilding society and an expanding economy. For two decades, during the Depression and World War II, construction of all types was thwarted; initially for lack of capital and then, during the war, there was a surplus of capital frustrated by a lack of materials. The fifties were the postponed gratification of twenty years of austerity. Madison Avenue was not lax in helping to establish the anthem; "There is a Ford in your future!" That future became the present in the Eisenhower years. American cities had changed during the war; rural exodus from agricultural reorganization, combined with urban employment, brought American cities to their greatest and densest populations ever. Popular, middle-class sentiment was that the cities, changed, had to be rechanged. The modernist cry of sunlight and air and open green spaces gave credence to the suburbs and an image to the urban renaissance. Architecture was the visible evidence that governments and corporations were involved in building the future. The open space of Seagram's Plaza was a "gift" to Manhattan. It did not matter that it was a *quid pro quo* for a zoning variance of greater height for the Seagram's Tower. Ignored in this era of middle-class and corporate affluence, of urban demolition and frenzied construction, was the popular anti-business sentiment created by the Depression. This sentiment still had credence with the poorer classes who resided within the urban renewal zones and within the highway easements. Now, however, it was the state as the instrument of urban renewal that bore the backlash.

Postmodernism, Commodity Reification and Symbolic Capital

The prosperity of the Keynesian city had considerable costs which reached crisis proportions in the late sixties and early seventies. This period defies a short description. The Civil Rights Movement, the Vietnam War, urban riots, the anti-war movement and the student revolts, all had complex and subtle consequences in urban politics. Notions of neighborhood and community became central in the formation of resistance to continued urban transformation. Resistance was not limited to the neighborhood conservation struggles of the besieged urban poor. Suburbanites pushed for "limits to growth." The production of space became impeded by a sensitivity to *place*. The final ravages of urban renewal is not so distant that it needs to be recounted here. In short, the future that was promised proved unacceptable. Much of the modernist vision that had been constructed was experienced as barren and fragmented landscapes; one more form of alienation in a society and time almost awash in strife and angst. Modernism seemed exhausted at the same time as the economic engine faltered. The postwar strategies of the Keynesian program eroded as revived world trade increased foreign competition in durable and consumer goods. Inflationary financing temporarily assuaged the falling capacity of the economy to absorb further investments. In the search for the highest rate of return, a wave of international lending that culminated in the weakening of the dollar and the international debt crisis of the eighties.

54   It bears repeating that the inherent and ineluctable character of capitalist urbanization is flux and that crisis is a significant mode of transition for capitalism. The recession of 1973, the "stagflation" of the late 1970s, and the "Reagan" recession of 1981-82 have produced subsequent phenomena of shrinking commercial markets, vast unemployment, rapid shifts in the global division of labor (indicated by plant closings, "deindustrialization,"[22] capital flight, and technological and financial reorganization). Harvey is an excellent observer and commentator on the effects of this crisis on urbanism and the built environment:

When monetary policy was tightened in response to spiraling inflation in 1973, the boom of fictitious capital formation [e.g.: land speculation] came to an abrupt end, the cost of borrowing rose, property markets collapsed..., and local governments found themselves on the brink of...the traumas of fiscal crisis. Capital flows into the creation of physical and social infrastructures...slowed at the same time as recession and fiercer competition put the efficiency and productivity of such investments firmly on the agenda... The problem was to try to rescue or trim as much of that investment as possible without massive devaluations of physical assets and destruction of services offered. The pressure to rationalize the urban process and render it more efficient and cost-effective was immense.

And to the degree that urbanization had become part of the problem, so it had to be part of the solution. The result was a fundamental transformation of the urban process after 1973. It was, of course, a shift in emphasis rather than a total revolution...It had to transform the urban legacy of preceding eras and was strictly limited by the quantities, qualities, and configurations of those raw materials.

The question of the proper organization of production came back center stage after a generation or more of building an urban process around the theme of demand-led growth.[23]

Harvey addresses the question: In the 1980s, how can urban regions, blessed largely with a demand-side heritage, adapt to a new supply-side world? He lists four current practices, none of them mutually exclusive, none without serious political ramifications and economic risks and none without some requisite form of destruction and re-creation. The following is a synopsis of Harvey's descriptions.[24]

First, cities can aggressively compete within the spatial division of labor to improve their productive capacity. Efforts in this regard are to attract new industry to an area. Typical of this competition are the recent lobbying of state governments vying for the location of domestic production plants of foreign automobile manufacturers. The overall, long term effect of this type of competition is seldom beneficial. Typically, the concessions granted to entice an industry to relocate are considerable, with short-fall gains and long-term liabilities.[25] A vast repertoire of resources is necessary for successful enticement of industry: infrastructure ranging from highway and transit systems to quality academic institu-

tions, capital resources and finance opportunities, and finally, a surplus of skilled labor power. Labor often has not benefited from this competition since union contracts and innovative, labor-saving technologies are often included in the negotiations of concessions.

Second, urban regions can seek to improve their competitive position with respect to the spatial division of consumption. This entails more than expenditures made by tourism, considerable as they may be. Demand-side urbanization has, since the end of World War II, focused energy and investment upon significance of life-style, the construction of "community," and the organization of space in terms of the signs and symbols of prestige, status and power. This urbanization has constantly expanded the opportunities for participation in such consumerism while concurrently distinguishing its class exclusivity, since recession, unemployment, and the high cost of credit forecloses participation by significant numbers of the population. This form of interurban competition is incredibly risky as investments that establish a prestigious living environment, and that seek to enhance "quality of life," are anything but cheap. In this endeavor, image is paramount. Examples abound: Ghiradelli Square in San Francisco, Faneuil Hall in Boston, Harbor Place in Baltimore, Union Station in St. Louis, Renaissance Center in Detroit. Even recent corporate headquarters, the Humana Tower of Louisville or the Proctor and Gamble Expansion contribute to this urban competition of status and consumer attraction. An example, as yet unresolved, is that of Oakland, Phoenix, Memphis, Jacksonville and Baltimore, who are all petitioning the National Football League for franchises. Baltimore, in efforts to retain its baseball team and to obtain a NFL team, has proposed a $200 million, two stadium, 85-acre development near its downtown inner harbor.[26] It should be clear that this urban clamor for prestige and life-style is not a new trend (consider the Sydney Opera House, or even the Paris Opera House). However, particularly telling is the linkage to overall, urban economic health and the competitive anxiety that has fostered these recent constructions. The result is an inner urban dichotomy of the construction of locales of conspicuous consumption within a sea of insidious austerity. Indeed, the Paris Opera House is the true precursor of this malaise.

Third, metropolitan areas can compete for those key control and command functions of conglomerates, high finance and government that embody immense power over all manner of activities and spaces. This competition fosters and protects centers of finance capital, of information gathering and control, and of government decision-making. Competition of this sort demands a careful strategy of infrastructure provision. Within a worldwide network of transport and communication, centrality and efficiency are paramount. This necessitates immense expenditures in airports, rapid transit, communication systems. Adequate office space is a requisite for this competition and it depends upon a public-private coalition of property developers, banking financiers, and public interest groups capable of anticipating and responding to possible needs. Here, also, architectural image is significant. The consolidated locations of the electronics industry are exemplary: Silicon Valley in California and the redevelopment of Route 128 outside Boston. This bicoastal domination was recently challenged by the efforts of the state of Texas to establish Austin and the University of Texas as the major American research and development center of electronics.

Fourth, the Keynesian program is not entirely gone. Huge expenditures on redistribution, the defense budget chief among them, present opportunities for regional and urban competition. The federally-financed, multi-billion, super cyclotron is one current example of the awards possible from this type of competition.

The Postmodern City

Cities are following the path of these four trends. The resulting shifts—some radical, some subtle—in spatial constraints and in the production of urban space have allowed geographical redispersion of production, consumption, and speculative investment on a very large, national and, at times, international scale. The net effect is an exacerbated state of intra-city, inter-city, inter-state, inter-regional and inter-national competition. Such fragmentation is realized within a skin of desperate utopian imagery. All these traits were present before the 1970s and 1980s However, the speed, appearance and general character are newly distinctive. The flexibility and alacrity of corporate and state bureaucratic institutions and small entrepreneurs to adapt and respond to, and even promote, the rate of change is unique to the present. Harvey has called this current period of late capitalism the era of *flexible accumulation*.[27]

Concurrent with flexible accumulation, aesthetic production has become more integrated into commodity production. As Fredric Jameson argues, there is a frantic economic urgency to produce more environments with the appearance of novelty at greater rates of turnover.[28] This is the structural role of postmodernism: aesthetic innovation and experimentation to support flexible accumulation.

Flexible accumulation is subsumed in postmodernism and this reflects the demise of the welfare state and of the architectural credos of modernism. The naiveté of universal norms and of ideal environments for living and working is lost. There is little security in this process because flexible accumulation makes long-range planning horizons unrealistic. "Creative destruction" no longer advances under the single umbrella of a grand, unified ideological system. Postmodernism is a cultural equivocation that allows for divergence and heterogeneity.

The term signifies a directionality, but no destination. Its architectural agenda suggests an antithesis. Modernism denied history, postmodernism embraces it. Modernism ravaged the landscape of the city, postmodernism respects the existing context and culture of urban life. Modernism disdained existing culture, postmodernism endorses it in all its "popular" forms. Modernism ignored vernacular prototypes, postmodernism elaborates typologies of all origins. It is difficult to give a comprehensive survey of postmodernism since its boundaries and strictures are so amorphous. However, postmodernism has a legacy from modernism it has yet to contradict. The current fabrications of architects are solitary objects divorced from their subjects. We may no longer be talking of the unadorned cube as the aesthetic model, but still remaining are fragmented social relationships, different and yet similar to those of modernism. "The alienation of the subject has been displaced by the fragmentation of the subject."[29]

The field is now one of stylistic and discursive heterogeneity that lacks any great collective project in an epoch of great collective need. Exchange-value has been exalted by such religious zeal that the very memory of use-value is tantamount to sacrilege.[30] The capture of exchange value (value realized only through the market system—speculation is one form) is preeminently the creation of image.

In the business of renting commercial space...developers must concentrate on attracting tenants from other buildings by providing a superior situation both physically and financially. The nature of their business tempts them to focus on short term benefits rather than long-term stability. Their buildings must be seductive, trendy, and as inexpensive as possible to build.[31]

With few exceptions, newer buildings age faster, but their tenuousness is due to more than insubstantial construction. It is also due to the vacuousness of image. Jameson uses the word "depthlessness," the virtual deconstruction of the very aesthetic of expression itself, to describe this condition. The "depth" models of modernism have generally been repudiated: essence and appearance, latent and manifest, authenticity and inauthenticity, and the opposition between signifier and signified. "Depth is replaced by surface or by multiple surfaces." The medium decries the lack of a message. As Debord comments: "The image has become the final form of commodity reification."[32]

Symbolic Capital

What *commodity reification* is to Debord is *symbolic capital* to Harvey.[33] Symbolic capital is the collection of luxury goods attesting to the taste and distinction of the owner. Symbolic capital describes little that is new. Yet, coupled with flexible accumulation, the term greatly enhances descriptions of gentrification (the usurpation of the place and his-

56 tory of "others"), the recuperation of "history" (real, fantasies, re-created, usurped, or assembled as pastiche), the idealization of "community" (real or as consumable commodity), and the role of ornament and "style" with which to establish codes and symbols of distinction. Creative destruction is integral to the pursuit of symbolic capital. This is true even with current projects of architectural rehabilitation and preservation where a structure is reconstituted but destroyed as a cultural and historic symbol.

Money capital itself became unstable in the 1970s due to inflation. Economic recessions forced the exploration of product differentiation, hence the desire to seek symbolic capital surged in the production of the built environment. The ability to convert symbolic capital into money capital is inherent in the cultural politics of the contemporary urban process.[34] Flexible accumulation has become the mobilization of image—the employment of spectacle within the urban arena. Disneyland becomes an urban strategy.

Despite the seductive images, and deference to the context in which they are placed, these Disneylands seem alien. They seem alien because they are components of an urban scheme that appears familiar, yet remains stubbornly vague; that appears vibrant in spirit, but aloof in engagement; and alien because our cities are becoming more and more fragmented with these postmodern visions. This fragmentation occurs because symbolic capital must distinguish itself. It must define its edges to protect itself as a symbol and to protect itself as investment. As such, it cannot be "infill" within the urban continuum. It has to be a separate event. The fragmentation of our cities is a result of multiple attempts to impose order, the success of which depends entirely on how geographically discrete the imposition is made.

This fragmentation of the landscape of daily life can have banal manifestations. Recently constructed shopping malls reveal the endorsement of, for lack of a better term, *one-way portals*. The entrances from the malls into the major anchors of the development, the department stores, are highly visible on the mall side. The doors typically are framed with heavy mouldings, are centered in a dramatically modulated wall and are usually axially located with the concourse, which itself expands in width in proximity to the entry. Few architectural tactics are ignored in celebrating the promise of the domain beyond the door. Once inside the door, the circulation of the department store tends to be a circular path that leads both right and left; the means of vertical circulation is usually not directly visible from this entry. Exploration is mandatory. Whereas the path of the mall is explicit and informing; now, within the store, the path is ambiguous. The circular track defies orientation. It occasionally jogs or splits around distracting display obstacles. Indeed, the entire path and environment is beguiling. To return takes effort. Not remembering having entered past the perfume counters (or whatever), the search

for re-entry back into the mall is difficult. The door you thought was the one you first entered leads to the parking lot. The exit doors are all remarkably similar. The architecture obnoxiously asserts that the department store is a shopping mall unto itself. Your return to the mall is obviated. The store's entry into the mall is judged not as important as the mall entry into the store. The portal to the mall which, on the mall side, has a high ceiling, has a low ceiling within the store. The wall it pierces is like many of the interior walls of the store, ladened with racks or shelves. On first encounter, the irritation is subliminal. The second time, the irritation is conscious and you learn the appropriate clues so as not to repeat the mistake. Our cities likewise render us lost. We travel their landscape awkwardly, our bodies invent and rely upon stutter-steps as we navigate the terrain.[35]

Postmodernist spaces, like modernist spaces, refuse to speak of what is "outside." They are secular spaces that depend upon the city, yet deny the inherent interconnectiveness of daily life within the city. One can walk to Faneuil Hall from the Boston Government Center or from the Financial District. As you cross the street into the commercial zone, the compression is almost palpable. Faneuil Hall is vibrant with crowds, the pace is immediately fatiguing. The human frame reacts with anxiety—to shopping, eating, working, or the throngs of tourists one has to negotiate. Does this anxiety stem from the fact that if you wish to participate in this place, or even linger here, you must spend money?[36]

Similarly, enter any of Portman's Hyatt Regency's. Follow the structure's perverted *marche* across the celebrated atrium that has all the charm and grace of a missile silo, enter the glass elevator capsules that beckon you upward for the view inward and outward. Upon your arrival you will be greeted by a host or hostess inquiring whether it will be drinks or dinner. Some may argue that you are being "served," but you are an object in this enterprise.

When Haussmann cut the boulevards through Paris, Baudelaire observed one interesting and vital aspect of the café culture that ensued: one could participate in the public realm and still maintain one's anonymity. With the privatization of the public realm that is occurring today, this is jeopardized. You are not anonymous when using your credit card. Nor are you anonymous if your social status is revealed by your inability to participate in the spending.

The Piazza d'Italia, with its St. Joseph's Fountain, has become an integral part of the identity of New Orleans, especially if you view recent cinema. Completed in 1978, designed by Perez and Associates and Charles Moore, the Piazza was heralded, for a while, as one of the major events of postmodernism.[37] The Piazza, a monument to the contribution of the Italian community to the cultural vitality of New Orleans, is an architectural Mardi Gras, seemingly a "Fat Tuesday" float permanently moored in a warehouse district near the central business district. Classicizing details run amok in this vibrant, dizzying, tumultuous construction. Historic elements that allude to the permanence of architecture are sliced and chopped and then reassembled into an ethereal, "depthless" pastiche of the Fontana di Trevi of Rome and possibly the Palace of Fine Arts of San Francisco. Pseudo-Corinthian columns have neon necking while adjacent columns with stainless-steel Composite capitals have water-jet "socks." The shafts of other columns are omitted and replaced by a cylinder of water flowing from the bottom of suspended Doric capitals. The space is animated with the dancing pet of the Piazza: water. Water spraying, spritzing, flowing, exploding, coursing, churning, the centerpiece of which is a eighty-foot long, three-dimensional map of the Italian peninsula with the island of Sicily at the focal center of the Piazza. The contours shimmer with the water of three fountains emanating from the locations of the Po, Arno and Tiber Rivers cascading down to two basins representing the Tyrrhenian and Adriatic Seas.

By 1985, when I visited it, the Piazza seemed aged well beyond its few years. Vandalism and graffiti testified that this was not the "people-place" it was intended to be. The stucco surfaces had weathered poorly and other elements were being eroded by the coursing waters of the fountains. The Piazza, with its fountains, was to be the initial investment of an urban renewal scheme to revitalize an "underused" area near the central business district. The revitalization has not occurred and therein lies the fate of the Piazza. To its developers, it remains a rhinestone in the mud. As architecture, the Piazza is a fiction. Its choreography is without people. It has no resident neighborhood to occupy and nurture it and it has, as yet, no infrastructure to sustain it. Its proximity to the central business district is labored and it has fallen victim to the very context it was intended to change. The Piazza stands as the frustrated prophet of a redevelopment which it may not survive. Recently the Piazza has been a locale for two different movies, *Tightrope* and *The Big Easy*. Incredibly, in each movie a dead body is discovered deposited in St. Joseph's Fountain. Paradoxically, both of these police-detective stories—fiction—treat the Piazza more realistically, that is, as an empty place, than the architecture itself. It is more a potential space than a real place.

The fiction and mythology of postmodernism is not lost on its practitioners, some of whom are candid, yet unapologetic:

The people who live in these buildings are of course like everyone else running around earning the money to live in such places and they never really sit on the chair on the porch, gazing at the sea, anymore than you sit in the Piazza and look leisurely at the Duomo. You rush around and take two seconds for a cup of coffee, but those moments imagined, are the anchors which make it possible to survive. That is the price of our modern condition. We must have that memory and tradition, even if it has to become its own myth, if we are to survive in the present.[38]

To repeat, American cities are becoming more dominated by these potential spaces that will forever be denied the authenticity of *place*. The peristyle court of Kohn, Pedersen and Fox's Proctor and Gamble Headquarters expansion was celebrated as a wonderful addition of green space to the city of Cincinnati, whose overburdened Fountain Square was the only downtown, public outdoor space. The court, bifurcated by a busy city street, is separated from the Headquarters by a wide ceremonial drive and is, at its outer edges, divorced from the city by broad, heavy traffic avenues. This green apron serves neither as a physical extension of the headquarters nor as an oasis for the city, although both uses were promised by its promotion. It is an Arcadian view from corporate windows. The ambulatory of the trellised colonnades is raised several feet above the sidewalk and above the interior green. This grass surface, consequently, is not visible to a distant pedestrian. From outside, the effect is more wall than space. This is no accident of design. The court is a space of power, nothing else. This space is not for habitation; it is not for the city. The embroidered void is an appropriate symbol and, as symbolic capital, it is more symbol than capital. And, in case the message is not clear from across the avenues, the entries are frequently draped with stainless-steel chains barring passage. In a design that is adamantly aloof, the chain is not redundant. The spaces of power require defense.

Union Station, St. Louis, is the latest progeny of the Ghiradelli Square, "bread and festival," inter-urban, shopping emporiums. The station and its hotel have been lavishly restored and the train shed, reputed to be the largest in the world, now covers several concourses of shops and an additional hotel. The scrupulous restoration of the original station and hotel establishes the rich character of the redevelopment. However, as one ventures through the shops, towards the rear, the design loses the clarity that the original buildings establish. The lagoon and the stages are the awkward transition from the enclosed shops to the parking lot which occupies the majority of the sheltered area of the shed. The ethos of the grandiloquent station was as an entry to St. Louis. Despite its grandeur, it had a calculated deference to the city. It was a processional threshold to the city. It was part of the city. Now, the spirit of its redevelopment is the introverted specter of the suburban shopping mall. The outcome is confusion; one is always *behind* the station, not *at* the station. The parking lot, given prominent space under the shed, confirms that this mall has no center. The original station and hotel are reduced to a stage front, yet this architecture is so dense and majestic that it eclipses its own redevelopment. Here, as in other urban renovations of existing monuments, the rehabilitation of a significant building has stripped them of symbolism. The building remains, pristinely reclaimed, but its cultural identity is destroyed. It is history appropriated.

58   Surely at some time during the preliminary phase of the Union Station design, someone must have suggested that passenger train service be restored to the rear of the train shed, however diminished that service may now be. Then the ethos of the original design could be reclaimed and expanded to the full length of the train shed. It would be a station, an entry to the city, a part of the city, not the fragmented island that redevelopment has made of it.[39] Just as surely, that idea must have been dismissed because those that now ride the trains are not the shoppers that the developers cared to entertain. The station, a monument to the industrial city and its ruling class, long vacant and devalued, has been reclaimed as symbolic capital for a new city and a new ruling elite, apparently less tolerant than the age of the robber barons.

A change in taste can devalue symbolic capital. One can tire of Disneyland. And what of "bread and festivals" when there is little bread to be shared? More festivals?

The Critical Value of Image: The Return of the Subject

We need more festivals, but not the urban placebos that are currently being produced. We need an architecture that initiates a movement toward human fulfillment, not an architecture that accommodates human existence in a less than humane world. Creative destruction must be harnessed to a vision in which harmful mystifications and legitimations are destroyed and potentialities for human growth are created.

Postmodernism, as an ideology, purports to embrace history, respect context, endorse "popular" forms of culture, and elaborate vernacular typologies. Certain questions are troubling: Whose history? Whose notion of context? Whose vernacular? Whose "popular" culture? A result of genuine tradition or another product of a consumer economy? These questions, and others, have not been asked, and, having not been asked, the drafted line will never negotiate the potent issues they address. The quality of architecture must be premised upon a critical and attentive exploration of the instances of creative participation that are typically labeled "disorder."[40] "Any theory of the city must be, at its starting point, a theory of social conflict."[41] We need to reestablish the pure terms of the class struggle, an often maligned and misunderstood Marxist term, yet a powerful and potentially joyous term. This struggle must recognize the truth of the present moment, that is, the truth of postmodernism—i.e., that ours is a world of multinational corporations and flexible accumulation. We cannot retrieve aesthetic practices that were responses to historical moments that

no longer exist. With struggle and participation, architectural objects can have an authentic subject. The image can be liberative, it can have critical content and allow for pluralist interpretation. And the operations that govern architectural production are open to productive questioning.

These are easy truths to some, heresy to others, and bombastic irrelevance to many. In a world needing radical change, perhaps not everyone needs to be a radical (although I would certainly welcome more radicals). Nevertheless, even the conservative position can acknowledge the interconnections of architectural and economic history. Quite often, architects are the vocal critics of the current condition, within the very creation of which they are tremendously instrumental. The profession must become an arena of discourse that engages with, and beyond, itself. This can begin in our schools, in our studios. But it cannot end there; the discourse must become architecture.

Criticism of our current condition must be expressed in architectural forms, rather than words. What is necessary is to establish a new conception of architectural quality. If an elegant design collapses the liberating potentialities of human and social behavior, if a formal or technical discovery does not improve the material conditions of human society, if an architectural event, though technically pristine and artistically emotional, fails to contradict the fragmentation of daily life...it is not architecture.

Notes

[1] David Harvey, *The Urbanization of Capital: Studies in the History and Theory of Capitalist Urbanization* (Baltimore: Johns Hopkins University Press, 1985), p. 16.

[2] David Harvey, "The Urban Process Under Capitalism: A Framework for Analysis," *International Journal of Urban and Regional Research* (1978), p. 124. Also in Harvey, *The Urbanization of Capital*, p. 25.

[3] Giancarlo deCarlo, "Legitimizing Architecture," *Forum*, (April 1972), p. 9.

[4] Marshal Berman, *All That Is Solid Melts Into Air* (New York: Simon and Schuster, 1982), p. 99.

[5] Fredric Jameson, "Postmodernism, or the Cultural Logic of Late Capitalism," *New Left Review*, (July-August 1984): 60- 62.

[6] David M. Gordon, "Capitalism and the Roots of Urban Crisis," in *The Fiscal Crisis of American Cities*, ed. Roger E. Alcaly and David Mermelstein (New York: Vintage Books, 1977), p. 99.

[7] See Frederic Engels, *The Condition of the Working*

Class in England (Moscow: Progress Publishers, 1973); Enid Gauldie, *Cruel Habitations* (London: Allen and Unwin, 1974); G.D.H. Cole and Raymond Postgate, *The Common People 1746-1946* (London: Methuan and Company, 1971), pps. 129-142. For a vision of the social costs born by the middle class in Chicago of the same period, see: Richard Sennett, *Families Against the City* (New York: Vintage Books, 1974).

8 Gordon, "Capitalism and the Roots of Urban Crisis," pp. 100-103.

9 Theo van Doesberg, "Towards a Plastic Architecture," in *Programs and Manifestoes*, Conrads, ed., p. 78.

10 "The idea of 'economic efficiency' does not imply production furnishing maximum commercial profit, but production demanding a minimum working effort." CIAM "La Sarraz Declaration [1928]," in *Programs and Manifestoes*, Conrads, ed., p. 109.

"The new architecture is *economic*; that is to say, it employs its elemental means as effectively and thriftily as possible and squanders neither these means nor the material." Theo van Doesberg, "Towards a Plastic Architecture [1924]," also in *Programs and Manifestoes*, Conrads, ed., p. 78.

11 Colin Rowe and Fred Koetter, *Collage City* (Cambridge, Massachusetts: MIT Press, 1978), p. 11.

12 Alexander Tzonis, *Towards a Non-Oppressive Environment* (Boston: in press, 1972), p. 87.

13 Manfredo Tafuri, *Theories and History of Architecture* (New York: Harper and Row, 1980), p. 103.

14 Gordon, "Capitalism and the Roots of Urban Crisis," p. 102.

15 Manfredo Tafuri, "The Disenchanted Mountain," in Giorgio Ciucci, Francesco Dal Co, Mario Manieri-Elia, Manfredo Tafuri, *The American City from the Civil War to the New Deal* (Cambridge, Massachusetts: The MIT Press, 1979), pp. 390- 391.

16 Nicole Pertuiset, "The Lloyds Headquarters: Imagery Takes Command," in Thomas A. Dutton, ed., *Icons of Late Capitalism: Corporations and Their Architecture* [Proceedings] (Oxford, Ohio: The Department of Architecture, Miami University, 1986), p. 87.

17 For a detailed history of the political and aesthetic evolution of the American skyscraper, see Tafuri, "The Disenchanted Mountain."

18 Harvey, *The Urbanization of Capital*, pp. 202- 211.

19 Gordon, "Capitalism and the Roots of Urban Crisis," p. 107.

20 Harvey, *The Urbanization of Capital*, p. 211.

21 *Ibid.*, p. 211.

22 For an extensive description of the phenomenon see: Barry Bluestone and Bennett Harrison, *The Deindustrialization of America* (New York: Basic Books, 1982).

23 Harvey, *The Urbanization of Capital*, pp. 212- 213.

24 *Ibid.*, pp. 215-218.

25 How Volkswagen came to western Pennsylvania is representative of the costs expended in these competitions. See: Ron Chernow, "The Rabbit That Ate Pennsylvania," *Mother Jones* (January 1978), pp. 18-24; Robert Goodman, *The Last Entrepreneurs* (Boston: Simon and Schuster, 1979), pp. 1- 31.

26 Susan Schmidt and Robert Barnes, "Maryland Stadium Foes Lose in Court," *The Washington Post*, September 9, 1987, front page-A8.

27 David Harvey, Lecture given at "Developing the American City: Society and Architecture in the Regional City," a symposium at the Yale School of Architecture, New Haven, Connecticut, February 6, 1987.

28 Jameson, "Postmodernism, or the Cultural Logic of Late Capitalism," p. 56.

29 *Ibid.*, p. 63.

30 *Ibid.*, p. 66.

31 Derek Drummond, "Identifying Risks in Corporate Headquarters," in Thomas A. Dutton, ed., *Icons of Late Capitalism: Corporations and Their Architecture* [Proceedings] (Oxford, Ohio: The Department of Architecture, Miami University, 1986), p. 74.

32 Guy Debord, *The Society of the Spectacle*, quoted in Jameson, "Postmodernism, or the Cultural Logic of Late Capitalism," p. 66.

33 Harvey, Lecture given at Yale, *op cit.*

34 That symbolic capital can indeed be liquidated is best illustrated by the sale by U.S. Steel (now U.S.X.) of its Pittsburgh headquarters for $250 million dollars in 1982. The corporation now rents its office space. Ralph Nader and William Taylor, *The Big Boys* (New York: Pantheon Books, 1986), p. 30.

Another example is the sale of $1 billion in assets, including its 611 acre headquarters site in Danbury, Connecticut, by Union Carbide Corporation, after it was "heavily pummeled by industrial accidents and a hostile takeover offer." Daniel F. Cuff, "$1 Billion Asset Sale by Carbide," *The New York Times*, April 8, 1986, section D.

35 For a detailed discussion of architecture and human response and body sensibilities, see John Knesl, "Foundations for LiberativeProjectuation," *Antipode* 10, no. 1 (March 1978).

36 In the movie *Charly*, of the early 60s, there is the briefest of scenes in which Claire Bloom and Cliff Robertson shop - without anxiety - for groceries in the open-air stalls of Faneuil Hall obviously some time before its redevelopment. The scene shows the grit and the casualness of the urban market which is an undeniable part of the city. The scene foretells the redevelopment. In the background rises the nascent forms of the Boston City Hall construction.

37 Martin Filler, "The Magic Fountain," *Progressive Architecture* (November 1978): 81-87.

38 Robert Stern at the lecture in Verona, *Art & Design* (April 1987): XI.

39 I would like to thank Frank Ferrario of St. Louis for this critique of the Union Station redevelopment.

40 Giancarlo deCarlo, "Legitimizing Architecture," p. 19.

41 Manuel Castells, *The City and the Grassroots* (Berkeley: University of California Press, 1983), p. 318.

SHARON WILLIS is an assistant professor in the Department of Foreign Language, Literature and Linguistics at the University of Rochester, New York. She is the author of a book on Marguerite Duras, *Writing on the Body* (1987).

Spectacular
Topographies:

Amérique's
Post
Modern
Spaces

CAUTION. Objects in this mirror
may be closer than they appear.

Photography by Marco Diani

The familiar admonition, lettered on side-view mirrors of our newer cars, stands as the epigraph to Baudrillard's *Amérique* (1986), a series of exhilaratingly manic passages between the mythic poles, Los Angeles and New York, an elegiacs of velocity traced in long trackings across the desert or the sky. Baudrillard's *auto*-motivated journey begins with a loss of perspective, inscribed through figures of post-modern mobility and specularity in a perpetual circulation of intensities. America is the name of post-modernity, the pure spectacle and simulation that confound imaginary and real, where all distance collapses, where specific differences are homogenized under a permanent, totalizing play of non-signifying differentiation.

"America" is the arena in which Baudrillard discovers the most extreme articulation of the hyper-reality he theorizes in his well-known *Simulations*. It is a space that performs the simulation effects he studies: "simulation corresponds to a short-circuit of reality and to its reduplication by signs" (*Simulations*, p. 48). For Baudrillard, simulation is a sort of apotheosis of the age of mechanical reproduction, where reality collapses into hyperreality. "From medium to medium the real is volatilized," he writes, "it becomes the real for the real, fetish of the lost object, but ecstasy of denegation and of its own ritual extermination: the hyperreal" (p. 141-142). Through this volatization, the real comes to be defined through reproducibility: "At the limit of this process of reproducibility, the real is not what can be reproduced, but that which is already reproduced, the hyperreal" (p.146).

As it examines this process at work in "America," however, Baudrillard's text performs its own kind of simulation. Its textual travels propose to map America, but instead, they seem to territorialize it, to claim that territory as a model of simulation. This process is embedded in a general spatialization of temporality; the "age of mechanical reproduction" becomes a space, a zone where historical time no longer pertains. Such spatialization, Baudrillard wants to claim, is an effect of the end of history. Yet, on close examination, *Amérique* shows itself to be a machine for spatializing history, evaporating it in spatial simulation.

In producing a kind of "short-circuit" between the imaginary and the real through this spatialization, the text performs and celebrates the very "loss of perspective" that it attributes to post-modern hyper-reality. Inscribing, rather than describing, a topography of post-modernism, Baudrillard's text exhibits its own tendency to construct a lost object to be recovered, a fetish to be adored. This tendency is accompanied by an underlying presupposition that loss of perspective entails an inability to hold a position—analytically or politically.

Composed as a series of tracking shots on the US, *Amérique* forgets that its seamless passage records the movement of objects in and out of frame; we are losing some things, and holding onto others. At the very least, we're holding onto the frame, a mobile but defined perspective, and through it we are holding on to the imaginary place of the viewing subject. Objects may be closer than they appear. But they may also be farther away.

Baudrillard's touristic performance produces a theatrical short-circuit of specularity. The "effect of bewildered auto-referentiality (*d'auto-référence éperdue*)...a short-circuit that immediately plugs the same into the same," (*Amérique*, p. 74) parades a desire for excessive and disorienting proximity, a space exploded by radical and random promiscuity. But what it forgets is that the mirror is still framed. Reproducing exactly the effects it analyzes in "America," the text exhibits a powerful wish fulfillment: to evaporate history.

Such an evaporation of history is necessary to construct "America" as Europe's primal scene. "America is the original version of modernity, we are the dubbed (*doublée*) or sub-titled version" (*Amérique*, p. 151). As the locus of melancholy and nostalgia, "America" is Europe's "primal scene" and its utopian projection. Baudrillard's America can only become the primal scene when both Europe and America are catapulted outside of history. "At base, the US...including the spaces it opens to simulation, is the only contemporary primitive society. And the fascination is to cross it like the primitive society of the future...but without a past to reflect it, and therefore fundamentally primitive" (*Amérique*, p. 21).

Such a reformulation of the term "primitive society" coheres with one of the textual thrusts of *Amérique*, that of undermining traditional ethnography. However, *Amérique*'s post-modern travelogue unconsciously re-establishes the traditional parameters of Western ethnographic discourse, since the term primitive society, a metaphoric relay of "scène primitive," participates in an orchestrated sequence of metaphors. In *Simulations* metaphorization appears in the anti-ethnographic challenge: "We all become living specimens under the spectral light of ethnology...It is thus extremely naive to look for ethnology among the Savages or in some Third World—it is here, everywhere, in the metropolis, among the whites, in a world completely catalogued and analyzed and then *artificially revived as though real*, in a world of simulation" (*Simulations*, pp. 16-17). In simulation, we may all have become "living specimens," and traditional ethnography may be theoretically obsolete, but Western societies still practice it *upon* those whom they construct as "others." And the fact remains that when the white European or American is a specimen, he is not dominated, or annihilated, in the same way as is the object of ethnography. Metaphoricity reduces specific differences and relations of power to mere inflections of the scene, like the striking details randomly picked up in a tracking shot. If the stage of history is simulation and spectacle, the subject's own stubborn historical rootedness may all the more easily evaporate, as in this reframing of ethnography which denies the historical roots of Western theoretical traditions in colonialism and imperialism.

The capital of post-modernism, Baudrillard's *Amérique* becomes a utopia rooted in Europe's nostalgia for modernism and, at least implicitly, for the colonialism which coincided with it. It is the stage upon which troubling historical specificities are mastered in regulated differences, partial, and non-referential differences, so that unequal distributions of power may be read as accidental channelings of energy. Significant social-political domination and oppression, mapped upon racial difference, seem analogous in this "America" to random collisions of a multi-colored batch of marbles. In this spectacular performance of theoretical nomadism, our collective production of history as spectacle is exposed, but also reproduced; the US becomes the screen on which the traveler projects his own images, and fantasies, which circulate right back to him. But this exhilarating feedback circuit also discloses a stubborn referentiality. It reproduces uncannily familiar figures; these are the coded figures of imperialism, reinstating the poles of same and other through which it represents itself.

What is being left out of frame here, or brought in only to be constructed as the figure of the subject's own desires? Here is Baudrillard in New York:

Beauty of the Black women, of the Puerto Rican women in New York. Beyond the sexual excitement racial promiscuity (*promiscuité raciale*) offers, it must be said that black, the pigment of the dark races, is a natural make-up that heightens itself with artificial make-up to compose a beauty—not sexual: animal and sublime—that is desperately lacking in pale faces. Whiteness appears as an extenuation of physical adornment, a neutrality that perhaps for that reason obtains all the exoteric powers of the Word (*verbe*), but which will forever lack the exoteric and ritual force of artifice ((*Amérique*, pp. 35-36).

Baudrillard's fascination with America's "promiscuité raciale" and his commitment to spectacle, simulation and surface engage a set of figures firmly rooted in nineteenth century imperialist racial ideology: blackness is a mask, opaque and mute, the pure "primitive" celebrated as the height of post-modern artifice. An obsession with simulation converges with the production of history as spectacle, and an eroticized fascination with Third World people. By producing its own spectacle, and a subject for it, the text constructs a particular relation to history.

This aesthetic fascination with multiraciality effectively occludes any recognition that race and class are crucial sites in the organization of power, sites of its investment or radical dispossession. Replicating the ideology that reads black faces as a screen for white fantasies, that hears in them a voice-over of its own projected speech, Baudrillard leaves the "Word" to whites.

Curiously, even when the Other's speech might be heard, Baudrillard freezes the speaker as pure image: "The gymnastics of rap is a kind of acrobatic prowess, where one doesn't notice until the end that it is a dance, when he poses in an indolent, indifferent position…the rapper comes to a standstill in the hollow of his motion with a derisive gesture" (*Amérique*, pp. 42-3).

Baudrillard is talking about a break-dancer—at once recalling and repressing the musical poetics of rap music that emerges along with break dancing, and that frequently addresses the political life of a community. This conflation of break-dancing with rap music is telling. It is not neutral because it suppresses the voice; the political speech of popular music is converted into mute spectacle here. Why can't Baudrillard hear or understand the word of the black speaker? Is it that the speaker of rap music, perhaps a kind of collective subject, can't be consolidated into a pure reflecting surface for the white traveler's fantasies?

The fascination with North American multiraciality that underlies *Amérique* depends on imagining perpetual circulation without exchange between groups. What lures the subject seems to be a kind of radical alterity frozen as a spectacle of random differences, of heterogeneous equivalents. As Henry Louis Gates suggests, this construction of race as a figure is intimately bound to power: "Race has become a trope of ultimate, irreducible difference between cultures, linguistic groups, or adherents of specific belief systems which—more often than not—also have fundamentally opposed economic interests. Race is the ultimate trope of difference because it is so very arbitrary in its application" ("Writing 'Race' and the Difference It Makes," p. 5). Such a biologically based consolidation of race as a category and a figure of difference occludes its social encoding, the ways it becomes an instrument of domination. Indeed, Baudrillard uncritically follows American cultural practices that often stress this figure in order to avoid confronting the economic issues that operate upon and through it.

Within its cinematic metaphorics, *Amérique* forgets that power relations always ground simulation's feedback effects, which allow for the appropriation of the other as pure spectacle, as the screen for one's own projected figures. The text's celebratory post-modernist aesthetic is itself intimately dependent on precisely such forgetfulness.

Amérique persistently metaphorizes or fetishizes figures and events, which exemplify simulation effects, then appear as "accidental." A centrifugal machine of representation, *Amérique* continually throws off figures of white America's haunting others: Blacks, Hispanics, the homeless, and its own totem, the Indian. Much the same is true for events, like colonization and the Vietnam War, two major sites in several of Baudrillard's texts. In each case, Baudrillard fetishizes the figure as sign which fails to signify simulates.

While he can effectively read the figure of the

Indian as America's haunting totem—that is, as a figure recuperated by late twentieth century white mythology and mysticism as a kind of chthonic voice of ecological wisdom, a benign return of the repressed—Baudrillard falls for a newly created totem of post-modern urbanity: the bum. "One sees that everywhere here, it's the saddest scene in the world, sadder than poverty, sadder than a man begging, it is that of a man eating alone in public" (*Amérique*, p. 35).

Attempting to arrive at an effective metaphor to convey the "tragic" force of self-destruction he finds in the desperate isolation of joggers running within closed sound circuits created by walkmen, he offers this tableau: "The only comparable distress is that of the man who eats alone standing in the middle of the city. One sees that in New York, those derelicts who don't even hide themselves anymore to eat garbage in public" (*Amérique*, p. 77).

Now, this is hardly a comparison, except on an aestheticized level. But the latter problem is hardly reducible to aesthetics, except in the discourse of New York City's developers. In a real sense, Baudrillard here reproduces an effect he ascribes to simulation: "today when the real and the imaginary are confused in the same operational totality, the esthetic fascination is everywhere." Reality itself, he argues, is aesthetic and we relate to it through a fascination: "magnetized by the signs...by the anticipation and immanence of the code" (*Simulations*, p. 150). The perception of the social, then, is like the perception of art, a matter of reading, but of reading that is entirely fascinated by the code: "the reading of a message is then only a perpetual examination of the code" (*Simulations*, p. 119). This aestheticization, however, refuses to analyze the power relations underlying both the code and the spectacle it generates.

In instances like these, the text's claim that referential functions no longer hold appears suspiciously wishful. And if one acknowledges the stubborn referentiality that clings to the textual figures, one must read certain willful occlusions. To reduce the homeless to the figure of the bum is to provide a spectacle that covers over the systematic operation of which homelessness is an effect, disavowing the existence of non-spectacular homeless people, those who don't fit comfortably into a banal melodramatic scenario of the maladjusted individual: the former working poor who have been pushed into desperation by the movements of investment in urban centers. These homeless can't be seen in isolation, in a reality entirely "satellitized," without system or center, where power "is no longer occupied." Instead, they lead one to consider the systemic effects of domination and economic power. But because their very existence demands an analysis of systemic problems that must be treated politically and economically, Baudrillard apparently can not see them at all.

The theoretical apparatus generated by Baudrillard's earlier texts is unable to cope with the concrete examples *Amérique* selects. Consequently, a reading of *Amérique* begins to undo that very apparatus. Despite Baudrillard's insistence that metaphor is dead, his dominant textual gestures inevitably return to elaborate metaphoricity, to the production of figures. His figures continually generate other figures, so that signification is never fixed, but always fleeing in a metaphoric relay. But this hardly amounts to non-referentiality. Indeed, the utopia of non-referentiality Baudrillard projects looks suspiciously like a dream of escaping history altogether by refusing to acknowledge its specific effects.

Baudrillard's figures are perpetually disappearing into post-modern space, a space he characterizes as follows:

...thus the body, landscape, time, all progressively disappear as scenes. And the same for public space: the theater of the social and the theater of politics are both reduced more and more to a large soft body with many heads... Advertising in its new dimension invades everything as public space (the street, monument, market, scene) disappears...it monopolizes public life in its exhibition ("The Ecstasy of Communication," p. 129).

Post-modern space, in Baudrillard's assessment, is characterized by the disappearance of discrete scenes, and of the culture of spectacle that depended on a spatial arrangement framing an object and a spectator for it. These phenomena evaporate in "the ecstasy of communication": "All secrets, spaces and scenes abolished in a single dimension of information" ("The Ecstasy of Communication," p. 131).

While this reading of contemporary urban spaces has a kind of aesthetic and logical integrity, it falters each time it produces a specific example. Each "example" constitutes a "scene," however temporary, and thus betrays the logic of the "obscene" (for Baudrillard, the characteristic of post-modern space is to be beyond all scene). Further, these selected scenes serve to obscure the construction of that space of simulation, a construction whose material bases are none too mysterious.

Treating the same issues, and the same urban terrain in "Post-Modernism, Or the Cultural Logic of Late Capitalism," Frederic Jameson calls for an analytic exploration of simulation effects, one that would establish a possibility of critical distance, rather than succumb to the exhilarating fascination that accompanies absorption into spaces of simulation, traversed as they are by technologies of information: "If we cannot achieve some general sense of a cultural dominant, then we fall back into a view of present history as sheer heterogeneity, random difference, a coexistence of a host of distinct forces whose effectivity is undecidable..." (pp. 56-57).

Like Baudrillard, Jameson focuses on the relations of post-modern space and simulation effects to the global information network and the power relations underlying it. Yet, he recasts the fascina-

64 tion Baudrillard celebrates, determining it as an unconscious effort to produce an analytical frame, the possibility of positioning:

> Our faulty representations of some immense communicational and computer network are themselves but a distorted figuration of something even deeper, namely the whole world system of present-day multi-national capitalism. The technology of contemporary society is therefore mesmerizing and some privileged representational shorthand for grasping a network of power and control even more difficult for our minds and imaginations to grasp — namely the whole new decentered global network of the third stage of capital itself ("Post-Modernism, Or the Cultural Logic of Late Capitalism," p. 75).

In contrast, Baudrillard's entirely superstructural universe is built upon a "passion for the code," a passion that denies not only referential residues, but the power relations, labor and production. His texts fall silent about issues of material power, preferring to remain enraptured with an apparently vertiginous circulation of information in globally connected networks. Fascination with the network, however, displaces an analysis that would examine its systematicity, rather than its randomness, and that would uncover the power structures with which information is embedded. Mike Davis argues strongly for an analysis to accompany such post-modern fascination, suggesting that "the crucial point about contemporary capitalist structures of accumulation" is "that they are symptoms of global crisis, not signs of the triumph of capitalism's irresistible drive to expand" ("Urban Renaissance and the Spirit of Post-Modernism," p. 109). Baudrillard participates in exactly this kind of celebratory fascination with capital, whose drive to expand his texts implicitly encode as an irresistible tendency to implode in simulation.

In the spatio-temporal extension of post-modernism, for Baudrillard, spectacle and scene are evaporated in simulation. "In a subtle way, this loss of public space occurs contemporaneously with the loss of private space. The one is no longer a spectacle, the other no longer a secret" ("Ecstasy of Communication," p. 130). This is the sort of spatial implosion Baudrillard wants/finds exhibited in America. But in its self-seducing nostalgia for spectacle, *Amérique* also retroactively re-reads the ideological stakes underlying the previous theoretical work. This re-reading casts Baudrillard's post-modernism as that auto-effecting state of theory whereby it takes itself for an event. This theoretical position is evident in *Amérique*'s transformations of events into catastrophes, power relations into a play of signs, social differences into random heterogeneity, and history into a scenario. The spatial short-circuits with which the text is obsessed are paralleled by theoretical short-circuits which participate in a general move to aestheticize the political. *Amérique* unfolds a scene, a theater of desire, where theory becomes an event all by itself.

Indeed, the notion of hyperreality seems to accomplish precisely such aestheticization: "what was projected psychologically and mentally, what used to be lived out on earth as metaphor, as mental or metaphorical scene, is henceforth projected into reality, without any metaphor at all, into an absolute space which is also that of simulation" ("Ecstasy," p. 128). Both space and practice, in Baudrillard's view, were lived out, or experienced, only metaphorically. Necessarily, then, with the disappearance of metaphor in simulation, they implode in a kind of immediacy. Yet, this formation depends on rendering space and practice as purely discursive phenomena, and isn't that gesture itself a metaphoric one?

More problematic still is the extension of this utopic non-referentiality to history itself. "History isn't over, it's in a state of simulation..." "History has stopped meaning, referring to anything — whether you call it social space or the real..." "What interests me instead (but can you still call this history?) is the possibility of a pure event, an event that can no longer be manipulated, interpreted, or deciphered by an historical subjectivity" ("Forget Baudrillard," in *Forget Foucault*, pp. 68-9). This argument rests on a banal confusion: it would suggest that because history has no inherent meaning or because it doesn't produce immediately legible meaning, that we can not interpret it, or analyze its movements. Further, even in the face of an obstinate refusal to mean, characteristic of both "history" and the "real," we remain historical agents, inevitably bound to interpret and analyze the history we make.

The possibility of historical agency, as well as of resistance, is abolished when power no longer maintains a situation. Again, for Baudrillard this is a spatial problem: "there is no longer a scene of politics the way it was organized around the history of power relations, production, classes. Power is no longer an objective locatable process" ("Forget Baudrillard," p. 116). Imploding along with space in simulation, power is "itself eventually breaking apart in this space and becoming a simulation of power (disconnected from its aims and objectives, and dedicated to *power effects* and mass simulation)" (*Simulations*, p. 42). Power implodes, then, in a familiar process; in a space that can no longer be mapped, representation collapses into simulation, analysis collapses into fascination. This fascination becomes the pretext for foreclosing the materiality of practice: "It is no longer a question of the ideology of power, but of the *scenario* of power. Ideology only corresponds to a betrayal of reality by signs; simulation corresponds to a short-circuit of reality and to its replication by signs" (*Simulations*, p. 48). But where is the short-circuit, really? In reality and material practice, or in texts and theory? While one of power's aspects may be a scenario, power is always overdetermined, and we still live its effects quite concretely in the social field.

Further political repercussions of this theory emerge around the question of the pure event. In *Les Stratégies fatales*, the pure event is characterized as catastrophe, taken in its literal sense: that of a curve that produces the coincidence in a single thing of its origin and its end (p. 23). For Baudrillard, all events are now catastrophes: "Once the sense of history is finished...every event becomes a catastrophe, becomes a pure event without consequences" (p. 23).

Catastrophe is inextricable from sense-making activity: "The event without consequences is signaled by the fact that all causes can be imputed to it without anything permitting us to choose among them. Its origin is unintelligible, its destination is as much so" (*Stratégies*, p. 23). Because events are overdetermined, Baudrillard seems to argue, they are without cause or consequence. Their non-intelligibility would seem to entail non-agency as well here, but such an analysis denies any recognition that we participate daily in the unintelligible. In the implication that history is entirely random, our agency is abolished, as is the acknowledgement that we still produce history and live its effects.

But there is an underlying agenda, or scenario here. *Amérique*'s construction of America as a set of heterogeneous scenes traversed, joined and disjoined by short-circuits, presents that quintessential post-modern space as pure event. America is a catastrophe, a catastrophe staged textually. So the only pure events may be textual ones. "The real, all things considered, perhaps it exists—no, it doesn't exist—is the insurmountable limit of theory. The real is not an objective state of things, it is the point at which theory can do nothing...the real is actually a challenge to the theoretical edifice. But in my opinion theory can have no status other than that of challenging the real. At that point, theory is no longer theory, it is the event itself" ("Forget Baudrillard," p. 125).

Amérique's construction of historical events as either scenarios or catastrophes presents them as fundamentally *textual*. Its figuration of colonialism arises along with a nostalgia for modernism: "In its export, its hypostasis abroad, the ideal is expurged of its history, it is concretized, developed with a new blood and an experimental energy...colonization was in this sense a global *coup de théâtre* that leaves profound and nostalgic traces everywhere, even when it collapses" (p. 154). This passage provides only partial assertions, and refuses certain questions. If we offer a different frame—not a referent so much as another angle, not the truth but a contestation—we can admit the following questions. New blood? Whose? Nostalgia *everywhere*? For whom is colonization a source of nostalgia?

By rendering colonization as a global *coup de théâtre*, as spectacle without a referent or a destination, as a scenario, the text frames a particular, privileged spectator. Who are the actors and who is the audience in this scenario? Baudrillard's textual centrifuge never considers the address of signs, their arrival at destinations which are historically conditioned.

This discourse also immobilizes the Vietnam War as figure. Currently reconstructed as the haunting repressed of recent American history, Vietnam is increasingly rehearsed in our cultural productions, most frequently as an *American* nightmare. Now this construction of Vietnam as a crime to be expiated, catastrophe to be recuperated, or trauma to be exorcised is what permits its erasure, the trope of its burial as something properly mourned, tactics which foreclose the possibility of ongoing analysis, and of engaging politically with the causes and persistent effects of the war.

In his own critical work, Baudrillard has reconstructed Vietnam as a liminal figure, a monument to the passage of history into simulation, to the implosion of sense in a global network of information: "what sense did that war make, if not that its unfolding sealed the end of history in the culminating and decisive event of our age" (*Simulations*, p. 66). Now here, despite the vast territory his theoretical apparatus claims to traverse, the frame is just too limited. What sense did the war make to whom? Where? And when? Before, during, or after? It seems that what Baudrillard persists in calling the disappearance of history, its incapacity to make sense, is rather more his inability to acknowledge that history produces conflicting meanings for a multiplicity of interpretive positions.

While the Vietnam War marks the end of history, in Baudrillard's scenario another reading suggests that Vietnam marked the beginning of a new stage in global conflict and in Neo-colonialism. The first "televised war" demonstrated that imperialist aggression could operate through and upon representations and that rendering events as spectacle is, precisely, an effective strategy of both war and domination. But, for Baudrillard, the war itself was a scenario, culminating in a final montage that concealed the "real game." As he puts it, that war and all wars since can be characterized as simulacra: "behind this simulacrum of a struggle to the death of ruthless global stakes, the two adversaries are fundamentally as one against that other, unnamed, never mentioned thing, whose objective outcome in war, with equal complicity between the two adversaries, is total liquidation" (*Simulations*, p. 68). By reframing all events, aggression and resistance, as determined by and concealing the ultimate scenario of global deterrance, by saturating the historical field with analogy, Baudrillard has evaporated all historical specificity, and along with it, all possibility of resistance. Such a position obviously resides within the site of power; the suggestion that Third World resistance is simulated, or incidental to a larger scenario of power's implosion in deterrance, can only be enunciated in complicity with Western domination.

Further, the Vietnam War's particular relation to the media and representation marked the moment when Third World resistance movements began to exhibit their acute analysis of incipient post-modernism. Where war and domination are con-

66 ducted across representations, where the oppressor operates by turning the oppressed into spectacle, resistance necessarily needs to analyze and occupy representations, to deflect the specularizing force. Throughout the Third World—in Vietnam, Nicaragua, South Africa, and in Palestinian camps, for example—we see this kind of analysis of the media, the occupation and staging of spectacle as a weapon against the West's urge to construct its opponents as objects of spectacle. Isn't the seizure of spectacle a response to and a reading of Western post-modernism? Further, couldn't it be the case that it is precisely these repeated struggles in the domain of spectacle that have helped to shape theoretical discourses like Baudrillard's? That is, perhaps he has learned something about post-modernism from the Third World resistance for whom its analysis is precisely a matter of life and death?

While Baudrillard's theoretical apparatus provides a means for analyzing the relation of representation to history in Western capitalist systems, as well as of their ability to occlude the politics of material practices, his own work reinstates that occlusion. On this view, it appears that Baudrillard reproduces precisely the effects he analyzes. His many theoretical short-circuits generate a crucial one: between perspective and position. Within the vertiginous fascinations of post-modern space, traditional "perspective," both literal and figural, dissolves, but this mobility of perspective does not necessarily preclude either political analysis or position.

Baudrillard's textual logic of simulation, infinite reproducibility, in which the message is never more than an analysis of the code, works as analysis of cultural production and circulation of signs in the west. But even though it is impossible to "isolate the process of the real or prove the real" (*Simulations*, p. 41), we must consider the real, the limit of theory, as exceeding theory and conditioning it, and as having to be lived nonetheless. There may be "noevents," but only their "signs and reproductions," no power as such, only "power effects"; yet these signs and effects do have historical effectivity. While the "event" may seem to us to exist only elsewhere, to happen to someone else, it has its effects, and we remain its subjects. And it remains true that these effects differ—some profit from them, some lose. Everything may be counterfeit, but counterfeit versions differ, and they are instrumentalized in different ways.

What we need, then, in post-modernism, is not to re-establish "perspective," but to theorize and inhabit a mobile, shifting analytical perspective—a series of positions that always temporarily fix or install a relation and a reference, out of which analysis emerges. To fail to do so is to give oneself over to Baudrillard's short-circuits, refusing reference and situation in a social field, in history. Rather than bask in the seductive effects of our own post-modern specular fascinations, as Baudrillard's work encourages us to do, we need to interrogate these fascinations and their relation to the social field they traverse. Baudrillard's critical discourse offers theory as a lure, the lure of escape from positionality. It preserves the integrity of theory in a relation of mutual saturation with the field it claims to analyze. But in so doing, it only disclaims the historical agency and troubled referentiality which always inhabit theory. And it disclaims these in a world where, if one believes Baudrillard's glib assertion that power can no longer be occupied, this theory is highly susceptible to occupation and instrumentalization by precisely the powers it refuses to analyze. The final question such theory leaves unanswered is: whom is this version of post-modernism for, whose interests does it serve?

Works Cited

Jean Baudrillard, *Amérique* (Paris: Grasset, 1986).

Jean Baudrillard, "The Ecstasy of Communication," in *The Anti-Aesthetic*, ed. Hal Foster (Port Townsend, Washington: Bay Press, 1983).

Jean Baudrillard and Sylvére Lotringer, "Forget Baudrillard," in *Forget Foucault* (New York: Semiotext(e), 1987).

Jean Baudrillard, *Simulations* (New York: Semiotext(e), 1983).

Jean Baudrillard, *Les Stratégies fatales* (Paris: Grasset, 1983).

Mike Davis, "Urban Renaissance and the Spirit of Post-Modernism," *New Left Review*, 151 (1985), 106-113.

Henry Louis Gates, "Writing 'Race' and the Difference It Makes," *Critical Inquiry*, v. 12, no. 1 (1985), 1-20.

Frederic Jameson, "Post-Modernism, Or the Cultural Logic of Late Capitalism," *New Left Review*, 146 (1984), 53-92.

PALIMPSESTS

PETER EISENMAN, FAIA, was the founder and former Director of the Institute for Architecture and Urban Studies in New York City, and a former editor of *Oppositions*. He practices architecture in New York, teaches at Cooper Union and is a visiting professor at the University of Illinois at Chicago. His books include *House X* (Rizzoli), *Moving Arrows, Eros and Other Forms* and *Fin d'Ou T Hou S* (both published by the Architectural Association).

Architecture as a Second Language:

The Texts of Between

To be able to read off a text as a text without interposing an interpretation is the last form of inner experience...
                              Nietzsche, Will to Power

With the influx of non-native English speaking students to American colleges and universities, it is now possible to see college course offerings entitled "English As A Second Language." The idea behind the title is that this course will be offered to students whose first language is not English. The word "second" in this context does not mean merely to come after in a temporal sense because the idea of a first language or mother tongue implies an originary and even moral value. Thus the idea of a second language suggests the absence of these values as a negative condition.

The idea of temporality and original value becomes key if this notion of "second language" is transferred to the idea of architecture. In one sense, "second language" would suggest that architecture is always a second language even to those who speak and read it. In another sense, the term second language could suggest that architecture is grounded in other disciplines, that it is secondary to philosophy, science, literature, art and technology. But finally, there is a third possibility for the idea of a second language in architecture; that is, architecture as text.

While the term "text" is at present quite fashionable, its value as an idea is almost obscured by its intellectual currency as a catchall for anything related to meaning. The concept of a text has a very precise and necessary condition as a strategy for dislocation in architecture, and more precisely for dislocating what is thought to be the natural or "first language" of architecture itself.

For the purpose of this discussion a more specific use of the term "text," which incorporates two recent developments, will be used. As a result of these two developments, text is no longer a vague and generic term for meaning, but is in fact a term which always dislocates the traditional relationship between a form and its meaning.

In the first of these developments, text is not so much the representation of a narrative but rather the representation of the structure of the form of the narrative. In the second, text "is no longer something complete, enclosed in a book or its margins, it is a differential network. A fabric of traces referring endlessly to something other than itself." In this latter sense, text "displaces the conventional" or the "natural" idea of the literary work. Whereas the concept of text as the structure of the work referred inwardly to the work itself, text in this sense is a fundamental condition of displacement; it depends on no terms of internal reference such as structure. It is neither a complete work nor a metalanguage. It is not a "stable object" but a process, a "transgressive activity which disperses the author as the center, limit and guarantor of truth..."

What do these developments of the idea of text mean for architecture? What is an architectural text and how can it inform a strategy for dislocation? First it must be understood that the extended idea of a text, whether in architecture or not, is the idea of essential multivalence. It does not cancel or deny prior notions of narrative or structure nor does it necessarily contain them, but exists simultaneously with them. Text never allows a single signified. Everything is shown to mean more than one thing.

Architecture, because of its presence, its here and now, its time and space specificity, was traditionally seen as necessarily univocal. Thus, it would be resistant to the dislocating multivalency of text. The implications for an architecture of texts would be the same as that of the second language, in other words, non-originary and unnatural. Thus in architecture it is possible to say that text is what always exceeds the immediate response to a visual or sensory image, i.e. that which we see on the surface as the story, or that which we see as the beautiful. This is the heart of the matter.

Since the terms of the natural in architecture have always been thought to be the specificity of time and place, it might be useful to examine this textuality, the dislocation of time and place, in another medium. Film is a discourse that is constantly impacted by a "second language." Film is the *sine qua non* of a dislocated place and time because it always has at least two times and two places: the actual time and place of watching, and the narrative time and place. In its early history the fact that film moved in linear time was thought to mean that the narrative moved in chronological time. However, when sound was introduced into film in the 1930s, this coincidence of linear time and chronological time was brought into question; textual time, that is the multivalence of time, developed out of chronological time.

For example, in David Lynch's film "Blue Velvet," the story, but not the text, is about an average young American couple in a small town in North Carolina in the fifties and their adventures related to a bizarre murder in the town. But "Blue Velvet" is not only about this. It is not about the fifties as a temporal narrative but, among other things, it is about *time* as text. In fact it is about the dislocation or the dissolution of narrative time in film seen as a natural or first language. All of the icons which are used in this film in a seemingly innocous and straightforward way set up a condition whereby the space of narrative time in the film is dissolved. This is accomplished particularly, though not exclusively, through the sound track. For example, the lead song "Blue Velvet" is from 1951 when it was sung by Tony Bennett. It was restylized by a group called the Statues in 1960, and that version was covered by Bobby Vinton in 1963 (which is the version used in the film). So there is already a first temporal dislocation in the sound track itself. In the film the star, Isabella Rosselini, sings the same song in a nightclub over a microphone which is certainly of a 1940s vintage, if not earlier. Another major song in the film, "In Dreams," by Roy Orbison also dates from 1963. Further, the convertible car that Jeffrey drives is a 1968 Oldsmobile, and when he first visits the Lincoln apartments, a single 1958 Fleetwood Cadillac is conspicuously framed in the film. Equally, to drink a Heineken beer in a local Southern bar before the late fifties is clearly anachronistic in the film, as is the earring in one of the male character's ears.

"Blue Velvet" is textual in that one of its intrinsic "image" components, sound, is not about the film's narrative structure of a time and place in the fifties. The complex and intentional tissue of superpositions of future and past create a temporal dislocation.

While those images and sounds are present so are their displacements. In other words, the text of the film is about something else. And yet, the film is crafted so as to render the gap between these disjunctions as virtually natural. This is an example of a text of "between"—between, but not a structure of between—where time is out of focus and interstitial. Textual dislocation comes about from the juxtaposition of two structures of sound and image, a narrative one and a chronological one, neither seen nor heard as dominant or original. One does not know what the "truth" of these sounds and images is. They do not appear to be related to the narrative but to something other than narrative, some other structure of relationships outside the film's structure. This "something other" than the narrative is the text between. The dislocating play of sound and images is uniquely possible in the temporal play of the film medium.

Such an idea of a text in relationship to a narrative or representational form such as a plot becomes a condition of a second or non-natural language. The dislocation of narrative time in "Blue Velvet" is exemplary for the case of text in architecture for two reasons. First because it illustrates another text in an aesthetic medium, but more importantly because of its dislocation of the concept of an internal time or time of narrative. Film, the media par excellence for displaying internal time, is used in "Blue Velvet" to dislocate the very phenomeneon of narrative time supposedly natural to it.

Architecture, unlike literature or film, has never had the capacity to contain or display a linear or internal time. This has problematized the concept of an architectural text. Despite the critique made by Colin Rowe and Bob Slutzky, much is still made of Sigfried Giedion's notion of space, time and architecture, that is, the potential of new materials and new spatial organizations—in particular, glass and the free plan—to collapse time in such a way that the user could experience different aspects of a plan or its facades from a single vantage point, this is still time as an aspect of the experience of the subject and not internal.

The question of how time could be introduced into architecture itself, rather than merely as the experience of our response to architecture remained unanswered. Architecture, because it was thought to have the single temporal dimension of the now, and because the static object of architecture was incapable of displaying a multivalent time, was thought not to be textual. However, architecture as text does not reside in the aesthetic or functional presence of the object, but rather as a state of between. Therefore, textual time can be introduced into architecture to produce an architecture which dislocates not only the memory of internal time but all the aspects of presence, origin, place, scale, and so forth. The potential for this textual time was always there and it was always hidden by matching narrative time with chronological time as in early films.

A dislocating architecture confronts originary or authorial value; it does not represent an original source of imagery or figuration; nor does it represent the uses of an object or even an outside discourse. Dislocating architecture displays its multiple meanings by *representing* the various relationships *between* other texts, between an architectural text and *other* texts. The nature of these other texts is the subject of the remainder of this paper.

A dislocating text is always a second language. In retrospect, the potential for a dislocating text in architecture can be found at least since the Renaissance. Alberti took the form of the traditional Greek temple front, which by the fifteenth century had become almost a banal vernacular form with an internalized icononography, and synthesized it with the triumphal arch of Septimius Severus in Rome to form the facade of Sant'Andrea in Mantua. This synthesis conflated the symbol of the sacred (the Greek temple front) with the symbol of man's power (the triumpheral arch). Although this architecture did not dislocate the "isms" of occupation—the rituals of the church remained intact—one can find in it the operation of a text between; it displayed a between of the theocentric world and the anthropocentric world and its references were spatially between Greece and Rome and temporally between the present and the past. But the actual superimposition of two formal systems or types, one of which remained dominant (that is, symbolizing the church), produced an incipient betweenness, but no dislocation.

Any interpretation of a text which is thought to be natural to the discourse of architecture can be called a text of authority, that is, given correctness and value by architecture itself. Architecture is constantly writing texts of authority without realizing that it is engaging in this activity. For example, representation is a text of authority. Representation is a false authority that suggests some sort of correct truthful relationship between the object of architecture and what it is signifiying. The apparent truth of architecture is in its claims for the univocality of the representation of the architectural object, that is, that object which has an immediate aesthetic and a function that it represents in its presence. The idea of presence and the representations of presence represses all other interpretations, represses textuality. The idea that the classical orders or a functional type is natural to architecture is an example of the representation of presence.

The dislocating text attacks the terms by which presence is represented, that is that origin, beauty, function, truth are "natural" (i.e., authentic) and not conventional to architecture. The dislocating text does not deny function or beauty but denies their authority and thus shifts the perception of them.

A dislocating text in architecture confronts this idea of originary (or what is thought to be the originary) or authorial value; i.e., that there is a correct way to read the object. Text, therefore, is not an originary source of imagery or figuration; it is not the representation of use or the aesthetic of an object. These are texts but are not dislocating. A dislocating text is or *represents* the various relationships between these other texts. In this sense, text is always a strategy which seems to be dislocating and thus a second language.

In a dislocating text the object is seen and read as different, as between its abstract and necessary object being and some known iconic form, which in its iconicity contains the traditional architectural text. Dislocating texts refuse any single authoritative reading. They do not appeal to the logic of grammar or the reason of truth. Their "truth" is constantly in flux. Although they are directed they are authorless. They are directed in the sense that they suggest a way of reading which seems to be internal to the object. But, at the same time, they deflect any single reading.

Text is then perhaps a term that can be used for any and all strategies and conditions which dislocate architecture from its authorial or natural condition of being; that is, the detaching of what architecture looks like from the need to represent function, shelter, meaning and so forth. It is not so much that the look of architecture will change (architecture will always look like architecture) but rather the style and significance of its look will be different. The idea of text is not in opposition to the reality of architecture, just as the imaginary is not the opposite of the real; it is an *other* discourse. Text surrounds reality at the same time that it is internal to reality.

The *Romeo and Juliet* project for the castles of the same name outside of Vicenza in Montecchio for the Venice Biennale of 1986, because of its already having in place an *other text*, that is the play by the same name, presented an ideal opportunity to present an architectural text that was no longer guaranteed by the tradition of architecture. Here, for the first time, there was a text of between; a fabric of images referring to something other than itself in order to create a dislocation in time and space. Traditional textuality (which includes the modernist idea of dispersal, incongruity and fragment) is ultimately projected to return the system to closure. The textuality of the *Romeo and Juliet* project is as a set of fragments which are internally incomplete. They signal the impossibility of a return to more traditional forms of text in architecture such as the relationship of form to type or form to man. The object is no longer identical to a substance.

In the *Romeo and Juliet* project, the texts are made to close on themselves by insisting on a condition of self-similarity which countered any single authoritative scale and detached this analogous process from the pursuit of a geometric ideal. It is this closure potential afforded by superposition which opens the possibility for a text between. Within the project, a process which moved towards closure, rather than end, guaranteed that there was some-

72 thing yet to be written before the reality of the castle sites in Montecchio and after the narratives of the Verona of Romeo and Juliet. This yet to be written is a temporal dimension outside of the present tradition of architecture, yet exists within the specific project. The design process is no longer governed by a teleology which moves it from an origin to a final goal of truth, but rather is an open ended series of superpositions.

The *Romeo and Juliet* project also necessarily confronts the traditional authority of architectural representation. Traditionally, architecture is represented in a set of drawings and models subservient to and depicted by a single object. Thus this representation in its singularity mediates and separates text from object. In *Romeo and Juliet*, on the other hand, each manifestation differed from the other creating the between, the figuration united with discourse to create text.

Romeo and Juliet is an example of what Jeff Kipnis calls an immanent text. An immanent text is one that is not authorized by architecture. It is a text which is authorized by the program and by the site not in architecture but rather is using this idea of text to denote a strategy for the dislocation of traditional ideas of time and place in architecture.

Using this idea of the superposition of two texts to generate a strategy for the dislocation of time and place in architecture also can be seen in our project for the Via Flaminia in Rome. In this project, the first text was the actual site in Rome, and the second text was the dislocation of the sites along the Via Flaminia in time, place and scale. Traditionally an axis such as the Via Flaminia represented a linear progression in time, a continuous and indifferent movement between two or more points, which in themselves have a meaning and a relationship because of the axis. Again through a process of superposition of elements of a different scale and place, similar to the one used in *Romeo and Juliet*, the elements of such an axial progression are continuously dislocated, appearing to be simultaneously in a different place.

This was achieved by superposing the endpoints of any three different length segments (in this case the segment of the Via Flaminia from the Ponte Milvio to San Andrea, and from San Andrea to Piazza del Popolo, and the entire segment from Ponte Milvio to Piazza del Popolo) and thus making them the same length. In this way their analogous relationship, as end points of different segments of an axis, is revealed. While these segments become the same length, they obviously become different scales. This in turn dislocates the traditional notion of a dominant scale typically generated by the human body or the aesthetic preferences of the eye. Each of these segments now loses its real dimension, location, place and time; ultimately the whole notion of the axis as a form bound to linear time with its implicit hierarchy and continuity is subverted. More importantly, because elements along each of the axes are relocated, they begin to also superpose

other elements to reveal unexpected correspondences, the architectural analog to the rhetorical figure *catachresis*, which in their former state would have remained unexpressed. What is revealed from the initial superpositions cannot be predicted.

These superpositions result in a dislocation of origin and destination, of time and space. By incorporating in an end point of the Via Flaminia, such as the Piazza del Popolo or the Ponte Milvio, an assemblage from disparate but analogogus elements of other sites on the axis, such as Vignola's Church of Sant'Andrea, the two figures occupy origin and destination contemporaneously. At the same time movement along the axis of the Via Flaminia toward a destination (supposedly the Piazza del Popolo) seems to result in a return to origin, the beginning of the axis at the Ponte Milvio.

In this way, the idea of a place along the axis of the Via Flaminia is both reinforced and denied. While new places are created, the traditional notion of place is undercut because each place is actually many places at once. The result is a text which displaces the traditional notion of time and space. It does not deny traditional and privileged ideas of context and aesthetic presence as modernism attempted, but subverts them.

While the elements of the site seem to be in their original position, that is they seem to be located according to their previous condition of formal structure (events at the beginning, middle and end of such axes), they in fact are not. Origin and destination are perceived contemporaneously while movement toward the destination results in a return to origin. The perception at one point of all the elements of the progression, rearranged in scale and distance, dislocates the relationship between time and space. In the same way, one might proceed along the axis encountering the same elements several times. Time and space, figure and form, are thus collapsed as interdependent entities. This allows these elements—time, space, place, form, figure—to be deployed in a system which contains its own contradictions, the meaning of space and time is freed from a linear symbolic representation. The definition of time as linear or circular, and of space as dynamic or static, now has no meaning in the traditional sense.

Most importantly, the received system of meaning, i.e. the cultural significance of a form is denied without denying the form: but now the forms in themselves have neither transcendental nor *a priori* meanings. They are cut off from the authority of their former singular significance. The architecture is between the signs.

The two conditions of text thus far described maintain the idea of text and reading within the tradition of architecture. However, there is yet another condition of text, of a text between, which in its displacement does not return to the authority of traditional architecture. The idea of a text between requires an initial condition of two texts. The texts themselves are not dislocating. The dislocation or condition of between is the result of the texts being seen, initially, as two weak images, that is not having a strong aesthetic iconic or functionally recognizable image. This weak image in itself leads to an idea of reading as dominant.

In the Frankfurt Biocentrum Project, two texts, one not from architecture and one not from biology, but rather between both, were used; neither was strictly authorized by the project. Here the form of the biology building was the result of the superposition of two texts, one displaced from biology and the other displaced from architecture. In the former, three aspects of the DNA's protein production were articulated as the processes replication, transcription and translation. These three processes were seen to have analogous processes in three dimensions in something called fractal geometry which is also outside of architecture's Euclidean or topological geometries and is, interestingly enough, a "between geometry"—that is, its forms are between whole number dimensions.

At first, the question to be asked was why should a biology building look like or be the result of the processes of biology. But in fact neither the processes of DNA or of fractal geometry are themselves the issue nor produce the form; they are merely the second text, from which the text of architecture generates the text between.

The question as to why the idea of text in general and more specifically, a dislocating text, has been resisted or repressed in architecture. Perhaps because this idea of text removes the restraint of morality, that is the responsibility of form to the traditions of architecture. What text demonstrates is that a building may function, shelter, be constrained by site, have an aesthetic and be meaningful without necessarily symbolizing in its forms these conditions. It can in fact do all of these things and still speak of something else. In a sense it radicalizes such formal concerns which in the past had been constrained by a morality without even realizing it, because formalisms assume such a morality to be natural and thus neither constrained nor morally impacted. When these constraints are removed then form can be read as a text, a text between as both outside the author's intentions and outside the authoriality of architecture.

Therefore the idea of a text between is necessarily dislocating. It does violence to the former celebrations of architecture as an object of desire (of an aesthetic pleasure); as a reification of man (anthropomorphism and human scale); as an object of value (truth, orign and metaphoric meaning). Such a between text is not place specific, time specific, or scale specific. It does not symbolize use, shelter or structure. Its aesthetic and history are other. Its dislocation takes place between the conventional and natural. Thus, what is being violated is the maintenance of the system as a whole.

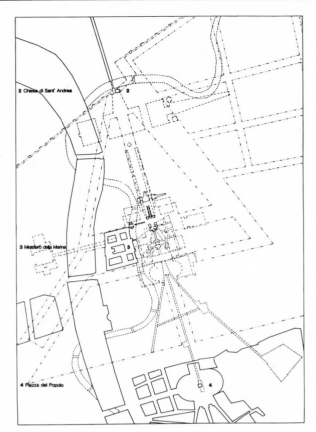

The dislocation of center: Superposition of EUR and the garden of Cardinal Montalto.

SIDNEY K. ROBINSON is an architect and associate professor in the School of Architecture at the University of Illinois at Chicago. Author of three books, *The Prairie School in Iowa* (coauthored with Richard Guy Wilson, published by Iowa State University, 1977), *Life Imitates Architecture* (University of Michigan, 1980) and *The Architecture of Alden B. Dow* (Wayne State, 1983), he is currently working on a book on the picturesque.

The Picturesque: Sinister Dishevelment

THE MAJOR MODE: National Archives, John Russell Pope, architect, 1935, Washington D.C.

Within this solid masonry cliff, a ceremonial cave safeguards the written words that sustain the nation. Classical, political, urban, this is the oracle of power.

THE MINOR MODE:
Studio of Alden B. Dow, architect, 1935, Midland, Michigan.

"Gardens never end and buildings never begin." Foliage, light and shadow on ribbed copper and beveled concrete block, reflections off the pond flicker and shift to produce a visual texture absorbing building and beholder alike.

Off to the side, or behind the familiar adjective ("Isn't that a picturesque scene?") is a noun—the Picturesque—capitalized even. A description is elevated into a category: a container with things placed in it, or leaking out of it as the case may be. The picturesque has been for two hundred years a fairly messy affair, more a mixed bag than a good, sturdy box with four corners and a lid.

The familiar picturesque is found on post card racks and in coffee table travel books. An image, a picture is already separated from the world out there and the adjective pushes it back even farther by diminishing the scene and making it immediately consumable. The eighteenth century used a device called the "Claude Glass," a darkened, concave mirror, to create the picturesque whenever one wanted. It was held up to capture a scene that actually lay behind the viewer. The natural scene was made picturesque first by turning your back to it and then reducing it to fit the hand.

The picturesque is a device for distancing, for refracting what is conventionally seen as whole. Why one would want to do such a thing is the subject of this essay.

The picturesque can be both trivial and disturbing. When it is seen as a mask covering up reality, it becomes a pejorative term. That is where we are today. Referring to an architectural design as picturesque relegates its creator to an infantile stage of development still intrigued by surface effects. The picturesque eye distracts from underlying structure and abstract concepts. To put the picturesque frame around something appropriates it and makes it ours. And once it is ours, we are free to discount it. Edmund Burke's categories of Beauty and the Sublime seem to make reference to things eternal or at least substantially beyond human creation, while the picturesque lies in the middle, partaking of both to some degree while being significantly compromised by the admixture of human artifice.[1] As a result one cannot take it too seriously. Framing something by the picturesque renders it innocuous or merely diverting.

To put a capital letter on such a frail idea as the picturesque seems the height of intellectual ostentation. And further, when one tries to trace the history of such a concept, if we can so dignify it, it proves the point by revealing so indistinct a cloud of references that one never knows quite what one is talking about. Making a list of what has been called picturesque seems all one can do.[2]

But the Picturesque, capitalized and made a category, is disturbing because taking the trivial seriously calls attention to an important transformation. Rendering something harmless, whether it is suppression or not, is an exercise of power.

In the late eighteenth century two writers, Uvedale Price (1747-1829) and Richard Payne Knight (1750-1824), argued for an aesthetic mode located in Edmund Burke's critical continuum between the categories of the Beautiful and the Sublime. They were less professional landscape gardeners than literary types who argued with Humphrey Repton, William Gilpin and others, and between themselves about the definition and intricacies of the new aesthetic mode. Price opened his discussion in public print with his book *On the picturesque* (1794). Payne Knight followed with his poem, *The Landscape* (1795). Later editions of Price's book included a 1794 letter from Repton and Price's reply as well as an instructive discussion among three parties directed primarily to answer Payne Knight's poem. Payne Knight's *An Analytical Inquiry into the Principles of Taste* came out in 1805.

The picturesque was caught in the middle of their arguments. It was not quite an independent entity having its own unmistakable rules. Price explicitly identified the picturesque as a "middle term" whose effect on the adjacent categories of visual experience is corrective, relieving the languor of Beauty and the tension of the Sublime.[3] It was supposed to be stimulating and energizing. Its reliance on novelty distinguished it from the predictable clumps and shaved lawns of the dominant school of landscape gardening whose master was Capability Brown. Whatever the genius of the place had provided, Brown saw possibilities to make it over in his own image.

As an extension of a much older notion of the pastoral, derived from the poetry of Theocritus and especially Virgil, the picturesque was initially proposed and practiced by English gentlemen whose use of the commonplace elements of the aesthetic mode: "roughness, irregularity and abrupt variation," was restricted to the country houses they retired to from their perfectly proper city houses in London. The idea of employing roughness in town filled these gentlemen with dismay. In town the major mode of the classical language of architecture does not give way the picturesque.[4] Although when the gentlemen were in the country, they certainly did not give up civilized conventions altogether.

The picturesque was a mode of seeing, building and gardening employed intermittently, not as a replacement for civic proprieties. It was dependent on the order and the support, both culturally and economically, of urban structures. The interaction between the city and the country within the experience of landed gentlemen of the eighteenth century occurred between the major mode of the city and the minor mode of their country houses. The picturesque is a position from which one looks back at the city. One packs a lunch and a good book or a box of paints and sets out for a day of ease on a hillside looking back to the city. Like the pastoral, it starts out to be a pleasant and diverting day in the country, but manages "under the veil of homely persons, and in rude speeches to insinuate and glance at greater matters."[5] That sideways glance seems to substantiate the charge that neither the pastoral nor the picturesque is serious and that they are, at the very least, escapist. But even the escape is only apparent. The safety found in the pastoral scene; its freedom from the unnaturalness and extravagance of the court, is illusory. Because it is subject to the dominant power lying beyond the hill, it is insecure.

These two modes: City/Major and picturesque/minor can be attached to numerous architectural examples illustrating their opposition, or rather their complementarity.

The major mode is communal, conventional, political. The minor is private, exotic and personal. These two points of view appear to tolerate the existence of the other. And yet they are hardly ever seen together and one is never replaced by the other. If we see these two modes as virtually independent today, one serious and one playful, it was not always so.

Uvedale Price, writing in the eighteenth century, looked beyond surface characteristics to connect the visual forms of landscape composition with political structures.

A good landscape is that in which all the parts are free and unconstrained, but in which, though some are prominent, and highly illuminated, and others in shade and retirement—some rough, and others more smooth and polished, yet they are all necessary to the beauty, energy, effect, and harmony of the whole. I do not see how a good government can be more exactly defined; and as this definition suits every style of landscape, from the plainest and simplest to the most splendid and complicated, and excludes nothing but tameness and confusion, so it equally suits all free governments, and only excludes anarchy and despotism. It must be always remembered, however, that despotism is the most complete leveller; and he who clears and levels every thing round his own lofty mansion, seems to me to have very Turkish principles of improvement.[6]

When the picturesque was being hotly debated in the 1790s, it evidently assumed greater significance than we can give it today. The intersection of the major mode of politics and civic convention with the minor mode of individualism and nature occurs in their use of power. The one mode exercises it directly and openly; the other uses it indirectly and withholds its impact. In this distinction lies the origin of the mistrust and suspicion that are attached to the picturesque. The sinister aspect of the picturesque was identified early in the debate. William Marshall, author of *Planting and Ornamental Gardening: A Practical Treatise*, 1785, whose inclusion of excerpts from Horace Walpole's "Anecdotes on Painting" indicates he was no friend of the picturesque, criticized the picturesque in a 1795 review as manifestly impractical and misleading. Deception in painting is "ingenious," while the landscape requires an "open display of facts." The whole aim of the picturesque is deception and is to be "ever suspicious and suspected."[7]

Marshall's pragmatism does not allow the land to be subject to the manipulation of representation. The proper relation to it is for purposes of survival, not taste. The transformation, or "improvement," of the land—some of which was removed from common usage by the Enclosure Acts—for non-productive purposes has been identified as a major social and economic shift of the eighteenth century. The land so used was, for picturesque reasons, hardly the most productive and the inclusion of pastures in the picturesque view did not render it unproductive, only tricked the eye into thinking so.

The appropriation of compositions from painting to landscape itself, which is, after all, at the heart of "The Picturesque," imposes layers of abstraction onto something that is supposed to be beyond such manipulation. Nature is a given to be employed for purposes that draw us away from human weakness, not as one more stage to play out our whims. A landscape manipulated to look like time and neglect had been free to take their course was offensive to many. Price defended himself from the charge of doing nothing more than designing by neglect in his letter to Humphrey Repton included in the later editions of his *Essay on the Picturesque*: "The charge of improving by neglect and accident is not true."

Neglect or accident are usually the result of not being able to intervene and deflect the progress of nature's way. Not having the money or the time to correct the depredations of gravity, water, growth and decay is one thing. To cultivate them is another. A crumbling, water-stained wall on a poor man's hut may strike the eye exactly the same as the garden house in a gentleman's picturesque composition, but they are worlds apart. And power masquerading as weakness immediately raises suspicions. Being able to do more and choosing to do less involves a profound dissimulation.

Dissimulation was another charge leveled at the picturesque. Dissimulation, of course has a venerable lineage. Castiglione's *sprezzatura* elevates the appearance of ease into a courtly virtue. "Although he may know and understand what he does [in music] in this also I would have him dissimulate the care and effort that is required to do any thing well."[9] "The Courtier" must avoid bald facts. The effort and time expended in acquiring skill in music, poetry, fencing or whatever, should be concealed. A landscape that is in fact an artificial composition is another form of courtly dissimulation.

How one feels in the presence of such "misrepresentation" depends on one's part in the game. The discomfort felt is most acute for those who need to play all their cards just to keep up. "Strength in reserve" is disquieting if the opposition never knows how deep the reserves are. The bluffing is intolerable if one is toying with nature, that bastion of fact and truth. The picturesque is a physical arrangement that looks as though no expenses had been paid when in fact no expense has been spared. As an example, Painshill garden, created by Charles Hamilton in the middle years of the eighteenth century, drove him to bankruptcy in 1773 after having rescued a scruffy heath from nature's hold, and replacing it with a pond (whose water was borrowed from the River Mole), lawn and forested hillsides.[10]

But the picturesque is also a mental arrangement; a picturesque composition can be created on the ground or in the mind. Price and Knight argued that the picturesque was not accessible without studying painting and reading books. It took education and practice to look at a scene that would ordinarily suggest trimming, painting and fixing up and to find its neglect perfect. The point was not to be taken for a poor man but for someone in control of the landscape.

The use of power leads us directly into the realm of politics. And, as Price's analogy drawn between landscape composition and political composition shows, this association was present from the beginning. Further connection is found in the fact that both Price and Payne Knight were members of Parliament and, more particularly, followers of the Whig faction led by Charles James Fox. After their time at Eton, Price and Fox traveled in Europe together. Fox's whole political career, spent mostly in opposition, was based on a nearly endless fund of trust that England's resilient "mixed constitution" could weather any storm. The only serious threat, he felt, came from the systematized attachment to power, particularly by George III. Fox, hailed as a "man of the people," supported reforms of religious toleration, slavery, and, to some extent, Parliamentary representation. It would not be mistaken to draw an analogy between visual forms of irregularity, roughness and abrupt variation and the political persona of Mr. Fox. "Fox was never normal: whenever he did not rise above the accepted standards of conduct, he fell below them...He had no middle course."[11] "In him we beheld the massy materials of the scarcely finished structure" whose extraordinary fecundity of mind presented itself with felicity and humanness.[12] His political stance presupposed a political structure that his attacks were meant to strengthen, not destroy.

The question before the Whigs in the last decade of the eighteenth century was, how much liberty can be tolerated before license takes over? For Fox, the answer was, quite a lot. For the majority of the Whigs, quite a lot less. Fox's toleration was not without limit, however. It was a mixture, as he was himself.

The act of toleration implies a provisional suspension of judgement. Granting liberty to an opposing point of view is possible only if you know you will not be overcome by that position. Tolerance implies recourse. Intolerance allows no gap, no margin, no reserves. What you see is what you get. It allows the opposition to plan, to know what it is up against. It was easy for Fox to be tolerant because he felt he had an absolute fall-back position that would, in the end, prevail. The sustaining faith in such a fall-back position is absolute but on a different level than that on which the discussion, whatever it is, is being argued. Moral certainty is like economic certainty in its ability to retreat without losing place.

The issue of tolerance was much on Fox's mind as he responded to the appeals of the Dissenters against the Test Acts required by the established Church for participation in public life. He believed that toleration and moderate behavior on the part of members of the Church of England would be produced by their "being forced to hear the arguments of the Dissenters, by their being obliged to oppose argument to argument, instead of imposing the silence of the strong hand of power; by that modest confidence in the truth of their own tenants, and the charity for those of others, which the collision of opinions, in open and liberal discussion among men living under the same government, and equally protected by it, never fails to produce…"[13] The terms for exercising toleration not to suffocate, but preserve, mixture are clearly set out in this position.

When pushed by dangerous calls for dissolution of the mixed constitution of Britain, Fox stood staunchly behind the crown. When the stakes were high enough, as in debates over Parliamentary Reform, Fox would step back from a position urging greater liberty to argue that liberty was fine, up to a point. He firmly believed that the men of position and education represented all interest groups in the realm. "His objection to universal suffrage was not distrust of the decision of the majority, but because there was no practical mode of collecting such suffrage, and that by attempting it, what from the operation of hope on some, fear on others, and all the sinister means of influence that would so certainly be exerted, fewer individual opinions would be collected than by an appeal to a limited number."[14]

Fox's arguments introduce the very serious idea of preserving mixture, of valuing roughness contrasted with smoothness, of abrupt variation relieving smooth transitions, of irregularity breaking predictable regularity. The overlap in the two realms of discourse, politics and landscape gardening, is found in their common desire to provide a place for opposition and doubt; not to enshrine the latter, but to make a place for it.

The preservation of mixture so that liberty did not disintegrate into license, also guided aesthetic discussions regarding garden art. Price's devotion to the ideal of mixture and toleration is asserted many times in his *Essay* as he tries to answer critics who charged that he not only preferred picturesque scenes, but wished to exclude all others. In answering these critics, he allied his attack on Capability Brown's "system" of gardening with parallel systems of religious and political intolerance and despotism.[15] Even the partisans of the picturesque accused him of being a false friend when he dared to argue in favor of smoothness, neatness and convenience near a country house, while the partisans of smooth Beauty saw him as some sort of tiger "who passes his life in a jungle, with no more idea of the softer beauties of nature than that animal."[16] The position Price tried to establish is a slippery one. Ultimately it was not a question of smoothness or roughness but of preserving mixture.

As a commentator, Price did not assert a position that he hoped would replace the dominant mode with his own. "I should be very sorry to be suspected of having combated the despotism of others, in order to establish any arbitrary opinions of my own." When he wrote his commentary, had there been a rage for the picturesque, with its endless diversity of different heights and breaks, with odd projections and separations, he would have equally argued for grandeur, elegance and simplicity.[17] Price is engaging in the displacement of reference that is at the heart of the picturesque and that drives its opponents mad. The discussion is constantly being moved from one level to another. If it isn't the displacement of nature by artifice, or righting the balance between roughness and smoothness, it is preserving the relation between the major and the minor modes.

"Institutionalized picturesque" is a contradiction in terms. Attempts to make it the major mode quickly reveal its limitations. Its strength lies not in holding ground, but in moving about. It is perpetual guerrilla warfare, not pitched battles. Liberty, "moderately glowing, is equally distant from the oppression of government and the enthusiasm of the people."[18] Freedom left on its own quickly degenerates into licentiousness and government unchallenged slides inevitably into despotism. In visual terms the counterforce to tyranny is novelty or variety. It interrupts continuity and keeps attention alive. Of course "variety carried to excess produces uniformity."[19]

A common fear of "system" runs through Price and Payne Knight's commentaries on government and garden design. Early in his career, Price destroyed an "old fashioned," seventeenth century garden. He

78

came to regret it, and to realize that he could have mixed it with the modern style he substituted. He realized that he carried out its total destruction with the same sense of duty felt by many Englishmen reacting to the American revolution, men "of careless, unreflecting, unfeeling good-nature, who...chose to admit it as a principle, that whatever obstructed the prevailing *system*, must be all thrown down, all laid prostrate—no medium, no conciliatory methods were to be tried, but whatever might follow, destruction must precede...."[20] Consistency was the mark, the *sine qua non*, of oppression. (The terror of random violence was hard for these Enlightenment gentlemen to imagine.)

System, of course, clearly sets the terms for the connection of constituent parts. Discovering the rule explains everything. Picturesque "connection," on the other hand, is always in the process of being discovered. Saying what it is, finally, is not quite possible without reference to a level of abstraction which strikes one as begging the issue. Price knew this difficulty and tried vainly to close in on it.

Price ends his letter of response to Humphrey Repton with a declaration of "Connection" in both its aesthetic and political realms: "Although the separation of the different ranks and their gradations, like those of visible objects, is known and ascertained, yet from the beneficial mixture, and frequent intercommunication of high and low, that separation is happily disguised, and does not sensibly operate on the general mind."[21] This kind of connection is almost invisible. It is not obvious like the hierarchy of tyranny where all lines focus on a conspicuous center. Too much pruning of the overlays that have grown up around it would compromise its pervasive power. Complete neglect would obscure it totally. A "happy disguise" is one more oxymoron that apparently undermines the whole picturesque mode. Happy deception is sufficient evidence for some that the pastoral, as well as the picturesque, is a mask of "naturalism" covering up the reality of social and political power. Price recommended that the landscape gardener "conceal himself like a judicious author, who sets his reader's imagination at work, while he seems not to be guiding, but exploring with him some new region...There is in our nature a repugnance to despotism even in trifles, and we are never so heartily pleased as when we appear to have made every discovery ourselves."[22] Appearances can be deceiving and being deceived is hardly pleasurable when you do not even know that a game is being played.

Designing according to picturesque principles is a risky business; a "too hardy achievement for common hands; and tho' there may be more honor if they succeed well, yet there is more dishonour if they fail; and it is twenty to one they will, whereas in regular figures it is hard to make any great and remarkable faults."[23]

The connection is, at the least, obscure. It is hard to teach, hard to locate and slippery in its conditional stance once it has been found. Obscurity is almost by definition a bad thing. Its employment suggests that someone is manipulating power so as not to alert others to the fact. Obscurity emphasizes the accidental and the imperfect. But if time eventually converts a beautiful object into a picturesque one, why would one need to set out to create the picturesque? Does the inevitable really need partisans? Yes, because the inevitable is a notion rigged up to block analysis. The minor mode of the picturesque functions as a position of comment. As Charles James Fox was more effective in reply than in proposition, abrupt variation breaks the continuity of any dominant system, whether sensory stimulation or political organization, but it does not propose to set itself up as the persisting alternative.[24]

The struggle to avoid tyranny and system by habitually injecting "roughness, irregularity and abrupt variation" unites political and aesthetic ideals of the late eighteenth century. The virtues of perpetual contrast that stimulate sensory response and of liberty that constantly challenges the silence and smoothness of power were held up by both garden designers and politicians. But no sooner is this face of the picturesque presented than its obverse asserts itself.

The analogy between visual form and social organization connects agitation in visual compositions to individual anxiety supporting economic vitality. Peaceful complacency is not the goal. Differences of light and shadow are like differences in social status and justified in the same way: their stimulating variety contributes to an essential unity of process, not of condition.

Even toleration and incompleteness can become oppressive when the abstract exercise of power takes its clue from the artifice embodied by the picturesque and keeps the system obscured behind a benign image of informality and ease. As the isolated individual expects to be addressed in the relaxed posture of the minor mode, the picturesque becomes the ideal mode for manipulation and dissembling. Just as the cracked wall looks the same on the peasant's cottage and the gentleman's garden house, but is totally different in meaning, the picturesque was either revolutionary or counterrevolutionary depending where one stood. It justifies the way things are by reassuring the country gentlemen that they are in league with nature while they were at the same time exploiting the land and the people. It undermines stability, on the other hand, by its love of irregularity and abrupt variation. A character in Jane Austin's *Sense and Sensibility* spoke against the picturesque because it was cosmopolitan, non-English.[25] A straight, tall, flourishing England faced the threat of becoming crooked, twisted and blasted by reform.

Once the two sides of the picturesque are separated from each other: the benign and the sinister, and once the minor mode of the picturesque is separated from the major mode of the city, the balance is upset. Distortion results because the tension between the country and the city, between "nature" and artifice is loosened. The prolonged minor mode is surely as destructive as an uninterrupted major one. Turning away from the city and its conventions transforms picturesque reflection into irresponsible deflection. The ideals of novelty, surprise and relaxation depend on intermittency. Repetition renders them dull and inert. The trip into the pastoral countryside is for the purpose of looking back. If attention is permanently directed away from the city, only deformity results. And yet the perspective gained from the artificial nature of the picturesque keeps the city's conventions from devolving into tyranny.

One could attack the picturesque because it has contributed to the destruction of conventional unities, political and aesthetic, and to the substitution of free floating tolerance and uncontrolled liberty. In its desire to preserve "mixture," it employed dissembling and disguise. Natural objects were moved around to appear as if they actually occurred that way without human intervention. In such a situation, one could not be sure of what one was looking at. The eighteenth century attacks on the picturesque were directed at this point as they tried to retain some sense of unchanging reference by saying that the "natural" landscape should be left as it is, or that human intervention should clearly be identifiable. The picturesque mixed it all up, crossing lines, shifting levels of discourse, and producing a dangerously unstable situation.

But these features of the picturesque also have a positive significance. The picturesque requires a tolerance for doubt. And more than that, it demonstrates that such doubt is a good thing. Learning to operate with it, use it, and yet not succumb to it is what the picturesque mode shows us. The power of the contrast between rough and smooth, between even transitions and abrupt variations, between regularity and irregularity lies in the stimulation it provides in situations that can otherwise congeal into systematic despotism. The continual effort to keep the wall stained and cracked, but not ruined, may seem paradoxical, but it ultimately demonstrates that the picturesque preserves the untidy fringes of our compositions.

Notes

[1] Edmund Burke, *A Philosophical Enquiry into the Origin of Our Ideas of the Sublime and the Beautiful* (1757).

[2] David Watkin, *The English Vision* (London: John Murray, 1982).

[3] Uvedale Price, *Essay On the Picturesque* (London: 1842), pp. 79, 510, 98.

[4] Richard Payne Knight, *An Analytical Inquiry into the Principles of Taste* (London: 1805), p. 393.

[5] Puttenham, *Art of English Poesie* (1589), First Book, Chapter XVII.

[6] Price, *Essay on the Picturesque*, notes for p. 73, line 13.

[7] William Marshall, *A Review of "The Landscape" and an Essay on the Picturesque* (1795), p. 247.

[8] Price, *Essay on the Picturesque*, "Letter to H. Repton, Esq. from Uvedale Price, A Supplement to my Essay," pp. 417-472.

[9] Baldesar Castiglione, *The Book of the Courtier* (Garden City, New York: Anchor Books, 1959), p. 104.

[10] J. W. Lindus Forge, *Painshill* (Walton & Weybridge Local Historical Society, 1986).

[11] Christopher Hobhouse, *Fox* (1934), pp. 306- 307.

[12] *The Morning Post*, September 15, 1806.

[13] "The Substance of Mr. Fox's Speech on Repeal of the Test Laws," p. 34.

[14] *A Set of Slips...*, (1850), column 19, p. 108.

[15] Price, *Essay on the Picturesque*, p. 305.

[16] *Ibid.*, p. 455.

[17] *Ibid.*, p. 338.

[18] Crito the Euclidian, *A Letter to the Right Honorable Earl Percy, M.P. for Westminster Containing the Life of the late Right Honorable Charles James Fox* (London: A. Seale, 1806), p. ii.

[19] William Shenstone, "Unconnected Thoughts on Gardening," *Essays on Men, Manners, and Things* (1768), p. 95.

[20] Price, *Essay on the Picturesque*, p. 266.

[21] *Ibid.*, p. 471.

[22] *Ibid.*, p. 231.

[23] William Mason, *The English Garden: A Poem in Four Books* (London, 1783), Book the First.

[24] *The Morning Post*, September 15, 1806.

[25] Jane Austin, *Sense and Sensibility* (London: 1811), Part I, Chapter 18.

PATRIZIA LOMBARDO is an Associate Professor of French and Comparative Literature at the University of Pittsburgh. She is the author of *Edgar Allan Poe et la modernité (1985)*, and the forthcoming *The Three Paradoxes of Roland Barthes* (Georgia University Press). She has written extensively on architectural criticism and theory and is the coauthor of *Aldo Rossi: Three Cities* (1984).

Architecture as an Object of Thought

Carceri etching by Piranesi.

Our century has no shape of its own. We have failed to imprint the mark of our times on our houses, gardens, or on anything else. [...]We have something of every century, except our own—a phenomenon unheard of in any other era: eclecticism is our taste; we take all that we find, one thing for its beauty, another for its usefulness, and another one even for its ugliness; so that we live with nothing but fragments, as if the end of the world were about to come.

Alfred de Musset (1835)
La Confession d'un enfant du siècle

The Interplay of Theory and History

An artistic object can be studied in different ways: as an independent form structured according to its own laws and systems of relationships, as a form belonging to a history of similar forms, or as a form belonging to the intellectual history of a given period. The architectural object is particularly complex: it belongs to art and science, the history of technology, materials and symbolic forms. How should we approach architecture? How should we read an architectural object? Historicism and formalism have often been deemed contradictory, all the more in the structuralist period. But who can today believe in the truth of a given model, in the coherence of a theory? Poststructuralism, post-modernism: the terms defining our age are loosening the sharpness of a movement or intellectual position, while the temporal prefix multiplies possibilities. *Post*: the answers to the immediate past suggest scattered attitudes and eclectic solutions. The age of manifestos is followed by one of dictionaries and quotations.

Manfredo Tafuri was already facing the problem of pluralism in 1968 when he first published *Theories and History of Architecture* in Italy: there is no theory, but there are theories, in the plural, in a continuous interplay with history. Nevertheless, no history can be written as an accumulation of facts; concepts are necessary to select the material, to organize it, to put it in perspective. Criticism is always at work, or, in other words, theoretical activity is indispensable in speaking about any type of human production. Facts do not exist by themselves, as Nietzsche said. They are discursive activities, interpretation. In spite of his empiricism, the historian is consciously or unconsciously flirting with philosophy, or, as Paul Veyne said in his inaugural speech at the Collège de France in 1976, facts only exist by means of the concept informing them: "history only exists in relation to the questions we ask it."[1] Even more than the historian, the architect must flirt with the theories and history of architecture. Julien Gaudet suggested in his *Eléments et Théories de l'Architecture* in 1894 that: "The architect today is, or should be, a most manifold man: a man of science in all matters touching construction and its applications, a man of science also in his profound knowledge of the whole heritage of Architecture." If we move away from the firm ground upon which the architectural historian stood in the nineteenth century—to use Giedion's words[2]—and we read Gaudet's statement from the shaky ground of our century, we can say that the "whole heritage of Architecture" is both the far away past and the recent one. Every form is historical in the sense that it reacts or simply responds to the most recent heritage. Postmodern architecture has an identity only insofar as it opposes some of the assumptions of the Modern Movement.

When Robert Venturi wrote in 1966, in *Complexity and Contradiction in Architecture*, that architects "can no longer afford to be intimidated by the puritanically moral language of orthodox Modern architecture,"[3] he was assessing the historical consciousness of architects and their knowledge of the recent heritage. At the same time, he expressed a theoretical concern in his negation of past orthodoxy. History and theory are inevitably connected. Only a desperate attempt at purism can abstract ideas from time, from the network of synchronic and diachronic inputs. Therefore, for example, the ornaments of Philip Johnson—the gothic towers of the Pittsburgh Plate Glass building which recall the London Parliament, or the Greek quotations of the AT & T building in New York—can be read as expressing the historical awareness of those architects who reject the "puritanically moral language of orthodox Modern architecture" and prefer elements that are hybrid rather than pure. These monumental ornaments or quotations are historical in their refusal of the recent heritage, but are nonhistorical in that they treat references like a dictionary, cutting words away from the reality of the sentence, fictionally trying to reconstruct possible contexts of occurrence. But history returns as interpretation, and not simply as the background of knowledge fulfilling a useful purpose, the practice of the architect. The study of history becomes the critical eye capable of deconstructing intentions, ideologies and effects. Postmodern promiscuity is actually quite old. It is as old as the nineteenth century. We could very easily comment on several postmodern productions using this quotation from *An Analytical Inquiry into the Principles of Taste* by Richard Payne Knight, written in 1805: "The best style of architecture for irregular and picturesque houses, which can now be adopted, is that mixed style, which characterizes the buildings of Claude and Le Poussin; for it has been taken from models, which were built piecemeal, during many successive ages, and by several different nations; it is distinguished by no manners of executions, or class of ornaments; but admits of all promiscuously from a plain wall or buttress, of the roughest masonry, to the most highly wrought Corinthian capital."

History can be weak or strong: weak when it is a collection of references put together almost at random, strong when it is the understanding of the interferences and interventions between different levels of reality. History can be the whimsy of using ornaments that recall past styles, or the tragic knowledge of our condition in the world. Our actions, works and words do not belong to ourselves: they circulate and are stained by different ideologies and imperceptible facts, just as buildings are stained by the air. They exist in the density of past discourses and future ones, and inevitably accumulate different tempos, meanings and loss of meanings. Cities, monuments, streets, dwellings, and all our talk about them, briefly, all that we call architecture, bare the traces of history. No object is so visibly historical as architecture. Every architectural realization implies, in the most minimal sense, the discrepancy in time between project and construction. But the architectural object does not exist by itself; it relates to other objects. Aldo Rossi furthered the understanding of the city as existing in time, in a continuous interaction of past—many different pasts—and present. Rossi's well-known thesis in *The Architecture of the City*[4] is that architecture and the city are one. The "being there" of architecture—to use Heidegger's term *Dasein*[5]—is space in conjunction with time. The vision of the city as an heterogeneous historical space completely reversed the functionalist position. The *Casabella* group, which was Aldo Rossi's intellectual milieu in the late fifties and sixties, opposed the Modern Movement's basic assumption that the city was a juxtaposition of architectural objects.

Nevertheless we cannot simply affirm that any position contradicting the Modern Movement is postmodern. If we do so it is because the use of this label now acts as a pure exchange value; time has transformed it into currency.

Walking the streets of Manhattan, moving from

that monument of the Modern Movement transplanted to America—Sixth Avenue—to the postmodern skyline of Madison Avenue, one comes to the IBM building at 56th Street where there is an Exhibition called: "Postmodern Visions. Contemporary Architecture 1960-1985." Charles Moore, Robert Venturi, Philip Johnson, Robert Stern, Michael Graves...among the European architects, Aldo Rossi, with his project of San Cataldo Cemetery (1971). In 1971 the term "postmodern" was not yet in use. Did not Modern Architecture die in St. Louis, Missouri on July 15th, 1972, at 3:32 p.m., when Yamasaki's Pruitt-Igoe housing project was destroyed? Should Rossi's anti-functionalist idea of architecture be called postmodern? What do we do with his rationalism?[6] With his interest in Adolph Loos? How can we comprehend, under the same heading, the historicism of ornamentation and the tragic perception of history?

Perhaps the entire difference between the Modern Movement and what followed can be epitomized by the distance between one sentence by Le Corbusier and one by Aldo Rossi. I am thinking of the famous Cartesian statement by Le Corbusier: "Architecture is the masterly, correct and magnificent play of masses brought together in light." And of Aldo Rossi's statement in 1981[7]: "Thus the temporal aspect of architecture no longer resided in its dual nature of light and shadow, or in the aging of things; it rather presented itself as the catastrophic moment in which time takes things back." How far away Rossi's aphorism is from the programmatic statement by Venturi quoted at the beginning of this article: "Architects can no longer afford to be intimidated by the puritanically moral language of Modern architecture. I like elements which are hybrid rather than 'pure,' compromising rather than 'clean'...." Venturi's idea of complexity and contradiction in architecture is simplistic compared with Aldo Rossi's notion of the "analogous city": no hybrid composition can bare the density of a city that is both real and unreal, composed of personal intellectual recollections and collective memories derived from centuries of historical sedimentation. There is nothing vernacular or folkloristic in Rossi's relationship to the past of the cities he has in mind in his projects (like the balcony structure in his Gallaratese recalling the working class housing typology of Porta Ticinese, or his floating Theatre in Venice recalling the similar Renaissance constructions used in public festivals, or his San Cataldo Cemetery recalling the city of Modena and Ferrara and the whole urban landscape of the Po Valley).[8] Rossi does not mean to revive a popular tradition, nor does he copy quotations increasing their scale; he proposes an analogical operation, which is neither the playful imitation of already existing forms, nor the logical mastery of masses. Rossi's analogy is the intellectual equivalent of the personal experience of a city, which means some image of this city plus the sum of images and buildings and streets and seasons making this city real. Rossi's collage of 1976, *Analogous City*, is more similar to the perverse rationalism of one of Piranesi's projects than to any postmodern vision (above all because it is an image of an urban setting and not an isolated building).

An Historian of Architecture

Once we enter the world of promiscuous elements with pieces of the collage multiplying indefinitely, we express the need to clarify, make distinctions and identify specific experiences. In this regard, it is worthwhile to point out again the importance of Manfredo Tafuri's remarks in his *Theories and History of Architecture*. In the first edition of this seminal text, Tafuri stressed the positive value of "critical eclecticism" before World War II. The "courage" of critics like Pevsner, Benjamin, Giedion and Argan consisted in the fact that they did not derive "their analytical methods from existing philosophical systems, but from direct and empirical contact with the thoroughly new questions of the avant-gardes."[9] Because the poetics of modern art inspired their methods, these critics were capable of interpreting phenomena "in the light of an open process, of perpetual mutability."

This vindication of openness does not announce the variety, the casual, the non-rational implied in the very notion of postmodernism and the practice of postmodern art. Tafuri wrote *Theories and History* almost twenty years ago, when the term postmodern was not yet used to indicate an architectural or intellectual position. The eclecticism he put forward stood against both traditional art history and new structuralist models. Traditional art history is founded on a non-critical idea of history conceived as a peaceful continuity, while structuralism, in the sixties, became a recipe for reading any phenomena in linguistic terms. Speaking of architecture as a language, using Ferdinand de Saussure's concepts, should be only metaphoric. It cannot explain or address the complex phenomenona implicit in political, economic and aesthetic decisions that visibly shape human actions; the phenomena of space and time.

Both art history and structuralism, in spite of their difference, are grounded on eternal values—continuity for one and universal principles for the other. Critical vision and subversive consciousness reject any ideology of the eternal. Tafuri's history is Marxist in that it aims to unmask the ruling class ideology. As he wrote in *Architecture and Utopia*: "A coherent Marxist criticism of the ideology of architecture and urbanism could not but demystify the contingent and historical realities, devoid of objectivity and universality, that are hidden behind the unifying terms of art, architecture and city."[10] Tafuri intended also to put in critical perspective the intellectual illusions of the avant-gardes and the hopes of an architecture for a "liberated society." No liberation is fully possible, but this does not mean that the architect should be paralyzed and the critic condemned to nihilism or silence. This means, instead, that one must know the limits of any work, action, discourse, and use negative thought in order to be constructive and "transform bourgeois-capitalist crisis into development models."[11]

Tafuri's critical eclecticism is very different from the plurality of approaches Charles Jencks was speaking of in *The Languages of Post-Modern Architecture* (1977). As Kenneth Frampton wrote, "Jencks effectively characterized Post-Modernism as being a Populist-Pluralist art of immediate communicability."[12] Jencks was looking for a live plurality. Disturbed by the unifying label of "Modern Architecture," he pointed to the variety of architectural traditions, the full expressivity of subjective experiences. Jencks' search is vitalistic and vernacular, drawn to the immediate, and holding to an idea of totality, even if it is the small plenitude of a tradition or an individual feeling. Tafuri, on the contrary, is conscious of the many layers and mediations making communication if not impossible, at least difficult. Every word, every form, are like hard stones over which we stumble. Reality and language are not in an harmonious relationship; one is not mirroring the other, nor does one free the other. Discrepancy is their mode of relationship. And the languages, or rather the dialects, struggling over reality are multitudinous. How can anything be immediate with the many discrepancies and contradictions surrounding us, composing us? History neither offers reassuring codes, nor finally frees repressed voices by giving them their identities. History, like Freud's unconscious, is an endless repertory of utopias, failures, crises, betrayals.

In the introductory chapter of *The Sphere and the Labyrinth*[13], Tafuri stresses again a historical perspective founded on the negative thought of modern avant-gardes. It would be reductive to pinpoint the influence of Walter Benjamin (who, long before he became fashionable in the United States and in France, was studied in Italy, especially at the *Dipartimento di analisi critica e storica* of the School of Architecture in Venice, where Tafuri has been director for twenty years[14]). Moreover, "influence" is not the right word, since it supposes either a model or an organic dependence. I would say instead that Tafuri is related to Benjamin in the same way Benjamin was related to Baudelaire: through an illumination, a series of illuminations and reflections, those of the dark light of the metropolitan experience which demands the interiorization of the *choc*[15]; the rational knowledge that the time and space of reassuring correspondences are lost forever in modern life. The cultural frame of references for Tafuri is exactly the same as for Rossi. The big city is that network of multiple languages; that complicated reality made out of contradictions and scattered fragments that is the very condition of modernity. The big city is never a full, graspable object; there are always rests, margins, forgotten corners, unplanned

changes and unexpected transformations. And there is no return; after the experience of modernity one cannot go back to previous experiences.

There is nothing less American than the negative (anti-urban) metropolitan philosophy. Tafuri, together with Francesco Dal Co, Giorgio Ciucci and Manieri-Elia, identified several ideological aspects of the American city and urban planning: the regressive anti-urban utopia, typical of the nineteenth century fear of the big city and in the romantic transcendentalist tradition of Emerson, which shaped so many organicist dreams; the progressist tradition which focuses on the reforms of urban institutions and modes of productions (see Frederick Law Olmsted, Clarence Stein, Robert Moses).[16]

Baudelaire, the poet of Paris and modern life, could not describe the metropolis in its physical aspect; he could only project its disquieting and necessary effects (the word "only" echos the severity of his understanding and choice). Benjamin could not compose a critical method organically based on Marxism; he could "only" write essays that would stumble on the form of the critical essay itself. Tafuri cannot build like an architect, nor recommend the work of architecture that would realize its own ideal of composition and finally resolve its relationship to social practice. Such a work does not exist. Tafuri is a critic *maudit*, as Baudelaire was a *poète maudit*. He can "only" work and rework, endlessly, his "historical project."[17] It is a stubborn and patient analysis, in which he accomplishes the work Nietzsche spoke about in *On The Genealogy of Morals*. According to Nietzshe, there is a color which, to the genealogist, is more attractive than blue—the color gray, the gray color of human morality's past, of its many documents, its "long hieroglyphical text."

Tafuri is faithful to his conception of the multiplicity of languages: the techniques of structuralism, the ideas of Michel Foucault, as well as the Marxist critique of ideology. They are all instrumental in the elaboration of the analysis. This does not mean that the tension between the signifier and the signified is the same thing as the Foucaultian notion of discourse as the violence we do to things. This means that there are moments in the analysis when the critic will find it useful to employ a recognized terminology or theme. The fact that Tafuri sounds more structuralist in *The Sphere and the Labyrinth* than in *Theories and History of Architecture*, does not show a conversion. Tafuri keeps his distance from any idea of the primacy of language, such as the notion of the materiality of the signifier in Lacan. Language is not an absolute, although it can reveal a mentality.[18] The fact that Foucault has evidently been seminal in Tafuri's thought does not mean that Tafuri is absorbing every aspect of Foucaultian analysis; it would be sufficient to see how firmly Tafuri holds to the Marxist concept of ideology (while Foucault prefers the notion of discursive technologies, since it does not imply any

84 truth to unmask). Tafuri is engaged in unmasking illusions—precisely those illusions that produce ideas and facts—and watching the way in which any research is made, even his own. For this reason, the initial quotation of the introduction to *The Sphere and the Labyrinth* comes from Carlo Ginzburg's *Giochi di pazienza*[19], which makes the work of construction comparable to a puzzle, typical of historical research.

The puzzle is composed of several elements which must fit together. The first essay of *The Sphere and the Labyrinth*, "The Wicked Architect," is a perfect example of a puzzle in which the elements of historical information are combined with the most sophisticated tools of textual analysis. The historian of modern life knows that Babel is the everyday reality and that multiple levels of inquiry are required to look at any object. Tafuri's chosen object of study, Piranesi, is already provocative to the intentions of a book, which aims at the study of the relationship between the avant-garde and architecture. But the choice of Piranesi is confirmed by Sergei Eisenstein's study of the eighteenth century architect, which is the object of Tafuri's second chapter, "The Historicity of the Avant-Garde: Piranesi and Eisenstein." The level of the text is thus doubled. Besides this, at least three languages are immediately spoken: the one of written texts—Piranesi's *Magnificenza ed architettura de' Romani* and *Parere sull'architettura*; the one of non- realized architectural projects—*Campo Marzio* and *Le Carceri*; and the one of the architect's work—the reconstruction of Santa Maria del Priorato on the Aventine. The languages of the work are further multiplied in the readings of other critics, such as Wittkover and Körte. Like Nietzsche's genealogist, Tafuri follows the hieroglyphs of Piranesi—the mobility of his often hermetic statements, his perception of the universe as mechanical and artificial now and then contrasting with an organicist vocabulary, the inevitable hint of nostalgia for an original happy nature, the cruel breaking up of the architectural order. Piranesi's fragmentations, distortions and contaminations are too rich to be mere *bricolage*. They compose "a systematic criticism of the concept of space," allowing the historian to reinterpret mid-eighteenth century European culture.

Piranesi shows that architecture is "nothing more than a sign and an arbitrary construction," but, as Tafuri continues, "this is intrinsic to Piranesi's discovery of the absolute 'solitude' that engulfs the subject who recognizes the relativity of his own actions." The tragedy of history reappears, almost in the terms of *Writing Degree Zero* (1963), in which Roland Barthes described the solitary position of the writer who has to fight against coded language in order to find his own mode of writing. The weight of past literature crushes him; but once he has found his style, it is immediately integrated into the canon by history/time.

What is the solution to this situation with no escape? Silence? *La Littérature assassinée* (such is the title of one of Rossi's drawings, dedicated to Manfredo Tafuri)? Or, perhaps, the Sisyphian effort Barthes mentions so often. The solution is that of speaking many languages, like the historian with no illusions, who only by destroying himself can constantly renew himself. Even the understanding of our solitude can offer the ecstatic illusion of recuperating an experience of "interior time." Tafuri concludes his last chapter of *The Sphere and the Labyrinth* (called "The Ashes of Jefferson") with a quotation from Barthes' *The Pleasure of the Text*: "[in the text of pleasure] nothing is really antagonistic, everything is plural. I pass lightly through the reactionary darkness." However seductive, this quotation turns into a warning against the illusion of solitude, of refinding the experience of "interior time." "Upon awakening, the world of facts takes on the responsibility of reestablishing a ruthless wall between the image of estrangement and the reality of its laws." This is Tafuri's conclusion.

The world of facts: Venice is there, with all its stones, its past, its archives. The historian-genealogist is not afraid of being out of date, searching documents, reorganizing erudition according to new perspectives, finding new spaces of erudition, using different tools, displacing the map of his areas of interest. Here lies the lesson of the founders of the *École des Annales*, Marc Bloch and Lucien Febvre. The quantitative study of well-defined small economies should be joined with the awareness of mentalities. Tafuri's book on the avant-gardes and architecture from Piranesi to the 1970s—so clearly placed under the sign of new history with the reference to Carlo Ginzburg—already announced the project as something different from the avant-gardes, from modern architecture. Against the danger of the heroic solitude of the modern man, one can patiently build specific knowledge. Two years ago, in the middle of all the postmodern talk, Tafuri published his immense study on Venice and the Renaissance.[20]

Notes

[1] Paul Veyne, *L'Inventaire des différences* (Paris: Seuil, 1976), p. 9.

[2] "In the nineteenth century the architectural historian stood upon firm ground. An encyclopedic treatment of architectural history presented the student with a sort of inventory of the acknowledged masterpieces of architecture. A second inventory consisted of the classical orders and Gothic structural features; this was accompanied by all the details of entablatures, friezes, and other ornamental accessories." Siegfried Giedion, *Architecture: You and Me* (Cambridge, Massachusetts: Harvard University Press, 1958), p. 109.

[3] Robert Venturi, *Complexity and Contradiction in Architecture* (New York: Museum of Modern Art, 1966), p. 16.

[4] *L'architettura della cittá* (Padova: Marsilio, 1966). English translation (Cambridge, Massachusetts: MIT University Press, 1982).

[5] For a discussion on Heidegger's concept of space see Massimo Cacciari. "Eupalinos or Architecture," *Oppositions* 21 (Summer 1980): 106-116.

[6] For the reading of Rossi's rationalism, see Bernard Huet "Aldo Rossi or the Exaltation of Reason" in *Tre città* (*Three Cities*) (Milan: Electa, 1984), pp. 9-21. A lucid review of the modern-postmodern question is Bernard Huet's "Conversation autour de l'architecture urbaine" in *Architecture en France. Modernité Post-Modernité* (Paris: Centre Georges Pompidou, 1981), pp. 48-55.

[7] Aldo Rossi, *Scientific Autobiography* (Cambridge: MIT Press, 1981).

[8] Anthony Vidler very effectively used the term of "third typology" as characterizing Rossi's architecture where the traditional city "provides the material for classification, and the forms of its artifacts provide the basis for recomposition." See the editorial in *Oppositions* 7 (Winter 1976-77): 4. Anthony Vidler criticized postmodernism in "Academicism: Modernism," *Oppositions* 8 (Spring 1977): 1. For a discussion of Rossi's work, see, among many articles, Manfredo Tafuri, "L'éphémère et l'éternel" in Aldo Rossi, *Teatro del mondo*. (Venice: Cluva Libreria Editrice, 1982).

[9] Manfredo Tafuri, *Theories and History of Architecture* (New York: Harper and Row, 1980), pp. 5-6.

[10] Manfredo Tafuri, *Architecture and Utopia. Design and Capitalist Development* (Cambridge, Massachusetts: MIT Press, 1976), p. 179. Translation of *Progetto e utopia*. (Bari: Laterza, 1973).

[11] Manfredo Tafuri, *Theories and History of Architecture*, p. 6.

[12] Kenneth Frampton, *Modern Architecture. A Critical History* (London: Thames and Hudson, 1980 and 1985), p. 292.

[13] Manfredo Tafuri, *Il labirinto e la sfera* (Torino: Einaudi, 1980). English translation by Pellegrino d'Acierno and Robert Connolly, (Cambridge, Massachusetts: MIT University Press, 1987).

[14] Francesco Dal Co, Giorgio Ciucci, Georges Teyssot, Mario Manieri-Elia, Paolo Morachiello, Marco De Michelis are among the other historians. Massimo Cacciari and Franco Rella are the two philosophers in this inter-disciplinary group. I should recall also that Aldo Rossi and Massimo Scolari are teaching at the School of Architecture in Venice.

[15] I am obviously alluding to Walter Benjamin's essay "On some Motifs in Baudelaire," *Illuminations* (New York: Harcourt and Brace, 1968).

[16] See Tafuri, Dal Co, Ciucci, Manieri-Elia. *La città americana* (Bari: Laterza, 1973). For the anti-urban ideology, see Morton and Lucia White, *The Intellectuals versus the City* (Cambridge, Massachusetts: Harvard University Press, 1962) and Leo Marx, *The Machine in the Garden* (New York: Oxford University Press, 1964). One could quote endless passages from Jefferson, Emerson, Thoreau, Sullivan. For example: "No wonder you have neither sought nor found man! And still less wonder you had neither sought nor found, nor had curiosity concerning that spirit of Democracy...No wonder you have so heavy a countenance as you walk the streets of the Great City alone - bitterly alone, helplessly alone in amidst the shoals of faces, among the half-humans - who are moving swiftly or slowly towards nothing whatsoever but graves. Because brutally they have struck kind and smiling Nature in the face -- in return for her smile." Louis Sullivan, *Democracy -- a Man-Search* (Detroit: Wayne State University Press, 1961), p. 107. When I say that anti-urban thought is not typically American, I should point out the exceptional case of Edgar Allan Poe, so important for Baudelaire. An indispensable chapter of metropolitan philosophy is his short story "The Man of the Crowd," *Edgar Allen Poe. Selected Prose, Poetry and Eureka* (New York: Holt, Reinhart and Winston, 1950).

[17] Such is the title of the introductory essay of *The Sphere and the Labyrinth*.

[18] See Tafuri. "Réalisme et Architecture" in *Critique*, (January-February 1987): 23. (This was a special issue on architecture entitled *L'Objet d'Architecture*)

[19] Carlo Ginzburg and Andriane Prosperi, *Giochi di pazienza* (Turin: Einaudi, 1973).

[20] Manfredo Tafuri. *Venezia e il Rinascimento* (Torino: Einaudi, 1985). English edition translated by Jessica Levin (Cambridge, Massachusetts: MIT University Press, forthcoming 1988).

MARK JARZOMBEK is an assistant professor in the College of Architecture at Cornell University. An architectural historian, he received a research grant from the J. Paul Getty Center for the History of Arts and Humanities in 1986-87. His publications include "Mies van der Rohe's National Gallery, and the Problem of Context" (*Assemblages*, 1987) and a book on the literary and aesthetic theories of Leon Baptista Alberti (MIT Press, 1989).

Post-Modernist Historicism: The Historian's Dilemma

I know an animal that doesn't value itself,
And for which scratching its chin turns it alive.
Yet, even when it is finally dead,
It can scream ferociously.

—*Leon Baptista Alberti*

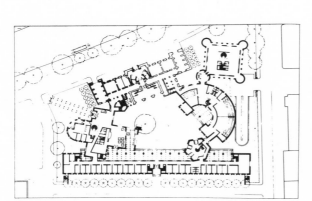

1. *James Stirling's Science Center in Berlin.*

2. *Arata Isozaki's Fuyimi Country Club.*

According to Charles Jencks, Post-Modernist Historicists are "reviving the classical languages to call up an idealism and return to a public order, but ... doing so notably without a shared metaphysics or a belief in a single cosmic symbolism."[1]

The notion that architectural theory was once under the spell of a "single cosmic symbolism" is, of course, a straw man, for obviously, a single cosmic symbolism never existed; the history of architecture ever since the Renaissance is the history of competing stances and ideologies, and not the history of a monolithic "classical" cosmology. Jencks' statement is plausible only when read within the context of a liberation mystique which focuses on the supposed evils of pre-liberation "oppressors" and in the process deflects criticism away from the "liberators."

Such attempts at legitimization are important in the development of architectural theory. What concerns me, thus, is not so much the defense per se of Post-Modernism, as a paradox inherent in Post-Modernist theory. The Post-Modernist Historicists, in their brave attempt to avoid a "single cosmic symbolism," have revived historical forms specifically to strip them of historiographic substance. In the process Post-Modernist Historicists may not have avoided coming under the sway of "a single cosmic symbolism"—that of art history.

In a sense Post-Modernism is the product of a debased version of late-nineteenth century Wölfflinian formalism, a "history without names," as it has been called, and a history without real issues. Wölfflin, attempting to hold in check questionable metaphysical speculation, singularly refused to regard anything outside the "frame" as relevant to his science of art, which was based exclusively on visual analysis. In its debased version, formalism not only denies the existence of complex relationships between art and culture, reducing historical forms to ahistorical signs, but creates a history based on monument-buildings and styles. This is not as benign as it seems, for it marks, perhaps, the end of architectural theory as it was known in the past; it certainly changes the way historicist architecture is designed and discussed.

Let us look at James Stirling's recent Science Center in Berlin, constructed around an existing nineteenth century courthouse. It is obviously a building lending itself to many "historicist" associations. (Illustration 1) One critic has commented that "the preserved [court] building is the Parthenon, the octagonal library is the Tower of the Winds, the amphitheater semicircle is the Odeon of Herod, the long institute is the Stoa of Attalos."[2] The most unusual feature of the plan, however, is the pairing of "castle" and "church" which seems to evoke a typical characteristic of the Ottonian urbanism of eighth-century Germany. Whereas the references to Athens seem farfetched, the references to medieval Germany appear to bring together images closer to home. The irony of choosing the symbolism of a distant medieval past in a city still conscious of its more immediate history is worth musing on. By scaling the forms down, à la Disneyland, Stirling even seems to be making a veiled political statement. The building complex also seems to offer a critique on the Modernist "cosmology," for the elegant fake church "apse," rising above the sculpture-garden wall of Miles' New National Gallery, makes it seem as if the Science Center is turning its rump provocatively against the great master of Modernism.

The Science Center lacks the ability to convince, however, because its historical references don't carry any significance beyond the whim of the designer. The "castle" is not treated as an architectural form with its own history but rather as a stereotype of "Germanness." By attaching himself to this cliché Stirling forgoes the possibility of evoking true regional forms. Furthermore, what any of the historical references, even the authentic ones, have to do with modern science remains a mystery.

I am not arguing that Stirling should have employed the historicist forms more "correctly." All historicism, beginning with the Renaissance appropriation of Roman forms, is "incorrect." Stirling's historicism, however, is not even "incorrect," since it is not guided by a vision of history. There is nothing necessarily wrong with that. But, let us not be fooled into viewing the building as

"historicist," or into thinking that it contributes to our understanding of ourselves and our past. Ironically, there are many buildings by Le Corbusier that are more "historicist" than this one and would serve much better as an example of history-conscious architecture. The references at the Quartier Moderne Frugès at Pessac to the Carthusian monastery at Galuzzo and the bastide towns of Southern France do not detract from the building's purism, for they are assimilated by a powerful imagination that sees through the forms to underlying principles.

Charles Moore's Italian Piazza (which alludes to the Trevi fountain), Venturi's Gordon Wu Dining Hall at Princeton (described as "Free Style Classicism"), Bruno Reichlin's Tonini House (and its neo-Palladianism), Robert Krier's Ritterstrasse Apartments (drawing on social housing projects of the Modernists), the First Federal Bank of Palm Springs (based on Corbusier's Ronchamp Chapel), are all excellent Post-Modernist buildings. But, there is no real historicism here.

Post-Modernist Historicists delude themselves and their clients into thinking that a reference to the past automatically confers historiographic depth on a building. Take Michael Graves' San Juan Capistrano Regional Library, for example, where lists of historical references become shallow substitutes for historiographic analysis. In the brochure advertising the building, the visitor is informed not about the obvious Spanish-Colonial aspect of the building or its reference to Santa Maria Regla in Hidalgo near Mexico City, but about the "architectural influences from ancient Egypt and Pre-Columbian America to classical Greece and the Renaissance." Where these influences are defies imagination; they have more to do with the attempt to legitimize the design within a scholarly realm.[3]

Arata Isozaki's Fujimi Country Club has also been designated a Post-Modern Classicist building.[4] (Illustration 2) This is because the architect, in his article describing the building, shows a minor detail of his building to be similar to a detail of a Palladian villa. Even though he throws in an elaborate Baroque facade for good effect, the connection between the Fujimi Country Club and its "precursors" remains elusive.[5]

Has Isozaki succumbed to the notion that historicist references must be tacked onto a building like medals on the chest of a decommissioned officer? Has Isozaki joined the rush into the library so that he too can be counted among the liberators?

Charles Jencks holds that Post-Modernist Historicists have a distinct advantage over their eighteenth-century counterparts in that they all have extensive slide collections at their disposal, which enable them to create revivalist forms with greater facility than those who had only sketchbooks and drawings on which to rely.[6] Perhaps therein lies the rub. Jencks' description of James Stirling's

3. *Leon Baptisti Alberti's S. Andrea Church, Mantua.*

4. *L. B. Alberti's S. Andrea Church, Mantua.*

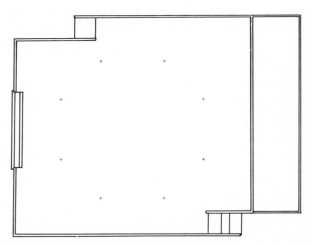

5. *Mies van der Rohe's New National Gallery, Berlin.*

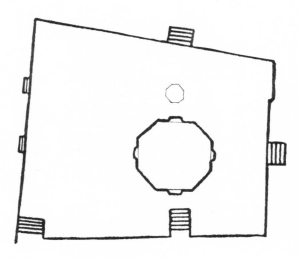

6. *The Dome of the Rock, Jerusalem.*

7. *The Primitive Hut, Frontispiece from Marc-Antoine Laugier's second edition of the* Essai sur l'Architecture.

Neue Staatsgallerie in Stuttgart is almost a parody of Post-Modern architectural "theory."

The sculpture court, a transformation of the Pantheon and Hadrian's Villa among other classical types, is a true *res republica* with the public brought through the site on a curvilinear walkway ... Cut off from the traffic and noise it also combines the profane piazza, reminiscent of De Chirico, with the sacred space of a centralized church. The oppositions continue with rustication set against metallic handrails, a sunken Doric portico opposed to an orange revolving door, and an implied ruin versus picture windows.[7]

The art of building has degenerated into the art of collecting one-liners; criticism into a self-conscious display of "learning." True historicism must be differentiated from One-liner Historicism. The former employs history to clarify the design process, the latter to mystify it, as in the following:

The size and most of the shape [of Philip Johnson's New Playhouse Theater Project] is Santa Costanza with a dash of Bernini at Ariccia and of Brunelleschi's Sacristy.[8]

The liberation argument proposes that historiography has been so abused by the "oppressors" that one must now search for a "clean" historicist architectural theory. Historicist architecture, though it has always been integrally associated with politics in one form or another, has, however, not always been shady in its commitments, despite what the "liberators" say.

Let us turn to Leon Baptista Alberti's S. Andrea Church in Mantua. As is well known, its interior draws on the volumetric monumentality of Roman structures and its facade is based on Roman triumphal arches. (Illustrations 3,4) These allusions were not chosen arbitrarily, nor were they as obvi-

ous as we might suppose. Mantua was certainly no unimportant power in the fifteenth century, but it was still very much a backwater, lacking not only a major ecclesiastic structure but especially Roman ruins (which Rimini had) that could tie it to the new Humanist culture. Though the city had been founded by the Romans it had little tangible evidence to show for it. The attempt by the Gonzaga rulers to bring the Renaissance to Mantua (an expensive proposition as it turned out) was ennobled by the circumstance that Mantua did have something that in contemporary eyes gave the town true cosmological significance: a vial containing the blood of Christ. Alberti's S. Andrea not only provided the proper architectural setting for the ritualistic display of the vial on the appointed day, but also "gives" to the city an artifically constructed "memory" of its absent historical origins by combining a Roman "triumphal arch" on the facade with an "Etruscan" temple for the interior.

Mies van der Rohe's New National Gallery is also a historicist building, despite appearances. The octagonal arrangement of the columns on the large expanse of the platform overlooking the city has an unmistakable precedent in the octagonal Dome of the Rock (A.D. 680), in Jerusalem. It too is on a platform reached by flights of stairs, and haunts the New National Gallery like an atavistic memory. (Illustrations 5,6) I find it ironic that a Mies building is more in line with historicist thinking than its "Post-Modern" neighbor, the Science Center.

Historicism can be employed in a meaningful way when it both informs society about present deficiencies, and semiotically points to something about past civilization that is worth preserving, whether formally or conceptually. Laugier's drawing is an ideogram that explicates this perfectly. (Illustration 7) The goddess, seated on the intricately carved ruins of a Roman building, points to

8. *The facade of the Rucellai Palace, Florence.*

9. *Detail of the Rucellai facade.*

90

the original grove-building; the act of pointing ties together the present and the past. Architectural theory today, lacking a real historiographic perspective, does not point to the past but rather gesticulates toward it. Thus it does not matter if Stirling's Science Center refers to the Tower of the Winds or to an Ottonian castle. They are both images employed to simplify the design process and lend it a pseudotypological mystique.

The proponents of Post-Modernism, despite their claims about history (and despite their impressive slide collections), have brought only meager insights into the origins of Post-Modernism. Until now, historicist movements have had mediators who stood between architectural practice and new concepts of history. Alberti, Laugier, Semper, Pugin, and Giedion are only a few who forwarded temporarily workable concepts of history, in an attempt to legitimize and define contemporary architectural practice. The strange thing about Post-Modern Historicism is that the symbiotic relationship between architecture and history has never developed much beyond the above-mentioned liberation mystique.

To explain the complex origins of the Post-Modernist discussion on architecture, one could, of course, discuss the cultural phenomena of displacement, or the anti-aesthetics of "pluralism" (in reality commercialism and egoism posing as egalitarianism to the naive); one might also suggest that the new architecture exemplifies the Post-Modern zeitgeist where everything is a self-conscious commentary on its own status as fiction. The real origins of Post-Modern historicism are more distant and less esoteric, pointing to the nineteenth century in an odd mixture of Wölfflinian Kunstgeschichte and English eclecticism. Unfortunately, the historiographic legitimization of eclecticism no longer applies. Nineteenth-century theories of eclecticism were based on a notion of cultural superiority. The ability to think and create eclectically

was supposed to differentiate architects in an advanced civilization from those in a lower form who are locked into one mode of articulation. Authenticity may be lost, but what is gained is an elevated horizon of knowledge. All this played into the hands of English colonial fantasies. Post-Modern eclecticism, embarrassed by such theories of cultural imperialism, now claims that eclecticism is a form of "democracy."[9] Instead of an architecture of cultural superiority it is an architecture of cultural freedom. But, can Post-Modernism escape from its own shadow? Perhaps that is why Post-Modern theorists seem to shy away from the nineteenth century. *Complexity and Contradiction in Architecture,* for example, discusses a wide range of buildings dating back to the Middle Ages, but only a handful are from the nineteenth century.

Concomitant with the strange discontinuity with its own past (rectified only recently by such historians as Mordaunt Crook in his excellent study *The Dilemma of Style*) is the widely accepted thesis that Post-Modernism, inasmuch as it is supposedly antithetical to antiquated theoretical rigor, picks up where "Mannerist-Classicism" (whatever that means) left off. Jencks, for example, perhaps thinking of Vincent Scully's argument that modern architecture begins with Piranesi, interprets Mannerism as a precursor of Post-Modernism.[10] Venturi makes a similar argument, going so far as to claim that because the Renaissance had not yet discovered Mannerist ambiguity, the facade Alberti designed for the Palazzo Rucellai in Florence, with Classical quoins incised on the facade, "brooks no ambiguity as to its symbolic and decorative function."[11] (Illustration 8) Unfortunately, there is hardly a facade of the Renaissance that is more ambiguous. The quoins, rather than terminating properly by a column, zigzag on into the last bay, giving the appearance that the workmen left for the day and never came back. (Illustration 9) This purposefully unfinished facade, meant to be read as only a few inches thick, is a mask, and can be interpreted as such from a purely architec-

10. Robert Venturi's Vanna Venturi House, Philadelphia.

tural point of view without even knowing of Alberti's theory of masking as expressed in his book *Momus* (The Greek God of Ridicule). Instead of criticizing the Rucellai facade as an example of rigorous Classicism, Venturi would be better to see it as a predecessor of the house he himself designed for his mother, which though formally very different exemplifies the same ambivalence between frontality and mask that makes the Rucellai facade and his own house so great. (Illustration 10)

The problem arises because so much of Post-Modernist jargon arises from a dead art-historical formalism that insists on such terms as "Mannerism" and "Classicism."

Paolo Portoghesi, one of the early European propagandizers of Post-Modernism, attempted to explain the liberation theory of Post-Modernism from a slightly more political point of view.

In the catalogue to the exhibition in Venice and Paris, called "The Presence of the Past," he argued that Post-Modernism represents a "new Renaissance," "a refusal, a rupture, a renouncement."[12] He points to the "fall of centered [political] systems" and the end of the modernist "prohibition" (the fact that it had been the *Renaissance* that saw the birth of "centered systems" in both politics and in architectural theory seems to be ignored). Portoghesi wants to link Post-Modernism with the "thirty years of free experimentation" that preceded the great "orthodoxy."[13] His surprisingly determinist thesis seems almost to mimic the Modernist's own search for "Pre-Moderns."

Before a Postmodern culture, there previously existed a "postmodern condition," the product of a "postindustrial" society. It was inevitable that sooner or later this creeping, underground revolution would end up changing the direction of artistic research.[14]

Modernism is viewed as a type of totalitarian evil that broke the flowering vitality of the Art Nouveau movement and Expressionism. Post-Modernism is a form of *glasnost* after the cold war. The link between Post-Modernism and the supposedly anti-totalitarian, freewheeling spirit of the *fin de siècle* does not solve the problem of Post-Modernism's historical origins. Art Nouveau and Expressionism were more than freewheeling formal experiments; they were valid protests against an inhuman industrial world. Post-Modernist architects utter not a word about the turn-of-the-century outcry against industrialism. In fact, they sidestep the issue by claiming that industrialism is a "spent topic;" its "impact of novelty is over."[15] In leaving the age of mechanical motion, they can enter the age of linguistic notions, "From Function to Fiction."

We have supposedly evolved from the corporeal to the mental, entering, so Portoghesi argues, a world of "taste cultures."[16] Of course, the world of "taste culture" suits the Post-Modernists just fine (Americans in particular). But it is, after all, just another form of mystification. Consumerism, Madison Avenue packaging, and even capitalist imperialism are all too easily hidden under the auspices of such euphemisms as "regionalism" and "pluralism." The worst examples of Post-Modern architecture can be explained away when framed against "the sudden impoverishment produced in architecture" by the Modernists.[17]

This "impoverishment" came about because Modernism denied the middle class the symbols that serve to differentiate it from the literally impoverished. Post-Modernism, so it seems, is correcting this. The impoverished still get their minimum housing projects, but the middle class can now have "distinctive" condo apartments though ignorant of the significance and meaning of historicist architecture. Jencks argues that Post-Modernist Historicists take Classicism and strip it of its class distinctions, creating a "classicism without tears."[18] But who expects to find tears in chic Post-Modern clothing stores and glitzy shopping malls?

The main roadblock to a history of Post-Modernism is the simplistic idea of caesura, which, once the legitimizing phase is past, will have to be dropped. Not only is modernism not what "Post-" Modernists claim, but Post-Modernism is a "condition" that stretches back in time at least to the Renaissance, as I have already tried to suggest. In removing images from their context, both in time and space, architects throughout the centuries have confronted and studied what Charles Jencks calls "irony, parody, displacement, complexity, eclecticism, [and] realism."[19] Alberti's facade at S. Andrea is a brilliant example of the Post-Modern aesthetic. The Roman triumphal entry is purposefully misapplied and pushed right up alongside an existing clocktower; it becomes not only an entry into a church, but also a covered street leading into a side courtyard. The facade was not to be read as a freestanding imitation of a Roman form, but as a monument integrally interlocked in the medieval urban fabric, much as Roman ruins were in other cities. Alberti was using a Roman form to simulate a medieval urban situation.

The Post-Modern aesthetic is thus not a specialized condition triggered by narrow-minded Modernists but a pervasive aspect of architecture since the Renaissance. If Jencks writes "that there is a freedom of interpretation allowed by the existence of ruins and by the incomplete and suggestive state of previous forms which is parallel to the plurivalence of interpretation inherent in eclecticism," he is right enough—provided he extends the "modern" backward far enough to include the Renaissance.[20]

One can go so far as to point out that the ambi-

92

11. *Villa Project published in* Leon Krier: Houses, Palaces, Cities.

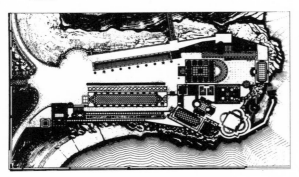

12. *Villa Project by Leon Krier (plan).*

Catholic town in 1440.

THE SAME TOWN IN 1840

13 and 14. *From Welby A. Pugin's* Contrasts: or a Parallel between the Noble Edifices of the Middle Ages and Corresponding Buildings of the Present Day; Shewing the Present Decay of Taste.

guities that are such a part of the Post-Modernist Historicist approach led to difficulties then as they do now. The unfamiliarity of historicist shapes—the calling-to-attention of the difference between the present and the past—cannot always be controlled to the satisfaction of the architect or the client. For example, Alberti's S. Sebastiano, also in Mantua, was never completed and left a contemporary puzzled: Cardinal Francesco Gonzaga could not figure out whether "it is supposed to be a church, a mosque, or a synagogue."

The irony of misplacement and misapplication that all historicists have to live with is destined to make their architecture fail if the nature of dislocation is not fully understood.

S. Sebastiano thus belongs to the list of "Post-Modern" failures along with Stirling's Science Center. The difference is that Alberti had a historiographic vision, but was unable to finish the building, whereas Stirling had only superficial historiographic understanding of the forms he brought into play.

Post-Modernist Historicists appear to be reawakening our understanding of history. They may be looking at the architectural history books that their "fathers" had thrown away. But there is little attempt to discover why the past is really so important to them. As a consequence, Post-Modernist historicists, even if they are good architects, make earlier historicists seem vibrant with Nietzschean vigor, for in the past, historicists have always defined themselves in healthy opposition to society. Alberti, for example, was not a slavish devotee of Roman architecture, nor a servant to his patron's wishes.

He saw his own buildings in relation to a society that he admonished for its excesses, its insanity, and its tendency to fragmentize the world, calling these phenomena collectively a "spectacle of frenzy." All revivalists of the subsequent centuries have shared this double vision: on the one hand they critiqued society, and on the other hand they argued for the necessity of historical forms or concepts in order to bring the criticism into context. Post-Modern Historicism denies for itself this traditional strong point of architectural theory, in favor of an uncritical alliance with mass culture that wants to neutralize history so that it doesn't threaten the day-to-day working of the world of marketing. Consequently, Post-Modernist Historicists, for all their supposed employment of historical irony, displacements, complexity, and so-called "critical" theories, have been so uncritical of their own culture that the question arises whether their claims to architectural theory are even valid.

There are some Post-Modernist Historicists who seem to maintain the traditional stance that links historical forms with a critical historiographic understanding. Leon Krier studies Rome to teach the simple lesson that Rome was a compact city of small elements. He suggests that if a city as large as ancient Rome could function without supermarkets, office blocks, and skyscrapers, perhaps we can too. While Beaux-Arts theorists went to Rome to study its monumentality, Krier went there to study the opposite. Thus, he points to something that might have been known all along, but was never appreciated as the basis for an architectural vision. (Don't expect to find in his publications actual drawings or sketches of Roman ruins.)

Unfortunately, Leon Krier opens himself up to easy attack. His work is filled with romanticist Hellenic fantasies and escapist self-delusions. (Illustration 11, 12) He critiques the simplicity of Modernism by envisioning a world without cars, without poverty, without the problems of social housing. His images have a sort of antiseptic Disneyland cleanliness about them that makes one wonder if he is fighting a quixotic battle with the Modernist windmill, while ignoring the dragon that terrorizes the city.

Krier's point of view is, however, not unlike that of Pugin, who pointed to the Middle Ages in order to awaken the consciousness of the present to the chaos threatening society. (Illustrations 13, 14) In *Contrasts: or a Parallel Between the Noble Edifices of the Middle Ages and Corresponding Buildings of the Present Day; Shewing the Present Decay of Taste,* Pugin compares a modern city with a medieval city. Both Krier and Pugin hold that industrialism has turned buildings, and indeed entire cities, into disposable objects.[21] The difference, however, between the real world as known by Pugin and his neo-Gothic fantasy is not as great as that between a twentieth-century city and republican Rome. Thus whereas Pugin's historiographic vision is at least workable, Krier's remains a utopian pipe dream.

Another architect who looks to the architectural past with a purpose in mind is Robert Venturi, who in many respects is a historicist of the old school. In his article "Learning the Right Lesson from the Beaux-Arts," he himself points out that while a student at Princeton he took Donald Egbert's course on the history of Modern architecture four times:

I sat in on it as a freshman, was a projectionist as a sophomore, took it for credit as a junior, and taught it as a graduate student assistant.[22]

Nobody can now accuse Venturi of dealing with history superficially, and indeed, in *Learning from Las Vegas,* he brilliantly turns the historicist methodology loose onto a history-less "environment" (as opposed to a "city"), forevermore changing our understanding of the American flatscape. Las Vegas has become an architectural pilgrimage spot, rivaling, as he himself points out, the attractions of ancient Rome.[23] (Illustration 15)

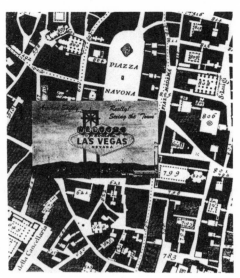

15. Robert Venturi's and Denise Scott Brown's "Collage, Nolli's Rome and Las Vegas.

16. Paul Letarouilly's drawing of the hall leading from the entrance to the main court of the Pietro Massimo Palace.

17. The balloon frame.

Yet, *Complexity and Contradiction in Architecture*, largely because of its tremendous impact, further secured the Wölfflinian-styled formalist analysis in the Post-Modern discourse on architecture. The argument is dependent on the art of "looking," and even though important things are discovered, the architectural past—ironically, but typically—is treated as passive and abstract. It awaits the illuminating gaze. Other forms of complexities, such as that of the relationship between architecture and society, of architects struggling to create or resist cultural conventions, of architecture and politics, never enter the discussion. "Learning from history" involves more than looking at it.

> Don't expect Post-Modernist Historicists
> To linger like Letarouilly
> In the corridor of history.[24]

(Illustration 16)

Ultimately, the question is: Can one have historicist buildings without historicism? Can one have historicist buildings when architects don't really love the architecture of the past—but see it all as so much stone, that can be much more cheaply imitated in sheetrock—and above all when architects deny historiography its determining role in forming an understanding of society? If one is a positivist, it might be possible to think so—and, indeed, the contemporary Post-Modernist Historicists are essentially positivistic in that the material object does not really point to its context. But this positivism, though it makes the design process more interesting, takes the meaning out of the design, because it takes the idea content out of architecture. Without the historiographic kernel to historicist architecture, forms lose their ability to resonate. It may be better to have non-historicist Modern buildings that have at least a certain amount of intellectual honesty to them.

The paradoxical absence of an historiographic understanding in historicist architecture is nowhere more apparent than when the discussion turns to architectural construction. As Post-Modernist Historicists have focused so relentlessly on forms and what they supposedly communicate, they have been unable to take hold of the traditional strong point of architectural theory; namely, construction. We seem to forget that Classicism was not a formalist exercise; Laugier's classicism, for example, was based on the notion that the column is the beginning of all architectural space, and that only an architecture that keeps faith with the structural integrity of the column can maintain itself over the tendency in society to turn architecture into mere objects of taste. In the thought of Laugier, the principles of architecture and a criticial social vision are united. In fact, his Classicism is as good an argument against naive, one-liner Post-Modern Historicism as one can find anywhere.

A regrettable shift toward One-liner Historicism can be found in the work of Frank Gehry. There was a time when he was the only Post-Modern architect I can think of who talked about architectural construction as the basis for theory. Whereas other architects were doing cute things with columns and pediments, Gehry was changing our interpretation of such homely contemporary materials as 2 × 4s, asphalt and chain-link fencing. Gehry's buildings talked about the origins of architecture in the common everyday materials of the American landscape. (Illustration 17) He looked penetratingly at the balloon frame, much as Schinkel looked at the Parthenon. He looked at an incomplete American house much as Alberti looked at the Roman ruins, with both fascination *and* irony.

In the Law School of Loyola, Gehry seems to have abandoned what I see to be his healthy beginnings in favor of naive historicism. As one commentator wrote:

> Its deep punched windows appear almost Neo-Rationalist, while the stair-to-greenhouse sequence is clearly Baroque, and the smaller buildings are Classical and Romanesque modules, albeit stripped of their archetypal simplicity.[25]

Gehry's architecture now provokes the sort of reading where buildings have to have a past legitimized by critics who tick off references like a salesperson rattling off the specifications of a stereo system. Unfortunately, when the historical references lack a commensurate vision, the message cannot be controlled, as we have already seen. It is difficult to associate the four thick concrete columns with either the democratic principles of Greek architecture, the ruins of the Roman forum, or De Chirico imagery. They look like exhausts for an underground garage. The influence of Rossi seems to be equally spurious. Rossi's architecture, empowered by powerful political and social visions, transposed to a Law School for future Yuppies might be a pun on Rossi's "seriousness," but I doubt it. Gehry has fallen victim to Post-Modernist self-infatuation.

In conclusion I propose a tripartite division of history (partially as a caricature and partially in earnest). With the Renaissance Historicists used historiographic arguments to legitimize historical forms (as we have seen with Alberti, Laugier, and nineteenth-century eclectics); Modernists used historiography to kill historical forms—still preserving the idea content in architecture (as we have seen with Mies). Post-Modern Historicists, however, use history to kill historiographic speculation, a much more dangerous proposition than either of the other two both from a design point of view and politically. There may not be much left to talk about when the next generation of architects comes along.

Notes

[1] Charles Jencks, "Introduction," *Architectural Design* Vol. 5/6 (1980): 5.

[2] Gerd Neuman, "James Stirlings Spree-Athen 'Eklektizismus;!-?.'" *Bauwelt* Vol. 14 (April 11, 1980): 575–577.

[3] This quotation comes from the brochure advertising San Juan Capistrano Regional Library.

[4] It was included in the *Architectural Design* issue dedicated to Post-Modernism (Vol. 5/6, 1980).

[5] *A. D.* Vol. 5/6 (1980): 83.

[6] C. Jencks, "Introduction," *10.*

[7] C. Jencks, *What is Post-Modernism?,* 17.

[8] Philip Johnson, *Speaking a New Classicism* (Northampton, Mass.: Smith College Museum of Art, 1981): 35.

[9] C. Jencks and Maggie Valentine, "The Architecture of Democracy: The Hidden Tradition," *Architectural Design*, Vol. 1 (Sept., 1987): 6–25.

[10] Vincent Scully, *Modern Architecture* (New York: George Braziller, 1961), 12–13.

[11] Robert Venturi and Denise Scott Brown, *View from the Campidoglio* (Cambridge: Harper & Row, Publishers, 1984), 112.

[12] Paolo Portoghesi, *Post-Modern* (New York: Rizzoli, 1982), 7.

[13] *Ibid.* 32.

[14] *Ibid.,* 7.

[15] *Ibid.,* 11.

[16] *Ibid.,* 10.

[17] *Ibid.,* 11.

[18] C. Jencks, "Introduction," 5.

[19] C. Jencks, *What is Post-Modernism?,* 15.

[20] C. Jencks, "Introduction," 10, 5.

[21] See "Salzburger Architektur Gesprache 1982," *Wege oder Irrwege der Architektur* (Vienna: Tusch-Druck), 7.

[22] Robert Venturi and Denise Scott Brown, *View from the Campidoglio,* 70.

[23] Robert Venturi, Denise Scott Brown, Steven Izenour, *Learning From Las Vegas* (Cambridge, Mass.: MIT Press, 1985).

[24] Letarouilly was one of the first to study the architecture and urbanism of Renaissance Rome and transport it to Paris along with an understanding not only of how the Renaissance transformed Roman forms to their purposes, but also of how contemporary architects can transform Renaissance forms.

[25] Pilar Viladas, "Form Follows Ferment," *Progressive Architecture* (February, 1985), 74.

Illustration Credits

1. *Architectural Design* (Vol. 5/6, 1980): 75.

2. *A.D.* (Vol. 5/6, 1980): 84.

3. Franco Borsi, *Leon Baptista Alberti* (New York: Harper & Row, Publishers, 1977), 264-265.

4. F. Borsi, *Leon Baptista Alberti,* 241.

5. C. Kutcher, *The New Jerusalem: Planning and Politics* (Cambridge, Mass.: The MIT Press, 1975).

6. Author.

7. Wolfgang Herrmann, *Laugier and Eighteenth Century French Theory* (London: A. Zwemmer Ltd., 1962), Plate 4.

8. F. Borsi, *Leon Baptista Alberti,* 68-69.

9. F. Borsi, *Leon Baptista Alberti,* 73.

10. Robert Venturi and Denise Scott Brown, *View from the Campidoglio* (Cambridge: Harper & Row, Publishers, 1984), 31.

11. *Leon Krier Houses, Palaces, Cities* (London: A.D. Editions Ltd., 1984), 122.

12. *Leon Krier Houses, Palaces, Cities,* 123.

13. Welby A. Pugin, *Contrasts: or a Parallel Between the Noble Edifices of the Middle Ages and Corresponding Buildings of the Present Day; Shewing the Present Decay of Taste* (Edinburgh: John Grant, 1898).

14. *Ibid.*

15. Robert Venturi and Denise Scott Brown, *View from the Campidoglio,* 116.

16. John Barrington Bayley, *Letarouilly on Renaissance Rome* (New York: Architectural Book Publishing Co., 1984), 46.

17. Luciano Rubino, *Frank O. Gehry Special* (Rome: Edizioni Kappa, 1984), 79.

PALENDROMY

JACQUES DERRIDA is a professor at the Ecole des Hautes Etudes en Sciences Sociales in Paris, and holds visiting professorships at the University of California, Irvine, and Cornell University. His books include *Speech and Phenomena* (Northwestern University Press, 1973), *Writing and Difference* (University of Chicago Press, 1978), *Of Grammatology* (Johns Hopkins University Press, 1974), *Positions* and *Disseminations* (University of Chicago Press), and *Glas* (Denöuel/Gonthier, 1981).

Why Peter Eisenman Writes Such Good Books

Translated by Sarah Whiting

This title barely conceals a quotation from another, well-known title. It lifts a fragment, or rather a person. By translating the title "Why I write such good books" (*Warum ich so gute Bucher schribe*), into the third person, by summoning Nietzsche's *Ecce Homo* to bear witness, I take it upon myself to clear Eisenman of all suspicion. It is not he who speaks, it is I. I who write; I who, using displacements, borrowings, fragmentations, play with identities, with people and their titles, with the integrity of their proper names. Has one the right to do this? But who will bestow the right? And in whose name?

By abusing metonomy as well as pseudonomy, following Nietzsche's example, I propose to undertake many things—all at once, or one by one. But I will not reveal them all, and certainly not in order to begin. Without giving away all the leads, the threads, I will reveal neither the route, nor the connections. Is this not the best condition for writing good texts? Whoever assumes from a simple reading of my title that I am going to diagnose the paranoia of some Nietzsche of modern architecture has mistaken the address.

First I propose to draw attention to the art with which Eisenman himself knows how to play with titles. We will take a few examples, among which, first of all, there are the titles of his books. They are made up of words. But what are words for an architect? Or books? I also want to suggest, with the allusion to Ecce Homo, that Eisenman is, in the realm of architecture, the most anti-Wagnerian creator of our time. What might be a Wagnerian architecture? Where would one find its remains or its hidden presence today? These questions will remain unanswered here. But isn't it true that questions of art or politics are worthy of being pondered, if not posed?

I propose to speak of music, of musical instruments in one of Eisenman's works in progress. It is unnecessary to recall the fact that *Ecce Homo* is above all a book on music, and not only in its last chapter, "The Case of Wagner, A Musician's Problem" (*Der Fall Wagner, Ein Musikanten-Problem*).

Finally, I propose to note that the value, the very axiomatics of architecture that Eisenman begins by overturning, is the measure of man, that which proportions everything to a human, all too human, scale: "Human, All-Too-Human, With Two Sequels" (*Menschliches, Allzumenschliches, Mit zwei Fortsetzungen*), to cite another chapter of *Ecce Homo*. Already at the entry to the labyrinth of *Moving Arrows, Eros, and Other Errors*, one can read: "Architecture traditionally has been related to human scale." For the "metaphysics of scale" which Eisenman's "scaling" attempts to destabilize is, first of all, a humanism or an anthropocentrism. It is a human, all too human, desire for "presence" and "origin." Even in its theological dimensions, this architecture of originary presence returns to man under the law of representation and aesthetics: "In destabilizing presence and origin, the value that architecture gives to representation and the aesthetic object is also called into question" (*Moving Arrows*).

We should not, however, simply conclude that such an architecture will be Nietzschean. We should draw from the *themes* or rather the *philosophemes* of *Ecce Homo* no more than a few characters, some staging and apostrophes, at most a lexicon, similar to those computerized palettes where colors may be summoned up by a keystroke before beginning to type. So, I take this phrase which in a moment you will read on my screen (I write on my computer and you well know that Nietzsche was one of the first writers to use a typewriter); it is from the beginning

100 of *Ecce Homo*. It concerns a "labyrinth," the labyrinth of knowledge, his very own, the most dangerous of all, to which some would wish to forbid entry: "*man wird niemals in dies Labyrinth verwegener Erkenntnisse eintreten*"; a little further on, there is a citation from *Zarathustra*, and then an allusion to those who hold "an Ariadne's thread in a cowardly hand." Between these two phrases, on my screen, there is an allusion to those bold searchers who "embark on terrible seas" (*auf furchtbare Meere*) and to those whose soul is lured by flutes towards dangerous whirlpools (*deren Seele mit Flöten zu jedem Irrschlunde gelockt wird*). In brief, let us agree that what we retain from the chapter "Why I Write Such Good Books" in *Ecce Homo*, is only this: the seduction of music, the musical instrument, the sea or the abyss, and the labyrinth.

A strange introduction to architecture, and especially to that of Peter Eisenman. In which hand must the thread be held? And firmly or loosely?

It is true that this is doubtless not my subject. I would rather speak of meetings and of that particular *meeting* which took *place* at the intersection of chance and design, of risk and necessity.

When I met Peter Eisenman, I thought in my naiveté that *discourse* would be my realm and that architecture "properly speaking"—places, spaces, drawing, the silent calculation, stones, the resistance of materials—would be his. Of course I was not so naive; I knew that discourse and language did not count for nothing in the activity of architects and above all in Eisenman's. I even had reason to think that discourse and language were more important than the architects themselves realized. But I did not understand to what extent, and above all in what way, Eisenman's architecture took its starting point from the very conditions of discourse, grammar and semantics. Nor did I then understand why Eisenman is a writer—which, far from distancing him from architecture and making him one of those "theoreticians" (who, as those say who do neither one nor the other, write more than they don't build), on the contrary opens a space in which two writings, the verbal and the architectural, are inscribed, the one within the other, outside the traditional hierarchies. That is to say, what Eisenman writes "with words" is not limited to the so-called theoretical reflection on the architectural object, which attempts to define what this object has been or what it ought to be. Certainly this aspect is to be found in Eisenman, but there is still something else, something that does not simply develop as a metalanguage on the basis of a certain traditional authority of discourse in architecture. This may be characterized as another treatment of the word, of another "poetic," if you like, that participates with full legitimacy in the invention of architecture without being submitted to the order of discourse.

Our meeting was indeed a chance for me. But the risk (*aléa*)—as with all encounters—must have been programmed within an unfathomable (*abyssal*) agenda which I cannot myself risk analyzing here. Let us begin at the point when Bernard Tschumi proposed to both of us that we collaborate in the conception of what was called, by convention, a "garden" in the Parc de la Villette, a rather strange garden in that it does not involve any vegetation, only liquids and solids, water and minerals. I will not elaborate here on my first contribution, which was a text on the Chora in Plato's *Timeaus*. The unfathomable (*abyssal*) *enigma* with which Plato speaks of the architect-demiurge, of his place, of the inscription that he carries within himself of paradigmatic images, etc.; all this seemed to me to merit a kind of architectural test, a rigorous challenge (*défi de rigueur*) to all the text's poetic, rhetorical, and political plays, with all the difficulties of reading which have resisted centuries of interpretation. But once again, I do not wish to speak here of what happened on my side, of the proposition that I put forward, even as I put myself forward with the greatest misgivings. What is important here is what came from the other side, from Peter Eisenman.

Things seem to have begun with words and a book; I must admit this quickly. Eisenman not only takes great pleasure, jubilation, in playing with language, with languages, with the encounter (*rencontre*) between many idioms, welcoming chances, attentive to risk, to transplants, to the slippings and derivations of the letter. He also takes this play seriously—if one can say this—without giving himself the principal, inductive, role in a work that one hesitates to call properly or purely architectural. Without setting up this play (*jeu de la lettre*) as a *determining origin* (such a thing never exists for Eisenman), he does not leave it *outside the work*. For him, words are not epigraphs.

I will cite only two examples.

After he had translated, or rather transferred and transformed, by himself and for himself, certain motifs appropriated from my Chora text in a first architectural project—a limitless palimpsest, with the concepts of "scaling," "quarry," and "labyrinth"—I insisted, and Eisenman fully agreed, on the need to give our common work a title, and an inventive title at that, one which did not have as its sole function the endowment of meaning, the production of those effects of legitimizing identification which one expects from titles in general. On the contrary, precisely because what we were making was not a garden (the category under which the administration of La Villette ingenuously classified the space which was confided to us), but something else, a place yet without name, if not unnameable, it was necessary to give it a name, and with this naming make a new gesture, a supplementary element of the project itself, something other than a simple reference to a thing that would exist without its name, outside the name.

Three conditions seemed essential.

1. That this title would be as strong, as subsuming, and as economical of the work as possible. Such

was the "classic" and normally referential function of the title and the name.

2. That this title, while designating the work from outside, should also be part of the work, imbuing it from inside with an indispensible motion, so that the letters of the name would participate in this way in the very body of architecture.

3. That the verbal structure should maintain a relationship to the risk (aléa) of meeting such that no semantic order could stop the play, or totalize it from a center, an origin or a principle.

Choral Work. This was the title invented by Eisenman.

Even though it surfaced at a moment when long discussions had already taken place over the first "drawings" and the overall scheme of the work, this title seemed immediately correct; by chance (coup de chance) but also as the inevitable result of calculation. No hesitation, no reservations were possible. The title was perfect.

1. It named in the most appropriate way, by means of the most efficient and economic reference, a work that in its own way interprets, in a dimension that is both discursive and architectural, a reading of the platonic chora. Further, the name chora implies song (choral), as in the word "choreography." Finally, in the l, choral, chora becomes more liquid or more aerial, I do not dare to say more feminine.

2. It becomes indissociable from a construction, on which it imposes from within a new dimension: choreography, both musical and vocal. Speech, which is song, is thus inscribed in the work, taking its place within a rhythmic composition. To give way to, or to take place is, in either sense, to make an architectural event out of music, or rather out of a choir.

3. In addition to being a musical allusion — see choreography in Plato's chora — this title is more than a title. It also designates a signature, a plural signature, written by both of us in concert. Eisenman accomplished what he said he would do. The performance, the happy efficacy of the performative, consisted in inventing by himself the form of a signature that not only signed for both of us, but enunciated in itself the plurality of the choral signature, the co-signature or the counter-signature. He gave me his signature, in the sense that one gives to a collaborator the "power" to sign in his place. The work becomes musical, an architecture for many voices, at once different and harmonized in their very alterity. This comprised a gift as precious as it was perilous, made out of coral (corail), as if water had naturally joined with minerals for this simulacrum of spontaneous creation in the unconscious depths of some divided ocean. Ecce Homo: the abyss of depths without bottom, music, a hyperbolic labyrinth. The law is at the same time respected and performed. Because the task that we had been given also prescribed this: only water and stone should be used for this pseudo-garden and above all, no vegetation. This was what had been created

with a single blow, with a wave of the magic wand, in two words, so close to silence: the magic wand is also the baton of the conductor of an orchestra. I still hear it now, like the masterpiece of a maker of fireworks, the explosion of a firecracker. How could I not be reminded of the Music for the Royal Fireworks, of the "architectural sense" we always admire in Handel, so influenced by Corelli.

The elements are thus brought to light, exposed to the air: earth, water and fire — as in the Timeaus, at the moment of the formation of the cosmos. But it is impossible to assign an order, a hierarchy, or principle of deduction or derivation, to all the meanings that intersect as if from a chance meeting, in hardly more than ten letters, sealed, forged (coined) in the idiomatic forge (forgery) of a single language. The "title" is condensed in the die, the seal or the initials of this countersignature (because to give a title was also a way not to sign while signing), and at the same time, it opens up the whole to which it seems to belong. Thus there is no principle role to be played by this title, itself open to other interpretations or, one might say, other performances, other musicians, other choreographers, or even other voices. Totalization is impossible.

We might draw together some other threads, other chords in this labyrinthine skein. Eisenman often refers to the labyrinth to describe the routes taken by certain of his works: "These superpositions appear in a labyrinth, which is located at the site of the castle of Juliet. Like the story of Romeo and Juliet, it is an analogic expression of the unresolved tension between fate and free will. Here the labyrinth, like the castle sites, becomes a palimpsest." Like the work it names, the title Choral Work is at the same time palimpsest and labyrinth, a maze of superimposed (surimprimés) structures (Plato's text, the reading of it that I have proposed in my text, the slaughterhouses of La Villette, Eisenman's project for Venice [Cannaregio] and Tschumi's "Follies"). In French, in a phrase that remains untranslatable, one says: the title se donne carrière. "Carrière" means quarry. But se donne carrière is also to give free reign, to appropriate a space with a certain joyful insolence. Literally, I intend here the sense of "carrière" which at once gives itself graciously, offering up its own resources, but belongs first and foremost to the very space it enriches. How can one give in this way? How can one give something at the same time as drawing away from it? How can one, while drawing away from it, enrich the totality of which it forms a part? What is this strange economy of the gift? In Choral Work and elsewhere, Eisenman plays the game of constituting a part of the whole en carrière (as quarry), as a mine of materials to be displaced for the remainder, at the interior of the same ensemble. The quarry is at the same time inside and outside, the resources are included. And the structure of our title obeys the same law; it has the same form of potentiality, the same power — the dynamics of an immanent invention.

102 For my second example, I must play another chord/string. This musical and choreographic architecture signals, as if incorporating or citing them in itself, both a poetic genre, that is, the *lyric*, and the stringed instrument which corresponds to this genre—the lyre.

The title was already given and we had progressed in the preparation of *Choral Work*, when Eisenman suggested that I finally take an initiative that was not solely discursive, theoretical or "philosophical" (I place this word between quotation marks because the reading of the *chora* that I propose perhaps no longer belongs to the realm of philosophical thought; but we will leave this aside). He wanted, with justification, our choir to be more than the simple aggregation of two soloists, a writer and an architect. If the architect signed and "designated," de-signed with words, I should for my part project or design visible forms. On returning from New York, in the airplane, I wrote Eisenman a letter containing a drawing and its interpretation. Thinking of one of the most enigmatic passages (to my mind) in Plato's *Timeaus*, I wanted the figure of a sieve to be inscribed in the *Choral Work* itself, as the memory of a synecdoche or an errant metonomy. It would be errant in the sense that no reprise would be possible; in whatever totality, it would figure as detached pieces—neither fragments nor ruins. For the *Timeaus*, in effect, utilizes what one no doubt calls abusively a metaphor, that of the sieve, in order to describe the way in which the place (the *chora*) filters the "types," the forces or seeds that have been impressed on it:

For the nurse of generation, moistened by water and inflamed by fire, and receiving the forms of earth and air, and experiencing all the affections which accompany these, presented a strange variety of appearances, and being full of powers which were neither similar nor equally balanced, was never in any part in a state of equipoise, but swaying unevenly hither and thither, was shaken by them, and by its motion again shook them, and the elements when moved were separated and carried continually, some one way, some another. As, when grain is shaken and winnowed by fans and other instruments used in the threshing of corn, the close and heavy particles are borne away and settle in one direction, and the loose and light particles in another. In this manner, the four kinds or elements were then shaken by the receiving vessel, which, moving like a winnowing machine....
Edith Hamilton and Huntington Cairns, eds, Plato *(New Jersey: Princeton University Press, 1961), pp. 1178-1179, 52d- 53a.*

This is not the place to explain why I have always found this passage to be provocative and fascinating by reason of the very resistance it offers to reading. This is of little importance here. But, as if to give body to this fascination, I thus wrote this letter to Eisenman on the airplane, a fragment of which I will cite here:

You will recall what we envisaged when we were together at Yale: that in order to finish, I would "write," so to speak, without a single word, a heterogeneous piece, without origin or apparent destination, as if it were a fragment arriving, without indicating any totality (lost or promised), in order to break the circle of reappropriation, the triad of the three sites (Eisenman-Derrida, Tschumi, La Villette); to break, in short, the totalization, the still too historical configuration, so that it would be open to a general decipherment. Nevertheless I thought, without giving any assurance on this subject, that some detached and enigmatic metonomy, rebelling against the history of the three sites and even against the palimpsest, would "recall" by chance, if one encountered it, something that was the most incomprehensible of all—the *chora*. For myself, today, that which I find the most enigmatic, which resists and provokes me the most, in the reading which I am undertaking of the *Timeaus* is, I repeat, the allusion to the figure of the *sieve* (*plokanon*, a work or braided cord, 52e), and to the *chora* as *sieve* (sieve, sift, I also love these English words). There is in the *Timeaus* a figural allusion which I do not know how to interpret and which nevertheless seems to me decisive. It refers to the movement, the shaking (*seiesthai, seien, seiomena*), the tremor in the course of which a selection of the forces or seeds *takes place*; a sorting, a filtering in the very place where, nevertheless, the place remains impassable, indeterminate, amorphous, etc. It seems to me that this passage in the *Timeaus* is as erratic, as difficult to integrate, as deprived of origin and of manifest *telos* as that piece we have imagined for our *Choral Work*.

Thus I propose the following "representation," "materialization," "formation": in one or three examples (if there are three, then each with different scalings), a *gilded* metal object (there is gold in the passage from the *Timeaus*, on the *chora*, and in your Cannaregio project) will be planted obliquely in the earth. Neither vertical, nor horizontal, an extremely solid frame will resemble at once a screen, a sieve, or a grill (grid) and a stringed musical instrument (piano, harp, lyre?: strings, stringed instrument, vocal chord, etc.).

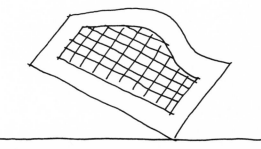

As for the grill, grid, etc., it would have a certain relationship with the *filter* (of a telescope or perhaps a photographic acid bath, or with a machine which has fallen from the sky having photographed or radiographed—filtered—an aerial view). This would be both an interpretive and *selective* filter which would allow the reading and the sieving of the three sites and the three strata (Eisenman-Derrida, Tschumi, La Villette). As for the stringed instrument, it would signal the concert and the multiple chorale, the *chora* of the *Choral Work*.

I do not think that anything should be inscribed on this sculpture (for this is a sculpture), save perhaps the title, and a signature might figure somewhere (i.e. *Choral Work*, by... 1986), as well as one or two Greek words (*plokanon*, *seiomena*, etc.). We should discuss this, among other things. (*30 May, 1986*).

One will note in this passage, the allusion to the filtering of a selective interpretation that evokes, in my letter, Nietzsche and a certain scene which is played between Nietzsche and the pre-Socratics—those same figures that seem to haunt the passage in the *Timeaus* (Democritus, for example).

So what does Eisenman do? He interprets in his turn, actively and selectively. He translates, transposes, transforms and appropriates my letter, rewriting it in his language, in his *languages*, both architectural and others. He brings another form to the developing architectural structure (a structure that is already quite fixed): that of a lyre, lying down at an oblique angle. Then, in a change of scale, he reinscribes in its very interior a small lyre within the large one which is the site. He is not content to create a metonomy within the abyss (*en abyme*) at the bottom of the ocean where coral is deposited in sediments, in order to destabilize the ruses of totalizing reason. Among all the stringed instruments evoked in my letter (piano, harp, lyre) he chooses one, whose play he reinvents in his own language, English. And in inventing another architectural contrivance, he transcribes his own linguistic reinvention.

What then takes place? First Eisenman adds another justification and another dimension to the open title *Choral Work*, which then finds itself enriched and overdetermined. Then, on all the semantic and even formal strings/chords of the word "lyre"—which is found in the same form in French and English—we hear the resonance of different texts. These are added, superposed, superimposed one *within* the other, *on* or *under* the other, according to an apparently impossible and unrepresentable topology seen through a surface; an invisible surface, certainly, but one which is audible from the internal reflection of many resonant layers. These resonant layers are also layers of meaning, but you can immediately recognize what is implied in a quasi-homophonic way, in the English word *layer* (*couche*) which takes its place in the series of layers I have noted and which also designates the totality.

The strata of this palimpsest, its "layers" are thus bottomless, since, for the reasons I have given, they do not permit totalization.

This structure of the non-totalizable palimpsest which draws from one of its elements the resources for its others (their *carrière* or quarry), and which makes an unrepresentable and unobjectifiable labyrinth out of this play of internal differences (scale without end, *scaling* without hierarchy), is then the structure of the *Choral Work*. Its structure of stone and metal, the superposition of layers (La Villette, the Eisenman-Derrida project, Tschumi's Follies, etc.) is then within the abyss of the "platonic" chora. "Lyre," "layers," would thus be a good title, overtitle or sub-title, for *Choral Work*. And this title is inscribed *in* the work, like a piece of the very thing which it names. It speaks of the truth of the work in the body of the work; it speaks of truth in a word which is many words, a kind of many-leaved book, but that is also the visible figure of a lyre, the visibility of an instrument which foments the invisible: music. And this is everything that the word *lyric* can imply.

But, for these same reasons, the truth of *Choral Work*, that which says, and does, and gives *lyre* or *layer*, is not a truth: it is not presentable, representable, totalizable; it never shows itself. It gives rise to no revelation of presence, still less to an adequation. It is an irreducible adequation which we have just evoked; and also a challenge to the *subjectile*. For all these layers of meaning and forms, of visibility and invisibility extend (lie, as in layers) *into* each other, *on*, or *under* each other, *in front* of or *behind* each other; but the truth of the relationship is never established, never stabilized on any terms. It always causes something else to be said—allegorically—than that which is said. *In a word*, it lies. The truth of the work lies in this lying strength, this liar who accompanies all our representations (as Kant notes of the phrase "I think") but who also accompanies them as a lyre can accompany a choir.

Without equivalent and therefore without opposition. In this *abyssal* palimpsest, no truth can establish itself on any principled presence or absolute meaning. In the labyrinth of this coral, the truth is the non-truth, the errance of one of those "errors" which belong to the title of another labyrinth, another palimpsest, another "quarry." I have been speaking about this other for some time now without naming it directly. I speak of Romeo and Juliet, and the entire story of names and contretemps about which I have also written elsewhere[1]; here, I speak of Eisenman's Romeo and Juliet, *Moving Arrows, Eros and Other Errors*. Have I not then lied? Have I not allegorically been speaking all this while about something other than that which you believed? Yes and no. The lie is without contradiction, both absolute and null. It does not mislead in error, but in those "moving errors" whose erring is at once finite and infinite, random and programmed. The "liar" is thus not to be found in this lie without contradictions. What remains "is" the unfindable, something entirely different from a signature, conscious and assured of its mastery, not a subject, but rather an infinite series of *subjectiles* and countersignatories, you among them, ready to take, to pay or miss the pleasure given by the passing of Eros. Liar or lyre, this is the royal name, and, for the moment, one of the best names, by which to signify the homonym and the pseudonym, the multiple voice of this secret signature, the cryptic title of the *Choral Work*. But if I said that we owe this to language more than to Peter Eisenman, you would ask me "which language?" There are so many. Would you rather say the *meeting* of languages? An architecture which is at least tri- or quadrilingual, of stones or of polyglot metals?

—But if I tell you that we owe this chance to Peter Eisenman, whose own name, as you know, embodies both stone and metal, would you believe me? Nevertheless, I tell you the truth. It is the truth that this man of iron, determined to break with the anthropomorphic scale with its "man the measure of all things," writes such good books! I swear it to you!

—This is of course what all the liars say, they would not be lying if they did not say that they were telling the truth.

—I see that you do not believe me; let me explain things in another way. What is it that I hoped to have shown, about the subject of the *Choral Work*, while proposing, on the other hand, an autobiographical description of my meeting with Peter Eisenman, in all of the languages in which he works? All of this in truth refers to two other works, the *Fin d'Ou T Hou S* and *Moving Arrows, Eros, and Other Errors*. What Jeffrey Kipnis correctly analyzed as "the endless play of readings"[2] is equally valid for these three works. Each of the three is at the same time bigger and smaller than the series, which no doubt also includes the project for Venice (Cannaregio) and several others. I had to find an economic way of speaking about all three at once and in the few pages allowed me. Similarly, at La Villette, we had little space, a single space which we had to accommodate. We had already multiplied it or divided it by three inside and we hoped to multiply it by three again in the future. For the moment we have to find a structure which multiplies within a given economy, "making an arrow," as we say in French, "all out of wood." When meaning is displaced like an arrow, without ever being allowed to stop or collect itself, we will no longer oppose the errors which it provokes, and which indeed are no longer lies, to the truth. Among *errors*, *eros*, and *arrows*, the transformation is endless, and the contamination at once inevitable and uncertain. None of the three presides at the meeting. They intersect like arrows, making a generative force out of misreadings, mispellings, mispronunciations, a force which speaks of pleasure at the same time as procuring it. If I had enough time and enough space, I would analyze the strategies played by Peter Eisenman, and what he should do in his books, that is to say in his works (*construction*) also, in order to fly like an arrow while avoiding being trapped by oppositions with which he nevertheless has to negotiate. The absence which he speaks of in *Moving Arrows...* is not opposed, and above all, is not dialectically opposed to presence, nor linked to the discontinuous structure of "scaling." It is a mere void. Determined by recursivity and by the internal-external difference of "self-similarity," this absence "produces," it "is" (without either being an origin or a productive cause) a *text*, better and something other than a "good book"; more than a book, or one book; a text like "an unending *transformation* of properties": "Rather than an aesthetic object, the object becomes a text..." That which overturns the opposition presence/absence, and thus an entire ontology, must nevertheless be developed within the language that it transforms in this way, in which it is found imprinted, what this language literally contains *without* containing. Eisenman's architecture marks this *sans*, which I prefer to write in English, *without*, with/without, within and out, etc. We are related to this "without" of the language, by dominating it in order to play with it, and at the same time in order to be subjected to the law, which is the law *of* the language, of languages, in truth of all marks. We are in this sense at the same time both passive and active. And we could say something *analogous* to the subject of this active/passive opposition in the texts of Eisenman, something also analogous to what he says about analogies. But one must also know how to stop an arrow. He also knows how to do that.

We might be tempted to speak here of an architectural *Witz*, of a new textual economy (and *oikos*, after all, *is* the house; Eisenman also builds houses), an economy in which we no longer have to exclude the invisible from the visible, to oppose the temporal and the spatial, discourse and architecture. Not that we confuse them, but we distribute them according to another hierarchy, a hier-archy without an "arche," a memory without origin, a hierarchy without hierarchy.

What there is there (there is, *es gibt*) is something beyond *Witz*, as in beyond the pleasure principle, if at least we understand these two words, *Witz* and *plaisir*, as implying the intractable law of saving and economy.

Finally, to raise the question of the book once more: sometimes we would wish to imply, gently, that the most innovative architects-theoreticians write books instead of building. It should not be forgotten that those who hold this position generally do neither one nor the other. In effect, Eisenman writes. But in order to break with the norms and the authority of the existing economy, he needed, by means of something which still resembled a book, *effectively* to clear a new space in which this an-economy (*anéconomie*) would be at the same time possible and, to a certain point, legitimized, negotiated. This negotiation takes place within time, and necessarily with the powers and the cultures of the moment. For beyond the economy, beyond the book, whose form still displays this encompassing mania of speech, he writes something else.

This something else would be a *topos*: monuments have often been compared to books. Eisenman's book-lets are, no doubt, no longer books. Nor are they at all "good and beautiful." They pass the test of calligraphy or of the *callistique*, this ancient name for aesthetic. I would not say that they are sublime. In its very disproportionateness sublimity is still a human measure.

Ecce Homo: end, the end of all.

Notes

¹ *L'aphorism á contretemps, in Romeo et Juliette, Le Livre* Papers, Paris, 1986 (to be published in English).

² "So an endless play of readings: 'find out house,' 'fine doubt house,' 'find either or,' 'end of where,' 'end of covering' [in the wealth of reading possibilities, two of an 'inside' nature that have recently arisen might be interesting to indicate. 'Fin d'Ou T' can also suggest the French *fin d'aout*, the end of August, the period, in fact, when the work on the project was completed. In addition, an English reader affecting French might well mispronounce the same fragment as 'fondu,' a Swiss cooking technique (from the French *fondu* for melted, also a ballet term for bending at the knee) alluding to the presence of a Swiss-trained architect, Pieter Versteegh, as a principal design assistant!] etc., is provoked by regulated manipulations of the spaces—between letters, between languages, between image and writing—a manipulation that is in every way formal, in every way writing, yet blatantly independent of the manipulations that the foundation (of French or English) would permit." Jeffrey Kipnis, "Architecture Unbound, Consequences of the Recent Work of Peter Eisenman," in *Fin d'Ou T Hou S*, p. 19.

³ Or the book to a monument. Hugo, for example, in *Notre Dame de Paris*: "The book will kill the edifice," but also "The bible of stone and the bible of paper," "the cathedral of Shakespeare," "the mosque of Byron."

Editorial note: This article was originally published in French in *Psyche* (Paris). It is republished here with the permission of the author.

JEFFREY KIPNIS is an assistant professor of theory and design in the School of Architecture at The Ohio State University, and an adjunct professor at Cooper Union in New York City. He has written numerous articles on architecture and theory, including "Architecture Unbound, Consequences of the Recent Work of Peter Eisenman," in *Fin d'Ou T Hou S* (The Architectural Association), and "Drawing a Conclusion" (*Perspecta* 22). He is the editor of a forthcoming book on the Derrida-Eisenman collaboration at La Villette in Paris.

Though
to my
knowledge

a writ has yet to be issued,

nevertheless,

the case is becoming well-known.

Daniel Libeskind's "Three Lessons in Architecture," better known as the "machines" (The Reading Machine, The Memory Machine and The Writing Machine) were his entry for the Venice Biennale, specifically—in that obliquely totalizing specificity which Libeskind alone authors in architecture—an "intervention" for the village of Palmanova. Created during the troubled denouement of Daniel's remarkable tenure at Cranbrook, the machines quickly disturbed the world of architecture, once again polarizing it into those oppositions that had become the familiars of his work: architecture/not-architecture, constructive/destructive, meaningful/meaningless, and so forth *ad taedium*.

Near the end of the summer of 1987 the machines, still shrouded in their travel cocoon, were destroyed in a fire at the Geneva Museum of Contemporary Art where they had only just arrived. As the story is told, at least in the States, the cause of the fire is somewhat clouded in mystery: arson? a mistaken effort at terrorism intended for a nearby target? Or perhaps some cause inexplicable, inevitable, metaphysical. It has even been said that "the truth of their destruction is unclear."

In the following, I consider some of the thoughts on architecture which can be solicited from the agitated birth, life and death of those wondrous instruments. I do so by wondering and wandering, with an unlikely agenda explicitly in hand, through a lecture about the "Lessons" which I heard Daniel give before their untimely demise, looking for the lessons to be learned from them. Occasionally I detour elsewhere—to *Unoriginal Signs*, Libeskind's preface to his *Chamber Works, an architectural meditation on the thought of Heraclitus* and to a published interview with the architect. Though this essay is fanciful, even far-fetched, I believe that it is written in a kindred spirit with that from which the machines emerged.

Daniel Libeskind's work plagues my thinking, irritating its complacencies most just at that moment when I strive most to irritate the complacencies of others, including Daniel. The "Three Lessons in Architecture" was an extraordinarily complex, disturbing and visionary irritant and it is for that reason that I mourn its loss. But my sigh of grief camouflages another sound, an irrepressible whisper. It hides relief's guilty sigh, the sound of relishing the removal of a source of anxiety. Perhaps, if it was as a source of distress that they taught most deeply, then relief is the better measure of the loss of the "Lessons" than grief. In either case, however, in relief or in grief, there is always a tone, or at least a tone meant. Allow me, then, to choose as a guide for this mourning after the fiery sacrifice of the "Three Lessons in Architecture" the English word *atone*. The history of this word, this sound/sight image, is a history of meaning, of course, but it is also a history of shape, sound and spacing—but we already know that these two, the history of meaning and the history of form, are always at one.

In his lecture on the "Lessons," Daniel stressed the work as a process, a "participatory experience," asking that we turn our attention towards his architecture on those terms and away from our habit of fetishizing the resulting object. "What I show you is not important. The objects I show you do not interest me. I think that the objects in architecture are only residues of something which is really important, the participatory experience." I will therefore not eulogize these lost objects, nor shall I apologize for them as objects by justifying them to that inordinate anxiety, that strong ambivalence which surged between awe and revulsion, which they engendered from the moment of their appearance. Eulogy and Apologea are inappropriate; they are forms for the mourning of objects. Rather then, will I grieve otherwise, obliquely, by guiding my guide through the words of the architect, taking him at his word, participating in it, writing anew its content.

The English word *atone*, which today means to make amends for, to reconcile with persons or gods who have been alienated, was born in the elision, the erasure of a gap. At the dawn of the 16th century, *At one*, after a brief life as *aton*, becomes *atone*, one atones to become again at one. A gap is erased to erase a gap arisen. Soon after, spawned by the change in tonality effected by the new shape of atone, the word *attune* appears. Attune, in effect, hears the new syllabic spacing of atone with both ear and eye, sees the sound of space in *atone* which sounds *a tone*.

At one: Atone, aton, a tone—these are my three instruments which in their differences construct one big Machine. (Daniel: "These are really one big Machine in three parts, which I cannot quite put together in one object.") The machinations of their spacing dances from the theological to the metaphysical to the aesthetic in a movement paralleling those of Libeskind's machines, i.e., a movement which cannot be frozen in any teleological "from…to" relationship, either in space, time or logic. Rather, movement as essence, movement as origin, originary movement. Daniel: "There is a space of space of the world [or did he say "word"?], which, on a permanent basis, one could even say eternally, produces a destabilized, let us say eternal movement of imperfections and differences."

One atones to become again at one. In Judeo-Christian theologies atonement, becoming again at one with God entails confession of guilt and sacrifice, the losing of an object prepared specifically to be lost. On Yom Kippur, the Jewish Day of Atonement, reconciliation with God is accomplished through confessional prayer, abstinence and fasting, the loss of loved objects. In earlier Hebrew traditions, animals which had been specially prepared were sacrificed on this Holy Day.

According to Christian theology atonement is made possible only with the loss, the sacrifice of Christ, who God gave to man in order to be sacrificed, a loss for which Christ was prepared. In early greek religion the huykan or animal prepared for sacrifice as a ritual scapegoat was termed a *pharmakos*. I would on that note inscribe here, in other words appropriate, Jacques Derrida's essay, *Plato's Pharmacy*, not only for its conspicuous discussion of the sacrificial *pharmakos*, but for all of its themes, which supplement this essay before the fact.

One atones to become again at one. A gap is erased to erase a gap arisen. This odd etymology, this visual onomatopoeia, if one can speak of such a thing, besides evoking and invoking its obvious theological tones, also strangely anticipates Freud's theory of mourning which is also his theory of ego growth, put forward in his *Ego and the Id*. In other words, Freud's theory of mourning is in actuality a theory of atonement, a theory of a gap erased to erase a gap arisen. Freud:

We succeeded [in *Mourning and Melancholia*, where melancholia is analyzed as grief with guilt] in explaining the painful disorder of melancholia by supposing that…an object which was lost has been set up again inside the ego [introjected]—that is, that an object-cathexis has been replaced by an identification. At that time, however ,we did not appreciate the full significance of this process and did not know how common and how typical it is. Since then we have come to understand that this kind of substitution has a great share in determining the form taken by the ego and that it makes an essential contribution towards building up what is called character…. It may be that this identification is the sole condition under which the id can give up its objects. At any rate the process [object choice, object loss, introjection, identification]… is a very frequent one, and it makes it possible to suppose that the character of the ego is a precipitate of abandoned object-cathexes….

For Freud, the ego reconciles itself to the loss of a loved object, a loss for which it always in part blames itself, by a process which culminates in an altering of that ego through an identifying with the lost object, that is, a becoming at one with it. The dynamic of the shape and tone of ego development is atonement.

Freud goes on to discuss the father as the object of the "first and most important" of these atonements. But there an uneasiness arises. How can the ego, which develops within this process, engage as an ego with a first object? The matter is further complicated when we consider Freud's earlier mention of cases of simultaneous object cathexis and identification. Freud proposes an uneasy and incomplete answer: "this is apparently not in the first instance the consequence or outcome of an object-cathexis; it is a direct and immediate identification and takes place earlier than any object-cathexis." In effect, he distinguishes between an original *becoming one with* and a subsequent *becoming at one with*, remaining silent on the conditions and terms of the first *at onement*. Yet it is the introduction of the original *at* into the process, with all of its incumbent implications of spatial and temporal difference and movement, that the ego as ego, as source and arbiter of same and other, as subject in the object world, begins.

This question of the origin of the ego's "at" cannot be decided, i.e., cannot be disentangled into any simple logic of spatial and/or temporal presences, since disentanglement into presences, into subjects and objects in the world, is always already an after effect of the ego as such. It seems therefore an illogical necessity of Freud's argument that an object is always already lost, introjected and atoned as the constitutional condition of its being chosen as an object, i.e., being constructed as an object by and for an ego. In other words, an ego's objects and the ego itself, and these are the same in their differences (movements), are always pre-pared, always already and at one, a unity divided.

Let me return, then, to read Daniel's texts with some questions suggested by these preliminary thoughts on atonement. To what extent, in and on what terms were Daniel's "Lessons" prepared (as *pharmakos*) to be sacrificed in atonement, or as ego objects already so lost. Prepared, that is, in order to teach architecture a lesson? To be sure, we will find that the machines were permeated in all of their regions and at every focal length of analytic resolution with the theme of atonement by fiery sacrifice.

In this brief reading I follow a somewhat gnostic path through the lecture, tracing a different though perhaps equally immanent route for the machines from the "curious path" prescribed by Daniel, for whom they were to journey from Detroit to Palmanova along a serpentine itinerary which moved from a medieval monastery to Camillo's France to Roussel's Africa to Venice (with excursions to Moscow and Dublin) to Geneva, where they were stopped before

arriving at their destination. I will leave the retracing of that route to the reader's own devices. Mine, on the other hand is not as concerned with geography and destination, though it cannot ignore these, as it is with destiny, the "to what end?" rather than the "to where?" for which the machines were destined. Yet it is not even this ulterior movement, this play which is the sum of my interest; it is not that which is at stake. What is at stake in tracing this second movement is a lesson for architecture.

One word, one moment of disclaimer before I proceed. Though I will have cause to take up the theme elsewhere, to demand a reopening of the case of Daedalus so as finally to accuse him and architectural theory after him of using his good name (*daidalos* in Greek means skillfully made, but also cunningly made) to conceal the horrible murder of his son, Icarus. Did not Daedalus attempt a second jealous defenestration, the attempted murder of his nephew and has not architectural theory always tried to kill the promising son before the son kills the father, moreover tried to kill him in the name of but also with craft? Though all of this must be heard it is not here where it sounds. I do not propose to accuse Libeskind of murdering his progeny, I propose to discover him preparing a ritual sacrifice.

Let us glance now at some of the preliminary evidence. Below are a few of the architect's words taken from his lecture on the Lessons:

Fulfillment and destruction in the modern world are intertwined, and it is in that moment of suddenness, prepared by the totality of the situation, that architecture is revealed and destroyed at the same time.

[The machines are] not one more thing which can be found in the catalog of the world. [They are] the one thing which can never be in any catalog of the world.

The purpose of this equipment is to release the end to itself.

These are pieces of metaphysical equipment because they do not do anything; they belong in another realm.

I tried to disengage the problem of architecture from the earth—to send it to its stellar source.

I must say something of what this thing is. It is an attempt to fill up the soul with memory so that one would finally obliterate it all together.

I have tried...to offer architecture as a sacrifice to its own possibilities of making a text.

In the process of sanctification one also destroys the text.

They wound up to be these small shrines and one had to have the ashes to put into them. So, it is kind of a ritual object I am showing you.

These are but a few of many moments in the lecture which cast a tone of sacrifice and obliteration onto the machines; which cast, that is, the machines into another world. The memory machine, for example, is modeled after a work by Camillo of which Daniel says, "the most interesting thing is that after Camillo made this machine two things happen—the machine disappeared and so did

Camillo," a circumstance with which the architect finds himself "absolutely enthralled." I confess the obvious. These words are in fact ripped from their context, even from their originally intended meaning. Nevertheless, can one deny feeling in them a sense of purpose, a palpable expression of the destiny for which these lessons were prepared?

Then what sin is atoned? Is it the sin of contemporary architecture's idolatry perhaps? In *Unoriginal Signs* Libeskind had already castigated today's neo-historicist vogue as worship of a Golden Calf, as the "false pleading the cause of reconciliation":

When the once potent truth of Architecture is reduced to a sign of its absence one experiences a parching, suffocating dryness: *"the psyche lusts to be wet..."*

When Time itself is rendered meaningless by reversing its irreversible presence, then the practice of Architecture becomes the false pleading the case of reconciliation.

A loss, a gap exists, a reconciliation is necessary, but idol worship is not the answer. Finding no true reconciliation to the loss of architecture's former greatness in the pretense that no loss has occurred, Libeskind adopts the only alternative with integrity that remains after the idols have fallen. "What remains for those who no longer find greatness in Architecture is either to deny it or create it..." Daniel atones not merely for the sin of idolatry but in order to reconcile himself as architect, caretaker of lost greatness, with himself as architect, aspirant to greatness. He atones not to any god, therefore, not to any outside authority who might return, as Heidegger hoped, to restore lost authority, but to "at one" his divided self as architect, as a first step in taking responsibility for architecture. He chooses to invoke some words of Nietszche as his own: "'I call myself the last philosopher because I am the last man. Nobody talks to me but myself and my voice comes to me like that of a dying person,'" though he might as easily have invoked Heraclitus: "I went in search of myself." He then declares his project: "The recourse to surrogates is only a habit which can be given up."

Besides his motives for sacrifice, we recognize in this text another aspect which assists us in specifying the terms of his preparation, for it is Heraclitus to whom Daniel dedicates this antecedent of the "Lessons." Heraclitus, philosopher of fire as first principle, philosopher of "the one" but not of the theological "one" or the transcendental one-in-the-many, rather, of the one as the "at one" of the many, difference itself as the one. It is of interest to note that English translations of key Heraclitian fragments often rely on the word "attune" to capture Heraclitus' meaning, as in "Men do not know how what is at variance agrees with itself. It is an *attunement* of opposite tensions, like that of the bow and the lyre." In any case, the ghost of Heraclitus in Daniel's past suggests that we read not simply for sacrifice but specifically for sacrifice by fire.

Another Daniel, of course, had already sent his hands, his three instruments, Shadrach, Meshach

and Abednego, into the fire on the issue of idolatry. Libeskind often speaks of his tools and instruments as not items for his hands nor even as extensions of his hands but in effect as his "new hands." But I am getting ahead of myself; I will return to the question of the hand, particularly the new hand. For the time being, though, let me look more closely at one Heraclitian fragment employed by Libeskind in a very idiosyncratic manner in order to effect a return to the "Lessons" lecture and to the interrogation there of fire.

When the once potent truth of Architecture is reduced to a sign of its absence one experiences a parching, suffocating dryness: *"the psyche lusts to be wet..."*

"The psyche lusts to be wet" is traditionally interpreted as a pejorative remark by Heraclitus in which water stands as the nemesis, the soporific of vital fire, at once the cause and the evidence of fire gone out. Thus the fragment speaks perhaps to the need for the thinking man to reject the lure of pleasure and the immediate gratifications of desire. This interpretation seems substantiated by other fragments, for example "...the dry soul, wisest and best" (which Libeskind also quotes) and "it is death to the soul to become water."

Yet Daniel seems to employ the fragment as part of a complaint of suffocating from a parching dryness in what amounts to a demand for water. Is this an intellectual lapsus, a mere *parapraxis*? But even that explanation, after Freud, is insufficient. Is it a quibbling with Heraclitus or a debate with the tradition of his interpretation? Or can it be imagined that it indicates the moment in which an architect of obsessive integrity realizes that the internal conflict of being an architect today can be resolved only in an unthinkably complex act of self-sacrifice, one which grasps fully the rich multivalences of all of the fire/water dualisms. In that sense it would foreshadow an act of simultaneous self-immolation and drowning which would capture the entire ambivalence between the Heraclitian fire/water structure of vitality/obliteration and the ritual fire/water structure of sacrifice/ablution. That would indeed forge a new tactic of difference, of a movement by which one could start again without starting over. But can that extreme interpretation find any support?

At the beginning of his "Lessons" lecture, Libeskind invokes water as a figure again, on this occasion in precisely the synthetic ablution/obliteration resonance we would need for confirmation. He employs an obscure [does it in fact exist?] text of Hegel:

It is the same with architecture as with the revolutionary state. We can think of the people as buried under the earth, above which there is a lake. Each intends to be working only for himself and the preservation of the whole by removing a piece of stone from above and employing it in the general subterranean construction. The tension in the air, the general elements begin to change. It produces a desire for water. Uneasy, the people do not know what it is that they are lacking, and to help they dig even higher in the belief of improving their subterranean construction. The crust becomes transparent. One catches sight of it and calls "water!," tears the last layer away and the lake rushes in and drowns them all by giving them drink. So it is with the work of architecture, the work of all. There is always one who brings it to its final completion by being the last one to work on it, and he is the darling of memory.

Libeskind remarks: "Fulfillment and destruction in the modern world are intertwined, and it is in that moment of suddenness, prepared by the totality of the situation, that architecture is revealed and destroyed at the same time. As Hegel says, the production of the desire for water unknowingly also produces the fulfillment of the tearing of the last upper layers, which by giving everyone drink also drowns them."

For the time being, then, allow me to hold out for further consideration the possibility that Daniel's phrase "the production of the desire for water" is elsewhere spoken by him as "fire."

The futile pursuit of permanence—in materiality, in aesthetic, in history, in the relation of building to the dream of a permanent and entirely self aware "man"—constitutes what many theorists today consider architecture's most persistent and notorious delusion. In an interview about the machines this architect seems to take up this theme as well, and positions himself in extreme opposition:

It is possible that there were many societies and cultures which did not leave behind themselves things that were lasting, *which did not make them lesser societies, in fact, quite to the contrary*. We do not know today certain cities of ancient India and China *because they were made out of wood and burned down*. [italics mine]

For Libeskind, impermanence, the opposite of the architectural canon of *firmitas* is not only not a flaw but, recalling Heraclitus, has the genuine virtue of being the only truth. The ideal of permanence and perfection in architecture is but another face of its idolatry, for which it must be taught a lesson. The machines, then, are they not that totality prepared for destruction by fire as the desire for water? At the very least Daniel assures us again and again in his discussion of each of the machines that they are made out of wood.

But there is no need to be elliptical. Sacrificial burning resounds throughout the lecture:

You may have heard of Giordano Bruno, who was burned in Venice…

Mossem is killed in Roussel's text by having a text burned onto his feet.

I discovered that being killed by burning an iambic text onto his forehead was St. Theodore…. So it began to make sense.

Angelica…was finally burned on a grid as St. Donatella.

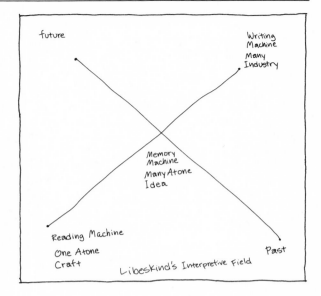

Finally, consider the Writing Machine, last of the three episodes that cannot quite be put together into one object, that are therefore never one but always at one with each other in a unity of differences, as it becomes, in an apparently unpredicated transformation, an ensemble of funerary urns. "They wound up being these small shrines, funerary urns, and then one had to have the ashes to put into them." But was that gesture in truth unpredicated within the lessons of the machines, or was it somehow foreshadowed by the first gesture of the making of the first machine? Daniel tells us that "the beginning was its end already." So, how did the first episode, the making of the Reading machine, begin? With the lighting of a candle. "We got up at the crack of dawn" and worked "with no electricity, just by candlelight."

But perhaps this solicitation of sacrificial atonement from Libeskind's text has gone too far, become too far-fetched, grown too dark, too morbid. Allow me then to return to my guide, *atone*, and ask it to seek sunnier residues in the "Lessons."

As was mentioned, for a brief period after its birth *atone* lived in the world as *aton*. With that shift of space, that shapeshift, we can change our tone and call upon a god of the sun to shed further light on Daniel's "Lessons."

In the 14th century B.C., Pharoah Amenhotep IV abandons the worship of the multitude of Egyptian deities and, taking for himself the name Akhenaton, establishes the obscure deity of the sun disc, *Aton*, as the sole god of Egypt, creating perhaps the first monotheism (at one!?) in recorded history. Even more remarkably, Aton, unlike the previous incarnate Egyptian gods, was intangible. In this pharaoh's new capital city, Akhetaton, The Aton was never depicted in human or animal form; he was never represented by an idol or a graven image in any inner sanctuary of a temple; instead, the Aton was worshipped outside under the sun. The architecture

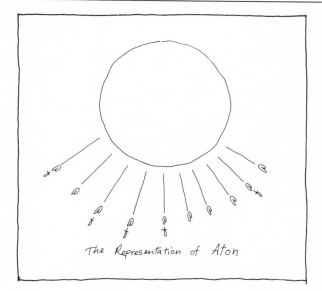

The Representation of Aton

for the Aton was of a new kind in ancient Egypt. Abandoning the ponderously massive solidity of the old buildings, Akhenaton called for lighter, smaller-stoned buildings, covered with energetic scenes and exaggerated forms. Egyptian art turned from a static statement of eternity to a dynamism both fascinating and frightening.

In Akhenaton's hymn to Aton we find the following invocation which might well have been written by Heraclitus: "He has a million forms according to the time of day and from where he is seen; yet he is always the same." Or consider Libeskind, in the interview on the machines: "I tried to make it singularly organized, revealing itself in different ways from different points of view, but really it is continuous."

It would be a delight to luxuriate in a lengthy diversion constructing analogies, some suggesting themselves already in the brief description above, among the Aton, Akhenaton, the Lessons and Daniel, even to speculate on the architect's fate through that of Akhenaton, whose vision was too extreme to sustain its remarkable energy. After his death, the Egyptians abandoned Akhenaton and return to their idol worship with renewed and well-known vigor. However, I wish now to turn attention to one aspect which connects the worship of the Aton to the "Lessons," the Aton's representation.

I have already said that the Aton was never represented as animal nor human, never tangible, wholly, that is, never by an idol. Instead, the god is represented by the constellation of a solar disk whose rays terminate in hands, some of which hold ankhs, the symbol for life. But is this not also both the very representation of each of the machines individually and, as well, the elusive totality which the machines as a divided unity represent beyond architecture — life: life as a wheel, life as a puppet theater, life as a complex of gears.

Each of those restless isomorphs of the circle, like the intangible Aton, engage the hand to hand it new

life, to transform it into a new hand. Hence that symbol is the representation of the Reading Machine, the wheel of craft which engages the hand at the hand-made book, *ankh extraordinaire*, whose very being is of the hand creating a new hand. It is also the representation of the Memory Machine, where the hand is engaged as by a puppet, as a pinocchio, who, though made lifelike by craft is only brought to life by truth, from the new hand as knowing and memory. It is finally the representation of the Writing Machine, whose complex machinations and gearings engage no longer "the hand" but the newest of new hands, the "at one" of many hands in the collective act as such.

But for whom did Daniel Libeskind's Aton shine? To whom did this sun, paradigm of the "at one," hold out its light, its life, its hand to create a new hand? To rekindle what light did the architect's *pharmakos* burn? Who shall atone, become at one with, introject and identify with the lost lessons? Whose soul will be "filled with the memory so that one would finally obliterate it altogether?" Daniel answers in the end, as at the very beginning: "I have tried to disengage the problem of architecture from the earth — to send it to its stellar source: to send it to 'the city which does not shine anymore, that star of Palmanova.'" Palmanova, whose stellar form, name (palma nova = new hand) and dimming (can one find it on a map?) are but a request for the machines, for Aton and for atonement. Perhaps it would be appropriate for Palmanova to fill its soul with memory, to honor the gap in the catalog of the world riven by the loss of the machines by taking up the gap of atonement, by becoming at one with the machines, by becoming Palma Nova. Perhaps then it will burn bright again.

I am near the end, but not quite finished; it remains to discuss the sound of my instrument, to raise a tone. Libeskind avows the importance of sound as a lesson: "I should say that sound is very important because the sound of equipment is important, and this is a piece of equipment to be used."

We might have, in the musicality of this moment, found riches in a meditation on the Second Viennese School, i.e., on atonal music. Thus we could have considered the parallels between its attack on the idolatry of the structure of the home and dominant keys, and those themes as they operate in the "Lessons." We even might have extended that reflection to the philosophies of home and domination in general, for surely lessons on those too can be found among the disturbances of the machines. But let us take more of a risk and set for ourselves a more specific task, the task of literally seeking the lesson of "a tone." We need then a single sound, one sound to guide us through the lecture and teach us yet another lesson of the machines.

In his lecture Daniel describes the three machines as three episodes, three movements of a totality of movement. He is careful to note that these are not movements in history, space, or any other linearity;

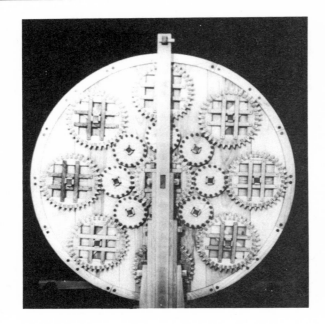

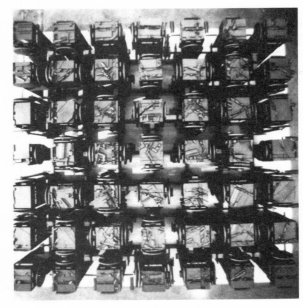

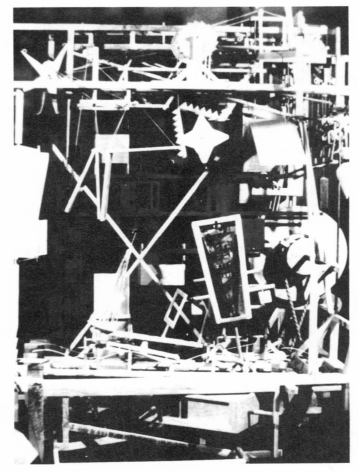

Daniel Libeskind's machines: top left, *Reading Machine;* top right, *Writing Machine;* above *Memory Machine.*

he draws a diagram (see diagram) which marks a two-axis field of interpretation for the machines. In this field, the Reading, Memory and Writing machines articulate movement from the One Alone, to the Many Alone, to the Many, but equally from craft, to idea, to collectivity or industry. Yet we understand, in the skew of the axis of the machines from the axis of history that this is a movement other than a "from...to." So, our single tone must move us without moving from craft, to idea to collectivity. In English there is such a tone, a unique sound which says those three movements as no movement, as movement itself. Moreover, in that single sound's fourth movement I find the last of the lessons for architecture.

What is such a tone? Among its images are *wright*, *right* and *write*. Their univocality outlines not a linear diagram, but a complex, concentric one: Architecture as to wright, to work as a true Craftsman; Architecture as to right, to work as an achiever of the Truth; Architecture as to write, to work as a Creator of truth; these are the machines. And in both their ritual making and their ritual sacrifice, we find the fourth dimension of this originary movement—Architecture as to rite.[1] From wright to right to write to rite—four laps of a four-dimensional Vicovian spiral in which each turn of the tone engulfs completely but not comprehensively the one prior in an unimaginable manifold. But also four stages in the fluorescence of that most dynamic of all objects, the man/woman, for these tones and turns articulate, do they not, that originary movement from the instinctual to the theoretical to the psychological to the ritual, which is man/woman in essence at any and every scale, from the individual to the collective.

Libeskind: "Architecture is involved in a meditative structure and always has been." As is well-known, in their work on the machines the architect and his colleagues adopted a different attitude of making architecture specific to each task at hand. They ritualized the entire scene of the making—becoming the medieval craftsman for the Reading machine, the Renaissance rationalist for the Memory machine, and the nine to five industrial worker for the Writing machine. In so doing Daniel and his colleagues provided architecture with a more important lesson than simply a critique of today's architectural idolatry, they provided a prototype for an alternative approach to architecture, the a-theological ritual.

Thus from Libeskind a new definition of architecture emerges as that unique ritual of wrighting, righting and writing the ground of the Living Present, the structure of the here and now. The "Lessons" can be seen as declaring that an architecture sufficiently courageous to address the complex present, complete with its forward-looking, can no longer be about or for any single surrogate, any one god, not even the ones called "man" nor "truth."

A distinction here is important: forward-looking is not dreaming of the future. Forward-looking is the difficulty of the problematic present; dreaming of the future, like dreaming of the past, is an escape

from it. An architecture which remains easily or thoughtlessly devoted to any surrogate source of authority or which dreams of a return to those sources forever passed remains fettered by that very idolatry which the forward-looking of the present seeks and must overcome. On the other hand, an architecture which is merely witty, ironic, or idiosyncratic for the sake of iconoclasm is escapist and therefore equally insufficient.

What is proposed in the thought and theory of the a-theological ritual, which is also the theory of the displaced text, is a meditative structure for architecture in which the approach to each architectural case is met with a specifically derived construction of a different ritualization of the making process, one which resonates without rest between identity and difference, between same and other, between lawful repetition and anarchic play. Such an architecture is without responsibility yet is never without law, because the a-theological ritual constantly rewrights, rerights, and rewrites law.

Such a theory and its architectures face serious difficulties; they raise important unresolved questions and engender much distrust. It is true that such an architecture will always be by definition *ad hoc*; it will thus always run the risk of producing something other than architecture or even worse, producing banality, impotence or mere style. But it is the only architecture today running a risk, and therefore the only architecture today aspiring to greatness, and therefore the only architecture today. This is the final lesson.

Notes

[1] After hearing Daniel speak of the movement from craft to idea to writing in his lecture, I turned to my friend, John Macsai, to comment on the analogous movement of the three homophones *wright*, *right* and *write*. True to his legendary, some would say punishing, wit, John immediately replied, "then the fourth stage must be *rite*."

Editorial note: Kipnis "responds" here to a lecture by Daniel Libeskind that is published, in a modified form, in this issue. Libeskind's lecture was delivered at the University of Illinois at Chicago, in the Spring of 1987.

DANIEL LIBESKIND is the Director and Founder of Architecture Intermundium in Milan, and the former Chairman of the Department of Architecture at Cranbrook Academy in Detroit. His publications include *Between Zero and Infinity* (Rizzoli, 1981), *Chamber Works* (Architectural Association), and the forthcoming *Architecture Works* (Electra).

Architecture Intermundium

Daniel Libeskind's machines:
top left, *Reading Machine;* bottom, *Writing Machine;* above *Memory Machine.*

I believe that practicing architecture today, teaching architecture today, being a student of architecture today, entails very different consequences than it did even a hundred years ago. I think all of us are in a different stage of possibility, of development of the modern world. I believe that architecture has entered its end. That is not to say that architecture is finished, but I would say that architecture has entered an *end condition*. I think that all those who practice architecture, whether knowingly or unknowingly, feel in some way that something has come to an end, but what it is, is very difficult to say since it is not in the realm of *objects*. Therefore, I will try to speak as clearly as I can of something about which it is not easy to speak, because it is not one more *thing* which can be found in the catalog of the world.

In any case, what I will try to speak about is a kind of *difference*, to use the word of Derrida. And I will try to make this difference apparent by saying only one thing: that if equilibrium could have been attained, it would have been attained a long time ago. Equilibrium could have been attained under two conditions only. One is that reality would have been indeterminate or indistinct, a kind of Heisenberg/ Mondrian postulation that equilibrium is achievable within a context of indeterminacy. This did not happen. On the other hand, equilibrium could have been achieved by postulating a global meaning of the world, a boundless but finite meaning, which is to say the meaning of Einstein, the meaning of mythology, the meaning of the centered world. But, needless to say, neither of these realities have been experienced, and they won't be. So what there is is the shape of space of the world which on a permanent basis produces a destabilized, let's say an eternal, movement of imperfection and difference. And it is this shape of space about which I would like to speak to you and explore in a very tentative manner because no language exists for it today. No language has been agreed upon in which to discuss such a phenomenon. I would like to draw a diagram for you to refer to, because it's a kind of schema of my small discourse here.

What I would like to illustrate with this diagram synoptically and synthetically is a schema of a project that I made with some friends some time ago entitled "Three Lessons in Architecture," and presented in an Italian urban setting. It's a project that I did for a problem in Venice. I did not choose to address this problem by simply providing another craft solution, another ideological solution, or another industrial solution I chose instead to present an alternative solution by exploring participatory reality and to present those who ask the question with a participatory experience in which the problem of architecture might come into focus on the one hand, and some part of it might fall into oblivion on the other. I chose to address the urban problem of Palmanova (a city which exists today in northern Italy in the Venetto region).

I presented the organizers of this program with a piece of equipment, really one big movement in three parts. I will show it to you in three moments of the machine—the moment of reading, the moment of remembering and the moment of writing architecture. And I will start at some point, and end at some other point, but please remember that I'm really addressing this diagram as a totality. One could in fact start anywhere and one could end anywhere. It's a big circle of interpretation, not necessarily a vicious circle, but a circle that by going through its own presuppositions in some sense destroys and obliterates the problem of the given as it also exposes other dimensions of architecture. The three lessons that I have offered here are the three lessons of architecture: A) reading architecture, and its equivalent, the reading machine; B) the lesson in the present remembering architecture, and the memory machine, C) writing architecture, and its equivalent, the writing machine. So these are pieces of metaphysical equipment (because they don't really do anything, they are in another realm) which propose a very curious path, because as I said earlier architecture was from its very beginning at its end. At the end it's possible to retrieve in some sense the whole past and future destiny, because the end of course is nothing in the future, nor is it anything in the past, nor is it anything in the present—it is simultaneously on all three levels. The three machines propose a fundamental recollection of the historical vicissitude, in particular of western architecture. They constitute a single piece of equipment and are mutually interdependent. Each is a starting point for the other. The purpose of this equipment is to release the end to itself, not to take the end, but to release the end to itself. I think the objects in architecture are only residues of something which is truly important: the participatory experience (the emblem of reality which goes into their making). You could say that everything we have is that kind of a residue. It is this experience that I would like to retrieve, not the object.

By the way, making machines, I discovered as I was doing this project, is an old task. Everybody needs machines. Vitruvius says that first of all an architect should make a machine—it is more important than making a city. Then he says you should also make theatre and other things. Alberti says this as well. When I read Vitruvius and Alberti and they said every good architect must first make a machine to do architecture, I thought that if I'm going to be a good architect I must follow the tradition to its end. So I tried to do it in a particular way. We wanted to retrieve reading architecture, so we made this first machine. I have to say what is involved in reading: to try to become a pure believer even in architecture. I know it's an experimental state. It's an experimental being I'm describing, not an experimental object. Try to become the pure medieval craftsman. That's really the object of this exercise. To make something in a way which is made only on one's

116 knees; which is made through complete faith in the transcendence of architecture, of the text, of reading; which is made by a total faith in the craft; which rejects all modern techniques and technology; which rejects modern thinking about architecture. So we did it that way. We got up at the crack of dawn, four o'clock in the morning. We built this machine in a small small place without any power tools, just with hand tools. With no electricity, just with candlelight. We went to bed early because with candlelight you can't work late. And we did it in silence because there is nothing to talk about when you work like that.

I feel it's the very notion of architecture. One always dreams, and I'm sure you have dreamed about it too, what it was like, and what it would be like to build this way. And of course, one must reconstruct this experience because how else does one make a circle without a ruler—with just a plumb line and the compass? I tried to make simply one circle, and to do it in that way, full of faith, and to get the experience as close as possible to this loaded experience of the monastic faith in the craft of making. Therefore, lesson A teaches the almost forgotten process of building, which really has not yet come to complete fruition. I would say that the medieval process is still coming to an end today, has not been finished. A certain technique was created, one which also brought a revolution of the word. A revolution of text. This archeological reconstruction (cities like Palmanova, military ideas in architecture and of engineering) and this will to power is disclosed by thinking about architecture and particularly by having no faith in its reality. I never knew about this weak point. Only when I started doing the project did I discover that the weapons of architecture and the weapons of the world did not originate in the Renaissance—they originated in the monastery. The machine gun and the parachute and the atomic bomb are not the inventions of Leonardo da Vinci, they are inventions of Thomas Aquinas and even earlier spirituality. I tried to become that architect who would be commissioned by a monastery and who would then deliver both the nonobjective and the objective counterpart of the purified, holy experience. So I made a gear. And then I made many gears. Please remember they are made with a chisel. It's hard to polish things without sandpaper. I made these detours because I would like for you to use these machines. Now, these machines were meant to be used since a machine is not something to look at. These are not aesthetic objects. I offered them to the citizens of Palmanova, the city for which I made the project. I suggested to the organizers of this competition that these three pieces of equipment be placed in the middle square of Palmanova, and that not just the architects but all the citizens who passed through this Piazza would use it. They could determine what the problem was and the possible solution to it.

I never did any work like this before. it was all new for me. And the experience of it is like that—you have to pull the wheel or push the wheel. That's important. And because the wheel is heavy it creaks. It's a big creaking wheel. And if you were to sit at it you would push it or pull it. This machine has many axles and many many gears which are both hidden and revealed. It has shelves and the whole mechanism is intended to support eight words. So there are eight words for which this mechanism is a support. Now the words are very very light because words are light. They don't weigh much. And especially these eight words are light because I sought words which are no longer readable in the text of architecture—words which cannot be remembered or written down. I placed these eight light words and made them into books to give them slightly more substance. I wrote eight books. I made the eight books by hand like the monks—made the paper, bound the books, and placed them into this big wheel. And what is interesting is that light as the books are, light as the words are, they actually completely crush the weight of these axles made out of wood. In crushing the weight of the axles they expose two things: they expose the reader and they expose the movement of the wheel, which of course revolves and then comes back to its own starting point, like all wheels do.

There are ninety-two wedges, and glueless joints, no energy of a contemporary kind. The machine seeks to represent the triumph of the spirit over matter, of candlelight over electrical light or darkness. It's made solely from wood as are the books. You will recognize that a wheel is always gigantic, no matter how small. This one is very big. It is a Vitruvian, Albertian humanistic wheel of fortune suitable for the diagonally crucified humanist of Raphael and Leonardo, for whom I really built it. The square intersecting with the circle. I would have liked to make it for Thomas Aquinas. Perhaps he would have bought this piece for himself. It's a device good for comparative reading of the architecture text. Rather than shuttling to your desk and looking for authoritative things like those monks always did who were looking for the right book to verify the eighth book or the first book, I placed the books in the wheel so that comparisons could be easily made. And in being easily made they could also reveal the tautological nature of the architectural text at its end. The text of architecture is a tautological text, which means that it says the same thing at the end as it said at the beginning because the beginning was its end already. In short, a chamber of revolutions. The word revolution is used here in its etymological sense: a revolutionary machine because it revolves, and with each revolution comes about the revolution of the text which is propelled by it.

It's difficult to show a book in a picture because a book is meant to be read. This is the first book that I wrote, and strangely funny because it was stolen. Five minutes after it was presented for perusal of the public, this book was stolen, and the exhibitors, the organizers of the Venice Biennale came to me and said: "Look, the book was stolen, but since it's a printed book, you have another copy of it." And I said: "No, I don't!" because if you are really a monk, you don't mass produce anything. You use the technology to do one thing only. So you print. You use the whole resourcefulness of that monastic faith to do a singular act only, and always the only one, the same singular act over and over again. So I don't have this book anymore. The book on ideas is missing, but there are still other books remaining and they are all different. They have different thicknesses. Some of the books are five hundred pages long. The pages are handmade and can be read. Someone asked me: "Do you read these books?" Yes, and I have seen other people read them. So there are eight books. Somebody said, why eight books? I discovered why while re-reading *Don Quixote*. You've read about the great knight, Don Quixote in his paper visor, going to fight against the injustice of the whole world. Cervantes says that Don Quixote met only one gentleman in his travels in Spain. In all his time (because he was old by the time he died) he met only *one* gentleman. He said it was the gentleman in green, and he was a gentleman because he travelled, and he travelled with a satchel of only eight books. Clearly Cervantes already had more books than eight, in the sixteenth century. And I certainly have more than eight books in my library. I made this project in order to get rid of my books, because I decided that I too, like the good knight, should reduce my library. It's hard to get rid of books. You can donate them to a church or a library, but really to get rid of books is an ethical problem, because one would have to rewrite them all. I still have more than eight books at home, but I am getting closer and closer to being Don Quixote's gentleman.

Here is an illustration of the kinetics of the machine. I must say that the *act* is the experience. The machine is not about the object, the object is just documented here—it's about the experience one has in participating in it. Of course, the act is different for the reader and for the voyeur, the onlooker, because the reader is involved in the undecipherable or in the completely transparent. But the voyeur, the one who looks on the reader, sees only a body bent over this wheel of torture, and he sees only a beautiful kinetic motion. When the wheels move and the little gears move, it's truly beautiful—the fascination of multiplying a circle. The experience one has is that the books on the top shelf, which are rotating, appear to be falling on top of you. This is what I was after. They appear to be falling on your head as you pull the wheel or as you read. It's a very uneasy feeling. And as you turn the wheel, the book which you've just left behind, which is going down, appears to be falling onto the ground. The books falling on your head and the books falling on the ground, but, at the same time, never falling on your head and never falling on the ground—always remaining in the same position because the axle rotates very very accurately, keeping them always in an ideal position to a hypothetical reader, a reader who isn't there.

That's the reading experience: one cog of the entire machine, not a starting point, but one element of the bigger machine. You will see it repeating itself in all the other machines.

Let me move on to remembering architecture. I've been told that when people die, (and I've also read alot about it), when one remembers one's life before committing suicide or when dying in a hospital, life reels rapidly in front of one's brain. And at the end things become quickly apparent. They very quickly pile up into the soul. In an end condition, then, things pile up rapidly in the memory of what architecture may have been. It's hard to know. But I set myself this task: to remember architecture, to construct an experimental being who could remember it. So lesson B is the lesson which is no longer in the arena of craft, in the arena of this future past, but it's in the arena of future eternal, of ideas. So we came out of the monastery. We didn't do this one with the notion of pure life on our knees, with our bare hands, praying that someone should save us; we did this in an ideological realm of politics, a kind of Renaissance notion of architecture. It's really the monks coming out with their weapons out of the monastery, and appearing on the stage of the theatre. Therefore, lesson B consists of that which can still be remembered of architecture.

As a historical program, architecture and its sight have been filtered through what can still be remembered. I modelled this machine after a very fascinating phenomenon to me: a small memory machine constructed in sixteenth century Venice by an architect called Julio Camillo. Julio Camillo was perhaps in his time the most famous architect. He was an opponent of Palladio in some ways. He was commissioned by the King of France to build a little machine which in a split second could reveal the meaning of the cosmos. I thought that was a worthy cause and a worthy memory. And apparently Julio Camillo, the architect, fulfilled himself nobly. This comes to me from his correspondence with Erasmus, who has always been very truthful about everything. Julio Camillo showed a small machine to the King of France in the sixteenth century. The King walked up to it (it was a small object, obviously), looked into it, turned around and said to Camillo: "Now I understand. I understand everything. You are an architect. You have revealed to me the meaning of all of it." The interesting thing about Camillo is that immediately after he made this machine, two things happened: the machine disappeared and so did Camillo.

Ever since I read about Camillo's machine I have been absolutely enthralled by it. I wanted to meet Camillo, and I wanted to know more about it because I'm also trying to remember what it used to be like, as he did. I went to London and discovered Frances Yeats who wrote a book on Camillo, and I found that nothing more is known about Camillo's theatre than what was written in her book: that it was made out of wood, had paper which was hanging, and

had rope in it. Those are the only absolutely objective facts about it—rope, hanging paper and wood. I tried in the presence of these ideas to remember through Camillo's mind: architecture.

I have designed only the backstage of Camillo's mechanism here as a model of the mind of the Renaissance in which equipment and architecture first comes to its own manifestations. The theatre, this little machine, is very very simple. It's made from many pieces of wood, paper and string, constituting the source of illusions of some olympic theater. I think I should tell you that the first machine with the books is already here in this machine inside of the wood. I should say that the sound is very important because the sound of equipment is important, and this is a piece of equipment to be used. The first piece of equipment was creaking; this machine clicks like a puppet theatre. You can use it, manipulate it, pull the strings. I guess it's a little puppet of memory—a theatre of architecture, rather than the architecture of a theater. And this too I read in *Don Quixote*. You might recall that there was a puppet show that he once saw somewhere in Spain. The King was vilifying the maiden and Don Quixote, being the good knight, the noble knight, pulled out a sword and cut off the King's head. And then the poor puppeteer jumped out from behind and said, "hey just a minute—this is not the real thing, this is only the play." It was too late. Clearly Don Quixote de la Mancha could not tell the difference between the puppet and reality, the representation and its source.

I have to say now that none of these machines were invented by me. The whole process is to get oneself out of it. One has put oneself into it historically, but one must, at some point, disappear. Well, this is my way, my three stages of the way out. For Kirkegaard it was 'either/or', but this is a more ambiguous process of getting oneself out. You can say out of the object and into the experience, out of the inanimate into the spiritual, out of the nonbeing into being. What I tried to do with the problem of architecture, to put it in another way, is to disengage it from its position on the earth. I was given a site in Venice, and rather than do what I think most architects are doing today, which is to engage the problem of architecture in the earth, in its own soil, I tried to disengage the problem of architecture from the earth—to send it into its stellar source. There were two stars I sent it to—two places where it all came from, I think. One is east, one is west. I think in the west it came from Dublin. So I sent back all of this project—everything from Venice, from Venetto, from the Renaissance, from Palladio, Camillo—back to Dublin c/o Mr. Joyce. Because I said in my program here that I would seek to release the end to itself. And then on the other hand I sent it back to Moscow, c/o Mr. Tatlin, because it also came from Moscow in some sense. Moscow and Dublin, two capitals, not of the nineteenth century. They are (?) capitals of the early twenty-first. So I sent this "odradek" (called odradek by Kafka and meaning in Czech "not to give any advice") back on the Moscow/Dublin route.

There are other things in this small memory machine to remember, there are little horses, little cloud machines, little wave machines, all sorts of instruments, measuring devices, because you may recall that in the first experience (the reading machine), the measurement came straight out of faith. But in the realm of ideas the measurement is a political measurement. It comes from an intersubjective dialogue. The text is also obliterated in another way as is the writing of the text, which is of course accomplished by writing architecture. This architecture is spread out and diffused or sprayed in a different manner across the screen of perception. The machine contains in it, by the way, the hanging papers seen by the King of France. An attempt is made to fill up the soul with memory so that one would finally obliterate it altogether. After a while there's really nothing you can remember anymore, only the process of storage. One more thing. There was a spiritual friend of Julio Camillo's. You may have heard of Giordano Bruno, the philosopher, the heretic, who was burned in Rome exactly in the year 1600. He was expounding Copernican theory all over Europe, but the church decided he was out. He was a type of spiritual architect. Bruno said that all his life he has been doing architecture. Well, he never built a building. He had been building the cathedral inside of himself. He said: "They're not building them anymore outside, so I'm building it inside." And just before he was burned at the stake he said, "I've almost completed it. I've got it completely inside. It's not necessary for me to have it outside." Well, look, not everybody's Giordano Bruno or Julio Camillo, but one has to try. So to put everything inside, this is what it would feel like, you see. It would be suspended over you; the suspension of architecture. It's not really grounding it at all. And I know how everybody wants to ground architecture and bring it back home with that misreading of Heidegger—to go back to the forest, to your little hut—but I think Heidegger was out of his world altogether. He's out of it altogether, with National Socialism and mythology and spirit and the black forest.

The first machine taught me how to make the wheel, then I had to make what is called the barrow. I tried to make a wheelbarrow—I had to remember how to make it. When you look at the twentieth century, you see a lot of architects photographed next to the wheelbarrow. Mies van der Rohe next to the wheelbarrow, le Corbusier next to the wheelbarrow, Behrens next to the wheelbarrow. But it's not quite believable that they are using it, since they are always in a suit or something like it. There's a beautiful photograph of Behrens in his tie and vest and top hat next to the wheelbarrow. So, I said, if I'm going to practice architecture I've got to get next to a wheelbarrow and *move it*. But it's hard to move

it because it sways alot (which is not really due to the weight). The problem with the wheelbarrow is that the stuff is so suspended in it that it is hard to propel it in one direction. But this is the second part. It's a sort of ideological bequest, and I can show you how the wheel and the barrow are engaged in a slightly more sophisticated whole: the written part both play in those pieces. Writing the book itself, by moving the barrow.

Now lesson C. I call this the writing lesson—not just the writing of anything but the writing of architecture lesson. This one teaches the artless and the scienceless making of architecture. I showed you the signs, the craft and the art of architecture. Now I would like to make architecture without signs and without art. Clearly signs and art are only stages on the way. I think it was Nietzsche who said that not only painting and music are beautiful pieces of art, but also the Prussian Army or the Jesuit Order. He would have been absolutely delighted to see the modern industrial state. This machine is the industrial part. First was craft: the "one alone," and in there were the "many alone" to remember it. Now I speak from the point of view that being "one alone" is not enough. Being "many alone" is not enough. One has to enter the full working force of the many: to do architecture without signs, without art, the way one would produce a pair of shoes. Now that I live in Milan I see a lot of shoe production, and I know what makes a good shoemaker there. They know how to put the nail in the right place. That's what it is. They know where to put it. The difference between the great and the mediocre shoemaker is the position of the nail. And that's what I tried to do. I tried to learn how to put a nail in without art and without science, in other words, to industrialize the process that I've been describing, to industrialize the poetic of architecture and to offer architecture as a sacrifice to its own possibilities of making a text.

The writing machine processes both memory and reading materials and is a cybernetic hinge because now it's a matter of mounting the gear and the axle and the text into an industrial propulsion, and to do it experientially as an industrialist would do it. So first one built by praying on one's knees, total faith. Second one built by being politically astute, through measurement and discussion. The third step brings one to a nine-to-five job. I thought I needed more experience in the nine-to-five. Maybe one has been working nine-to-five all along but hasn't really gotten enough experience, enough participation in the process. So how does one get it? I think one opens a little business, a little industry. I got myself a clock with my friends, a time clock. We tried to reduce the problem to its bare minimum, technique, and not to make it interesting at all—to have all our fun after five. During the procedure we agreed to work hard, speak only in "small talk," smoke cigarettes, dream about TV, but to try, in this project, not to contaminate it with other issues. That's what it's about.

I started mounting the gear onto this prototype. You know that once you make one gear you get a little more confidence. You can make one which is slightly more complex. You can engage that gear not just with itself tautologically, but you can then project it along these axes, back and forward, and maybe somewhere altogether outside of itself. I'd like to show you how it evolved. I built it out of wood. I continued with the gear. I opened a little factory making the little reading wheels. Then I used the books…I had to have a lubricant, fuel for the machine, and so I had to use the books. There had to be surfaces because it was not for one reader. To lubricate such a big industrial piece of writing one would need all the texts in the whole world, so I translated the books into forty-nine times four languages because seven words times seven is forty-nine cubes. The cubes are pinned on four sides revealing four faces which means forty-nine times four surfaces. Many many axles to lubricate; many languages. The first machine creaks, the second one clicks, this one I can assure you, whirls rapidly. A very very well-lubricated mechanism goes very very fast: in any language. Then the books were cut up slowly, and very particularly because the most poignant part of architecture is to use it all up. Because now one is making something that has to be very useful. Not just for those who are alone in the many, but to the many in one. And then I spliced the axles into intricate formations, like genetic codes, and all sorts of devices were invented in order to produce it.

Then came the problem of the housing unit, because this is an architectural problem. This is an entry for an urban design competition. I had to deal with the dwelling units, economics, commerce, etc., which means I had to deal with the memory machine. But I had to reduce it to scale. So I reduced the memory machine with its little windows to this small artifact. Now I'll explain how it works conceptually and practically. The idea is this: to rotate *this* handle, but to move *that* far diagonal cube at a different rate from your rotation. So let's say you move it to the right once, and you move the diagonal cube to the left four times with that one movement. Or you rotate the right handle twice to the right and you move these four cubes here on the left three times forward. That's the complexity of the gear movement. All about technique. In reality that's what industrial modernity is all about. It is to engage those reading cycles and those memory wheels into a kind of securing or stocktaking which would yield unexpected results. It's primitive, but Pascal made his little calculator, and Babbage made his little computer, and after all, the regular computers we have today are only based on two phases. They are just two-phased computers, one and two, right? They are so-called binary, black and white, which is what makes them so schizophrenic, because you always say either yes or no to everything, never maybe. I tried to make a quadripartite computer operation, which means to mirror the realm of decisions in a double of itself. One can say there are four parts. Perhaps they are the parts which belong to God and mortals, to the earth and to the sky. You can say they are the parts that belong to the four interchanges. So that's how I went about it with another prototype, in order to couple these configurations together into a rapid whirling movement.

Now you can see the little swelling units, the little houses; you can see the roof gardens on top and that's the city itself, and in the back you see the big piston that goes up and down. And by going up and down in the vertical it can turn it all. The horizontality can be transformed into the diagonal movement. Here is the kit which was manufactured for one cube. I didn't do it monastically because I realized that industry can rely on other industry, so one can get all industries to work together happily. The machine is very complex. It has 2,662 parts, most of them are mobile, so you don't see them, but everything—the text that you see on the bottom, the assembly of the machine, the mosaic of movement—is coupled. The first machine had one drawing, like the medieval masons who had only one drawing—the drawing of the circle. The second one had already two drawings. And this one has, once again, one drawing, but the drawing is more like a diagram than a drawing—it engages the binary computer system into the larger grid over there. I believe that the modern city has a good deal in common with military problems. The vulnerability of the modern city is closely tied with the invisibility of the threat to the city. I think when the walls came tumbling down in history and the city was revealed, it died, though it apparently continues to exist. And

I've often thought that the relationship between military vulnerability and the entity of the city as a visible organism, cannot be perceived in a visual attitude. It has nothing to do with the eye, because it is really the problem of equivalence between this particular configuration of a star and another particular star in the middle. The one in the middle is perhaps Houston, or maybe Chicago, or any city which is a new, right-angled, orthogonal star. But both of these stars don't shine unless one introduces a matrix in the back of them.

In the end, it's a problem of equivalance. Balzac said to comprehend is to equalize. So to equalize is here the task. I think all of us are equalizers, but in the process of equalization one also has ritual duties, primarily to protect the text. So the problem is to protect the text. It's like the mezzuzah in the Jewish tradition: that sacred text, the scroll—a bit of the Torah—which is pinned to each doorway of a household which makes the threshold a sacred threshold. I've often wondered why in the Jewish tradition they have to have it. I understood it when I became an industrialist. In the process of sanctification one also destroys the text, and one is then responsible in every way—I don't know, responsible to someone, to God himself—for protecting it. Everything became a technical problem. I had to wrap up time itself with words. When you get this kind of density of the text you've got to wrap it up very well indeed. You can see that the little wheels when they are coupled together are more efficient. And you can see that it gets busy. It gets very busy and nine-to-five is not enough: there is overtime. Immediately there is overtime. You know when you stack up these equivalences you stack up the two attitudes. You stack up the whole ending to itself. You get the matrix as stockpile. And then as you work on the housing, resources appear in these urns. They wind up in these small shrines, funerary urns, and then one has the ashes inside of them. It is a ritual object that I'm showing you. Not an old-fashioned ritual object, because these little shrines' ashes are not blown to the wind, nor stored in particular position, they are mounted on an axle to be rotated permanently.

The writing machine is a machine to write a single text. The single text which it seeks to write is a text that has already been written by a particular author of the twentieth century. It's a text by Raymond Roussel, a French writer who wrote a book called *Impressions of Africa*. What Raymond Roussel tried to do is to present in the text an experience which could never be had, either historically, or in the future. Many people were interested in Raymond Roussel. Picasso said that he painted because Raymond Roussel inspired him to paint. Duchamp, the antagonist to Picasso, said that his work was all a footnote to Roussel. Le Corbusier said that he did architecture because of Roussel. Giacometti said he became a sculptor because of Roussel. Proust said that Roussel was classical French literature. Cocteau said that he took opium because he read Roussel. I can enumerate the list on and on and on. It's all the heroes that I've got. But it's time to interpret Roussel's text yet how to go about it since the text of Roussel is made out of nothing? It's about experience that could never be had. For example, in Roussel, there are certain miraculous figures that appear and disappear. There is Mossem. I don't know where Mossem comes from, but Mossem is killed in Roussel's book by having a text burned onto his feet. It's an experience which could not be easily had. But then I discovered that St. Theodore of Constantinople in the seventh century was killed by burning an iambic text onto his forehead. So it began to make sense. Then I find Angelica who appeared in Roussel. Angelica with the grid, who was finally burned on a grid as St. Donatella, at a particular date in the third century A.D. Well, there are forty-nine empty boxes. They have to be filled with ashes of unknown saints. Fortunately there is a book of saints which can link up the impression of Italy, the impression of what can be said to be the end with the "Africa of the mind," a kind of uncolonized or about-to-be colonized last region. I would say that Roussel is great because he is the colonizer of the remote parts of the brain, which are just about to be imperialized. In any case that sort of equipment is not easy to explain but is easy to use. It helps to position the city in a spaceless space.

I should probably say what the four sides of this machine—this calculator are. It's a little computer I built. A calculator which is to prognosticate the written destiny of architecture. By becoming an operator you can stockpile information resourcefully, information which is linked with a prophesy made by Victor Hugo that architecture is doomed to die because of the text. Victor Hugo said that the book will kill the cathedral. So I tried to make this computer following Victor Hugo and Jonathan Swift's *La puta Voyage* into a pragmatic reality. Therefore the four sides of these funerary boxes contain the following: On the first side, the city which doesn't shine anymore, that star of Palmanova which doesn't shine anymore, intersected and congealed into the rectilinear star, let's say of Mies van der Rohe; the occult star of victory boogie-woogie; the white and black stars congealed into singular star. That's one side of the dwelling unit. The second one is just a piece of metal which is a reflection which shatters the mathematics of it. It's kind of a reflective order which disrupts the forty-nine times four sides. Side three consists of a geometric sign which is actually an architectural horoscope. I did horoscopes on all the positions of all the saints in all the spots of Palmanova in order to derive where to cut them up. One cannot cut them up arbitrarily. One has to study all the stars and all the horoscopes. That's the third side. And the fourth side is the enumeration of the forty-nine saints, the saints who are needed for the completion of the pilgrimage: the pilgrimage of Absolute Architecture.

UJJVAL VYAS is a Ph.D. candidate in the Committee
on the History of Culture at the University of Chicago.
He is writing his dissertation on Philip Johnson.

The Hidden I:
A Review of
Philip Johnson

Philip Johnson: Architecture
1949-1965. By Philip Johnson.
Published by Holt, Rinehart and
Winston, Inc., New York, N.Y. 115
pp. Illustrated. 10 1/4 by 11 1/4
in. $15.00.
REVIEWED BY PHILIP JOHNSON

It is always good in our
decadent world to see a well-
designed, sumptuous book
come on the market. This is
one. Paper heavy, lots of color,
generous type, excellent cover
design. Elaine Lustig at her
best. Cocktail tables look
handsome with it.

The importance of the
book, however, is other. It is
the latest in a line of architects'
books on their own work.
The genre deserves prop-
agation. Perhaps because
Johnson was an architectural
historian before he became
Mr. Johnson, a former director
of the department of architec-
ture and design at the Museum
of Modern Art, is also the author
of several important books and
essays on architecture. He co-
authored, with Henry-Russell
Hitchcock, the now-classic **The
International Style: Architecture
1922-1932**; and he is the author
of the first definitive monograph
on Mies van der Rohe, published
in 1947. The fact that he hap-
pens to be both the subject and
the critic of the present book is
not entirely coincidental: Philip
Johnson, it turned out, was the
only critic and scholar fully qual-
ified to review a book on Philip
Johnson's work.

an architect at the age of 36,
he thought it important for
some of his public (the few
who buy books) and espe-
cially for the future to have a
record made by the architect's
hand. How right he was.

All of which has noth-
ing to do with the quality
of Johnson's architecture.
Plenty of second-rate archi-
tectural works are also grist
for the architectural histori-
an's mill, as anyone going
through Avery Library can
judge. The value of this book,
for example, is the new way
of showing architecture.
Color photography beats
heliotype any day. And think
of the impossibility today
of the beautiful line draw-
ings of Schinkel's works or
Frank Lloyd Wright's 1910
Ausgefuhrte Bauten. No one
would ever do it. Marcel
Breuer's half-tone photos
and Saarinen's fuzzy gravure
seem pale next to Technicolor.

Whether color catches
on or not is less important
than that here is a book
which by its very existence
shows that someone (pub-
lisher?, architect?) cares
about the position of architec-
ture. Architecture becomes
as important a branch of
knowledge and life as, say,

Beautiful Meissen, or Wild
Life in Africa. And anything
that will raise the level of
public estimate of our hith-
erto lowly art is very, very
welcome.

The text is faultless. Henry-
Russell Hitchcock, the dean
of architectural historians of
the 19th and 20th centuries,
has produced a lucid, critical
essay that well might stand
as a paradigm for the mono-
graphs on living architects.
Although commissioned by
Johnson, he indulges in no
hyperbole. He *says* something
in each sentence, and what
he disapproves of, what he
finds positively ugly, he men-
tions not at all. He accen-
tuates the positive without
flattery or sycophancy. A
difficult piece of tightrope
walking. The result is packed,
objective, interesting.

Concerning the quality of
Johnson's oeuvre, I shall
have to hide behind what
Furneaux Jordan wrote. Per-
sonally I feel too close to
the trees to see the forest.
Contemporary architecture
is too near to let us judge. Mr.
Jordan wrote in the London
Observer: "Whether the work
of Johnson will eventually be
looked upon as a culmination,
a climax, in modern archi-

tecture, is for the future to
decide. It is certainly difficult
to see how his kind of archi-
tecture can be taken further.
There is more than one facet,
more than one technique, in
modern building."

Whatever Johnson's place
in history may be, it is a
plus for the historians to
have a book on his work.
Without any invidious com-
parisons to the great self-
publications, starting with
Ledoux and Schinkel down
to Otto Wagner and Frank
Lloyd Wright and the incom-
parable *Oeuvres Complètes*,
it might be said that Johnson's
book may encourage archi-
tects to bring out their own
books. For a minor reason,
it is fun to see what the artist
picks out to illustrate, also
how he wants to show it (think
of the difference between Le
Corbusier and Frank Lloyd
Wright in methods of self-
advertising!). Also interesting:
Why did they choose the
buildings they chose? Also,
why did they change styles
when they changed? Also
(alas, lacking in Johnson's
book), why does what they
say differ from what they do?

From: Architectural Forum, CXXV
Oct. 1966, 52-53

Suddenly we drew too near to something from which we'd been held at a mysteriously favored and measured distance. Ever since, corrosion. Our head-rest has vanished.

—René Char

What follows is an attempt at a certain kind of pathology. It is an attempt to take apart with care a dead body, while at the same time marveling at the structures that hold it together and make it work. In this particular case the body is a text, and the structures are a concatenation of meaning and rhetoric. Calling this a pathology does not mean necessarily that we seek sickness, but an articulation of differences from which interpretations must be made.

The career of Philip Johnson poses a challenge to the profession of architectural history and should open up questions concerning the so-called "canonical" histories of architecture. As is always the case, such strong challenges to the canon may always be disregarded as impudence from the uninitiated or put down with whatever institutional power is available. This essay attempts to chart out some peculiarities in a text of Johnson's that may begin to help us re-examine the canon and what the canon considers an acceptable text.

Philip Johnson has been called many things during his long and often cacophonous involvement with Modern Architecture. His alignment and disalignment with Modern and Post-modern Architecture has been going on for well over fifty years, yet he has always been enigmatic to his critics, whether they are peers, clients or cocktail conversationalists.

Philip Johnson occupies a unique position in the architectural world. A man of unequalled taste and sensibility, but one with no consistent idea of the kinds of buildings that he should be building, he has left a trail of admiration and confusion.[1]

Along with admiration and confusion, one must be sure to add invective, to which Johnson has replied in kind. He began his career as a polemicist for Modern Architecture. The story of his involvement with Henry-Russell Hitchcock and Alfred Barr in the creation of the Museum of Modern Art's Department of Architecture is too hackneyed to bear repetition, but it is a story of power, politics and rhetoric worth noting for those who believe the canon is given somehow from "on high." After this Johnson became a devout follower/practitioner of the Modern Movement and studied at Harvard mostly under Gropius. He later worked extensively with Mies. After that Johnson became a disgruntled follower of the Modern Movement (c.f. his article "The Seven Crutches of Modern Architecture"), and penultimately a peculiar anti-Modernist—peculiar since it could be argued that he was the most instrumental figure in creating the Modern Movement in America. Ultimately what he became, is...what?

Peter Eisenman calls Philip Johnson "an essayist, an anti-philosophe."[2] Tafuri has this to say about Johnson's work: "The abstract stylemes of Philip Johnson also make use of irony. But their meaning is rather that of a disenchanted game."[3] Johnson replies, "How often dislikes and personal preferences of aesthetic form can engender meaningless rationalistic criticism—an attempt to confirm personal taste through generalized logic."[4] Having established this heretical position many years ago Johnson continues to expound it with vigor. In 1975, in a written lecture delivered at Columbia University, he declared:

The day of ideology is thankfully over. Let us celebrate the death of the *idée fixe*. There are no rules, only facts. There is no order, only preference. There are no imperatives, only choice; or to use a nineteenth-century word, "taste."

Philosophically, it seems to me we are today anarchistic, nihilistic, solipsistic, certainly relativist, humorous, cynical, reminiscent of tradition, myth-and-symbol-minded rather than rationalistic or scientifically minded. What makes a building satisfactory—the word "beautiful" is more than ever treacherous--to Stern or Venturi, for instance, is bound to be different from what is satisfactory to me. *Vive la difference*, we live in a pluralistic society.

What a grand period for us to live in today! Contrariwise, what will all this sound like in ten years?[5]

Johnson's often anarchistic, aristocratic,and "careless" rhetoric has incensed many and has often caused him to be written off as a fop. Keeping Johnson's penchant for rhetoric in mind, let us turn to the problem at hand.

In October of 1966, Johnson wrote a review for *Architectural Forum*—normally an event of little note, but an event to which I wish to draw special attention. A taboo was broken in this review: the author of the review and the author of the book being reviewed were the same. Furthermore, the rupture of this taboo was sanctioned by the editor(s). The difficulties I wish to address now begin to emerge. Could this review be ironic? And what are the consequences of addressing this question? One cannot quickly answer yes or no. I myself am ultimately undecided concerning the question of irony in this review, but I can say for certain that I find this text peculiar and disturbing.

Virtually every paragraph of this review wrestles with the conventions of author/meaning. It seems to me that once the author is in question, difficulties in meaning necessarily arise and vice versa. The review begins with a clear indication of who the author is: "Reviewed by Philip Johnson."[6] Further confirmation is given by the commentary added by the editor(s) at the bottom of the first column of text. But as we proceed to the actual body of the text, the jocular and self-congratulatory first paragraph puts us on our guard, and we begin to wonder if this review is going to be "objective" or not.

If we have not yet begun to suspect the "quanda-

124 ries of authorship" in paragraph one, we are certainly presented with something like "quandaries of meaning." The very first sentence of the review has this disorienting effect: "It is always good in our decadent world to see a well designed, sumptuous book come on the market." Does this mean: the world is decadent (that is taste is declining) therefore this book is a tasteful, "well- designed, sumptuous book" i.e., not decadent, *ergo*, "it is always good...to see a non-decadent...book come on the market"? Or does it mean: the world is decadent, the book is decadent (that is, it participates in a world of hedonism, etc., ergo, "it is always good...to see a decadent...book come on the market"? If we begin to suspect the narrator of being ironic, this sentence could lead to even more convoluted oscillations of meaning. (Could Johnson be being ironic not only about "decadent" but also about "market," or maybe "always," or even in some way the reader can not guess?) What kind of a judgement is the narrator making when he says, "cocktail tables look handsome with it?" Is the world of people who buy these "picture books" and put them (to be seen conspicuously with others) on their cocktail tables being made fun of? Or is this book so "well-designed and sumptuous" that "Cocktail tables look handsome with it."?

The reader's puzzlement grows stronger when the relative certainty of the author suddenly evaporates in the middle of the second paragraph. Up to this point the tone might be described as conversational, with Johnson doing the talking. But suddenly and strangely the review shifts to the third person: "Perhaps because Johnson was an architectural historian before he became an architect...etc." Paragraph two then ends on the resounding, "How right he was." The tone remains conversational, but there emerges an ambiguity of subject(s) both spoken and referential. Is this Johnson playfully adopting the third person in order to speak about himself from some greater (more objective) distance? Is he being his witty and erudite self? It is hard to tell. The third person continues to reappear throughout the rest of the review, presenting us recurrently with this ambiguity. Was it this constant self-consciously produced ambiguity which led Eisenman to say, "Johnson is at his most opaque when he is speaking of himself?"[7] Johnson is well-known for defusing/diffusing the pomposity of critics, and often his own ego, with a barrage of self-deprecatory and highly self-conscious witticisms.

But why should Johnson choose to engage in such witticisms and games of authorship when the editors seem to have gone to the trouble to call attention to his authorship in the commentary? The question becomes even more difficult when we recall that Johnson, the editors tell us, "was the only critic and scholar fully qualified," to write this review. Are they suggesting that the author of a work (whether written or architectural) can criticize his own work with the most clarity?

Paragraph three begins: "All of which has nothing to do with the quality of Johnson's architecture." This is true enough, but we will look in vain to find anything having to do with the quality of Johnson's work in paragraph three or elsewhere in the review. It seems as though the narrator cannot speak about the "other" author/architect, let alone comment on the quality of this other author's work. The author/narrator will try again in paragraph six to deal with the question of quality, but in paragraph three the author/narrator seems to have confused the quality of book production and architectural reproduction with the quality (content) of the works exhibited in *Philip Johnson: 1949-1965*.

The relationship between the "narrator" and his subject, Philip Johnson the author of the book being reviewed, becomes especially puzzling in paragraph six: "Concerning the quality of Johnson's oeuvre, I shall have to hide behind what Furneaux Jordan wrote. Personally I feel too close to the trees to see the forest." These "I's" are the only two first person usages in the review. Is this "I" the same person as the narrative "voice" heard throughout the text? Why does this "I" have to hide when speaking about "the quality of Johnson's oeuvre" and not when the narrative voice makes assertions like:

Henry-Russell Hitchcock, the dean of architectural historians of the 19th and 20th centuries, has produced a lucid, critical essay that well might stand as a paradigm for the monographs on living architects. . . . A difficult piece of tightrope walking. The result is paced, objective, interesting.

If the narrative usage and this first person usage are not the same person, then, who is this "I"? And most importantly, why is the "I" hiding? Even if we maintain that both the narrator and this "I" are the same "voice," ambiguity is not avoided.

Paragraph six is the second attempt by the narrator to deal with the quality of Johnson's architectural work. His earlier attempt, in paragraph three, led us initially to believe the issue would be dealt with. But instead, the topic of paragraph three (if it can be said to have a topic at all) has something to do with photography, architectural reproduction and truisms of architectural historians casting about for publication fodder. All the while the narrator avoids broaching the topic of one particular subject's work, alerting us by this insistent omission. Why these "I's?"

If the whole question of authorship seems indeterminate within this review, there are also a series of other topics, opinions, assertions and meanings which seem indeterminate. That is to say, many of the things which the "author" says are puzzling and disorienting. Paragraphs four and five are no exceptions.

The second and third sentences of paragraph four put the first sentence (an assertion) into doubt. (This pattern of assertion and dissimulation seems to have some prominence in the technique of this review as well as in the architectural work of Philip Johnson.) Does it make sense that someone who "cares about the position of architecture" would wish to elevate it to the level of expensive knick-knacks ("Beautiful Meissen") and other cocktail table paraphernalia ("Wild Life in Africa")? Is raising the "level of public estimate" of architecture from the floor to the level of cocktail tables really a "very, very welcome" improvement?

"The text is faultless....The result is packed, objective, interesting." These two powerful assertions bracket paragraph five, but by the time one arrives at the last sentence of the paragraph both assertions have been put deeply into question, if not made completely farcical. For although the narrator tells us the "text is faultless," we are told that Henry-Russell Hitchcock's introduction was "commissioned" by Johnson and that "what he (HRH) disapproves of, what he finds positively ugly, he mentions not at all." What kind of a "tightrope" is this? And what could the word "objective" possibly mean here?[8]

Let us now examine briefly some aspects of the book being reviewed. Some of the connections between the book and its review are especially interesting since they further the entanglements of authors and intentions. *Philip Johnson: 1949-1965*, published by Thames and Hudson in 1966, has an introduction by Henry-Russell Hitchcock and illustrative plates of Johnson's work. The book continues a well-established tradition in twentieth-century architectural monographs: plates constitute the overwhelming bulk of the book, affirming the basic premise that buildings should (can) speak for themselves. Although photographs are still not as good as "being there," they are the next closest thing. One might say the book represents Johnson "speaking" his piece with pictures.

There are two distinct bodies within the book: the twenty-page introduction by Henry-Russell Hitchcock and eighty pages of examples of Johnson's work. Illustration of the work consists of photographs and ground plans. None of the photographs were taken by Johnson. The typographical work is by Elaine Lustig, as mentioned in the review, and all the written text is by Henry-Russell Hitchcock. We can see already a peculiar fact emerging. Johnson has not "written" anything in this book. Curiously enough, it seems that if we only looked at the book, we would have no idea of Johnson's part in its creation.

The book itself buttresses this incongruity. Johnson is neither listed on the title page nor the copyright page as the author, nor does the remaining body of the book refer to Johnson as the author. If Johnson is not the author of the book, but the subject of the book, then the editorial insertion in the review seems much less troublesome: "Philip Johnson...was the only critic and scholar fully qualified to review a book on Johnson's work."[9] But Johnson must be the author of the book. The editors of *Architectural Forum* tell us so, bibliographical references tell us so, Robert Stern's introduction of this review in a compilation of Johnson's writings tells us so.[10] The review acknowledges that Johnson clearly has some connection to the book besides being the subject—

but what connection?[11] If Johnson has done neither the text, nor the typography, nor the photographs, what has he done to make others confidently claim him to be the author?

To begin an initial sketching out of the answer it may be necessary to go to the "minor reason" mentioned in paragraph seven of the review. Could Johnson be the author because he "picks out" the photographs and illustrations? If this does make him the author, why is it only the "minor" and "fun to see" that is constitutive of Johnson's "authorship"? Before the publication of the review it would have been difficult to understand how this mode of authorship could have been claimed for Johnson (that these choices were made by Johnson is not indicated in the book). Why then, if there is no clear author should it be necessary to make the claim that Johnson is the author? There are, after all, books which have no clearly attributed authors or paintings without clear attribution. The relationship between the review and the book seems almost orchestrated. The review probably does little good for the book, the editors or Johnson. Could this be a big inside joke?[12]

Paragraph seven, with its series of rhetorical questions, seems to indicate the reviewer felt many of the most important questions were left unaddressed. But the most stunning of these questions, and certainly a most stunning way to end the review, is the last rhetorical sentence. Johnson knows very well that there is a difference between "what they [artists, and he in particular here] say" and "what they do." Johnson the writer/author realizes that there is no simple relationship available to him towards Johnson the architect. And even more pointedly, it is clear that the book will never reveal the *why*, the intention(s), "(alas, lacking in Johnson's book)," which keep apart the Johnson that "speaks" and the Johnson that "does." By this time it may be evident that not only are we as readers unsure as to what Johnson may be saying and doing, but Johnson too is aware of this constellation of ambiguities. Thus tentatively, I propose, there are at least four Johnsons within these two texts:

1) Philip Johnson the architect.

2) Philip Johnson the "author" choosing/picking/judging Philip Johnson the architect.

3) The narrator of the review commenting on the above two Johnsons while trying not to be either.

4) The hidden "I" of the review, allowing Johnson to escape/comment on/laugh at other Johnsons, readers, and editors/critics.

The more one considers this proliferation of Philips (fillips?), the more it seems that Johnson's rhetoric(s) is not to elucidate but to create the hiding place of the "I." That is, to avoid the appropriation of Philip Johnson.

Whether we decide that Johnson's review is ironic or not, it seems advisable to attempt an alternative reading of Johnson's writings (and work) in light of the difficulties encountered in this "review of a review."

126 At the very least a reappraisal should lead one away from believing that Philip Johnson "frankly bares his own intentions"[13] in either his writings or his work.[14] The extent and thrust of the revision will depend on how strongly one feels the difficulties to be present and what strategies are available for legislating adequate meaning in Johnson's *oeuvre*. That is to say, how will the historians stop the dissimulation of meaning and create a canon, with its attendant litany of Johnson "facts." I tend to believe the difficulties raised by this review pose radical problems of many types that infect the means of interpreting architecture in general. My desire is to address only two of the problems encountered here: a cursory examination of the idea of an "author" and the related topic of irony within a text.

Much recent work has concentrated upon the troublesome term "author" with unexpected and uncanny results. What is an author? We have not yet begun the oppositional posturings: actual author vs. implied author; good author vs. bad author; clear author vs. unclear author; psychological author vs. historical author; etc.... Who can be an author? What can I author?: a book?, a painting?, a theory?, another author!? May I author a painting in the same manner I author a book? These questions return insistently. Since the concept of "author" (and of meaning) depends so heavily upon assumptions about intentionality and is constructed by imputing intentions to a "self" (or to a "sign"), it should not be surprising that any ambiguity introduced into the intentional structure of a work (our review, a novel, a painting, or a building) would lead to an oscillation of the concept.

Let us suppose as an axiom that the desire for attribution is a desire for appropriation. In matters of art as everywhere else.[15]

This quote begins one unravelling of the positions of the "author." Since it has been difficult to establish exactly where or who the author of our review is—"the I that writes the text is never, itself, anything more than a paper *I*."[16]—it seems safer to begin with those who are certain the author of this review is a determinate someone with an appellation of Philip Johnson. The question of course is how did these individuals feel justified in determining Philip Johnson to be the author of this not-so-transparent review? Whose word is being taken? Only one possible systematics of this authority— how this attributive/authoritative mechanism may be operating here—will be of prime interest to us in what follows.

The editors of *Architectural Forum* leave little room for doubt that they are sure Philip Johnson has written a fitting review.

The fact that he [Philip Johnson] happens to be both the subject and the critic of the present book is not entirely coincidental: Philip Johnson, it turned out, was the only critic and scholar fully qualified to review a book on Philip Johnson's work.

But the shattering of this keystone of the review genre seems not to have produced the result the editors might have expected. In fact, it might easily be claimed that the review is singularly poor as well as breaking the rules. The reviewer speaks flippantly about the design of the book, the text, and all its other contents. The writing meanders and has several quizzical and opaque self-references. Clarity seems especially absent. In short, it seems as though the reviewer is not maintaining a *serious* disposition towards his task, something not easy to forgive. Given this alternative description, what prompts the editors to proceed as they do?

Let us imagine as a heuristic scenario that the editors are forced into this peculiar position. Thinking that maybe it would be of journalistic interest to have Philip Johnson review his own book, they contract Philip Johnson to write the review. To their great chagrin they find the submitted review sorely inadequate, but they are forced by circumstances to print it. In an attempt to recover from this situation an escape route is sought. There are several options:

1) The editors could say nothing to the reading public and just let the review appear without any intervening comments. This solution seems simple enough and adequate, but...they are haunted by the rupture that they have allowed to take place. To allow the review to appear without comment would leave the editors' and the journal's reputation open to charges of manipulation, loss of objectivity, or even stupidity. Some acknowledgement must be made of the situation to counter not only the rupture but also the unorthodoxy which has resulted. But what type of acknowledgement?

2) An *apologia* might be possible but hardly admissible. *Apologiae* tend to make pointing gestures at the unorthodoxy in question. Further, this is an inadequate solution since in conjunction with an apologia there is inevitably a question of culpability (apologia as disclaimer). Who is apologizing to whom, and why? Where is the guilt here that necessitates an apology?

The search to discover the place of residence for this culpability would lead to an even greater rupture in this genre. Are we to speculate that the author is guilty?, or maybe the editors are guilty?, maybe the person who drew up the contract between the author and the editors is at fault?, and what of the reader's own culpability? Or is culpability a misplaced word here? Should it be gullibility, that is, a trait of those that are guilty of easily being fooled by authors/meanings? These circumstances obviate the possibility of an apologia in any form, since to apologize would be to implicate oneself. As Derrida has remarked:

This chain [the loose entanglements give above] is heterogeneous; only the proper names, texts, and situations are different each time, yet all the subjects are inscribed and implicated in the scene that they claim to interpret.[17]

The editors are reduced to whistling in the dark, hoping that the creature they have created will let them pass.

3) Only one avenue seems open and it is an avenue with a great deal of traffic. The various parties involved construct the appropriate examples to legitimize their interpretation. This is, after all, the basis of all argumentation, and leads the editors to be aggressive in their legitimization.

At the moment when criticism (be it aesthetic, literary, philosophical, etc.) allegedly protects the meaning of a thought or value of a work...: it creates an example.[18]

The choice of an example is always both arbitrary and calculated at the same time: arbitrary inasmuch as there are, at least in principle, a multitude of possible examples for any law and calculated inasmuch as the choice of a particular example is already an interpretation (even a formulation) of the law it is meant to illustrate.[19]

In this instance the object of inquiry (Philip Johnson) is appropriated via examples in such a way as to make necessary the adequacy/legitimacy of the subject's (editors') construction. The claims of the reading, writing, or interpreting subject must make the interpretive construct a result not of its own idiosyncratic creation, but rather a construct imposed from without. "The reason of the strongest is reason by itself."[20] This imposition from without seems closely linked to justification via conscious or unconscious projection. While revelling in the rhetoric of "open-mindedness" in the text, "Giving the greatest chance to chance," the projection "reappropriates chance itself into necessity or fatality."[21]

The editors have taken this chance (maybe a *malchance*) and transformed it into an imposed necessity. "Philip Johnson, it turned out [by chance?] was the only critic and scholar fully qualified to review a book of Philip Johnson's work." It seems what the editors are doing is to make Johnson's review a prime example of their own proper and astute handling of the tricky situation. Instead of it being an improper judgement to have the author review his own book, the tables are turned to make it appear as if those who are astute and knowledgeable know that having Philip Johnson review Philip Johnson is an externally imposed and necessary move.

Is not the editorial insertion into the review a desire to attribute, to appropriate Philip Johnson to the editors' own uses? Is not this insertion, this breading of the skin of a review, of a review which breaks the skin of all reviews, making the author into an example? That is, an example of the propriety of the editor's choices? This "appropriation" as Derrida calls it, seems very much like Wittgenstein puts it, "At the end of reasons comes persuasion. (Think what happens when missionaries convert natives.)"[22]

The indeterminate author is made determinate only by appropriation(s), by a making of an example *for* something. The author, like a style or a signature, becomes part of a "game" of legitimation and propriety. This is a strategic game within which the appropriated determinate author (the example) is used to validate the examples of the critic. Most often the critic's goal is to show, paraphrasing Serres above, that the strongest author is the author by himself. When the "author by himself" cannot be found, things begin to go awry. What is most disturbing of course, is that there is no such thing as the "author by himself."

This returning of the author (or Reality) to an indeterminate status is disturbing, especially if one views meanings as residing in a property which can be bought or sold only with certain accepted currencies. Here one returns to the systematics between irony, gullibility and culpability. To be gullible in this case is to "take a wooden nickel," thus making one culpable for accepting the False. It makes little difference where one begins, for "this chain is heterogeneous..."[23]

It is here that the ever-present spectre of irony intrudes. Irony is the harbinger of the indeterminate author. For some reason the conventional, common and dear meanings constructed during apprehension (I prefer apprehension to perception) are cast into doubt. At the same time the acknowledgement of this ironic state of affairs is difficult, for it causes a breach in the world that assumes there is contiguity between Reality and accepted/acceptable modes of representing this Reality. What results is:

A crisis of representation, in which an essentially realistic epistemology, which conceives of representations as the reproduction, for subjectivity, of an objectivity that lies outside it—projects a mirror theory of knowledge and art, whose fundamental evaluative categories are those of adequacy, accuracy and Truth itself.[24]

Accepting that Philip Johnson's review is ironic, the requisite question becomes: How to proceed with the task of talking or writing about these ironies? Is it possible to choose to be ironic or not? Once the questions are asked, no simple closure suffices. The ironies in the review implicate not only all of Johnson's work but pose questions for interpretation in general.

Re-examining Johnson's work, we are no longer so easily convinced that judgements of good or bad apply in any simple way. In fact, if the intentionality of much of Johnson's work is put under doubt because of a certain self-reflexivity, it seems hardly possible for architectural history to make any sort of attempt at interpretation. Of course, this will not by any means stop the interpretations from continuing, since architectural history bathes in the glow of transcendental intentions, or, if one wishes to appear more liberal, the glow of intentionalities arising from the social, political, or economic history. What Johnson's review so clearly illustrates is the

128 difficulty of discerning intention in some "original" source. In many cases going to the author, architect, builder, etc., is no closer to the "truth." How could one ever trust the author, etc., knowing that his perspective is always unreliable? Are we not constantly surrounded by and participating in being unreliable witnesses, no matter how much we work to hide it through institutions or conventions?

Johnson has introduced into the fabric of architecture, with his writings and his work, a series of minute displacements, bringing a momentary but repeatable hiatus to the "mad dash" for attribution. The displacements in this body of work serve as a warning and an aperture. They are a warning to those that are already convinced of the efficacy of their modes of interpretation, and an aperture for those convinced of the opposite. Johnson forces us to wrestle not with his productions, although that may also come, but instead with the possibility of interpretation at all.

If Johnson jars our sensibilities, it is not so much because of his personality, or politics, but more because he refuses to acquiesce to our notions of judgement, morality and history. Playing the harlequin has allowed him to say things which would not easily pass without censure.

I have no faith whatever in anything. It neither hurts nor helps my architecture, though it may produce some rather funny results.[25]

If we are willing to suspend our initial judgments, these "funny results" may prove to be enlightening.

Notes

[1] John Winter, "Philip Johnson," *Contemporary Architects*, Muriel Emanuel, ed. (New York: 1980), p. 401.

[2] Philip Johnson, *Writings* (NY: Oxford University Press, 1979), p. 10. This quote is from the introduction by Peter Eisenman.

[3] Manfredo Tafuri, *Theories and History of Architecture* (New York: Harper and Row, 1976), p. 113.

[4] Johnson, *Writings*, p. 203.

[5] Johnson, *Writings*, pp. 260-65.

[6] All unnumbered quotes in this paper will come from the review under consideration.

[7] Johnson, *Writings*, p. 20.

[8] For that matter, what could any of these words "mean" if either the authorship or the intentionality required for the creation of standard "meanings" is put into serious question? Naturally the battle rages around this word "serious." It seems that either the meaning/author/intention is always already in question, or there must be systems of control which guard the legitimate parameters of meaning/authors/intentions.

[9] If the book was written by someone else, then for Johnson to review the book might have been a way for the editors to get a judgement of the book from the "horse's mouth," so to speak.

[10] Johnson, *Writings*, p. 254.

[11] C.f. especially paragraph two where Johnson says, "It is the latest in a line of *architects' books on their own work*," and "he thought it important for some of his public (the few who buy books) and especially for the future to have a *record made by the architect's hand*" (my emphasis). How exactly is it that Johnson's "hand" left a record?

[12] This raises several questions about the nature not only of American architecture, but of architectural journals, and finally the power that architectural journals exert upon the architectural scene. Johnson is quite aware that without "self- advertising" and repeated journal publication by biased editors and authors, Wright, Corbusier, Mies or Gropius would have amassed little or no power to change the then prevailing fashions in architecture. This ability to control the parameters of available information is of course applicable to those now playing the architectural game.

[13] From R. A. M. Stern's introduction to this particular review in *Writings*, p. 254.

[14] The ambiguity of Johnson's intentions especially leads to difficulties in scholarship where he is the principal source of information. For example, most of the work on Mies is heavily indebted to Johnson's monograph. This ambiguity should play a role in any future appraisal of Philip Johnson's work. Only Craig Owens, in his article "Philip Johnson: History, Genealogy, Historicism," has taken note of some of these problems.

[15] Jacques Derrida, "Restitutions of Truth to Size," *Research in Phenomenology* 8, trans. Johns P. Leavey, Jr., ed. John Sallis, (Atlantic Highlands 1978): 3.

[16] Roland Barthes, "From Work to Text," in *Textual Strategies*, Josue Harari ed. (Ithaca: Cornell University Press, 1979), p. 79.

[17] Jacques Derrida, "Mes Chances," *Taking Chances: Derrida, Psychoanalysis and Literature*, Smith and Kerrigan eds. (Baltimore and London: Johns Hopkin University Press, 1984), p. 19.

[18] Jacques Derrida, "La Parole Souflee," in *Writing and Difference*, Alan Bass trans. (Chicago: University of Chicago Press, 1978), p. 170.

[19] David Carroll, *The Subject in Question* (Chicago: University of Chicago Press, 1982), p. 37.

[20] Michel Serres, *Hermes: Literature, Science, Philosophy*, Josue V. Harari and David F. Bell eds. (Baltimore: Johns Hopkins University Press, 1982), p. 28.

[21] Derrida, "Mes Chances," *op. cit.*, p. 29.

[22] Ludwig Wittgenstein, *On Certainty*, G. E. M. Anscombe and G. H. von Wright eds. (New York: 1972) 81e, #612. The affinities between the work of Derrida and Wittgenstein have been noted by several authors.

[23] Derrida, "Mes Chances," *op. cit.*, 19.

[24] Jean-François Lyotard, *The Post-Modern Condition: A Report on Knowledge*, trans. Geoff Bennington and Brian Massumi (Minneapolis: University of Milwaukee Press, 1984): viii. The quote is from the introduction by Frederic Jameson.

[25] Johnson, *Writings*, p. 109.